Performance and Reward

Managing Executive Pay
to Deliver Shareholder Value

D0863380

Patrick Gerard

Performance and Reward

Managing Executive Pay
to Deliver Shareholder Value

Matador
9 De Montfort Mews
Leicester LE1 7FW, UK
Tel: (+44) 116 255 9311 / 9312
Email: books@troubador.co.uk
Web: www.troubador.co.uk/matador

ISBN 1 905237 38 3

Typeset in 11pt Stempel Garamond by Troubador Publishing Ltd, Leicester, UK

Matador is an imprint of Troubador Publishing Ltd

Contents

	Acknowledgements	vii
	About the author	viii
	Introduction	ix
1	Different perspectives on performance	1
2	Linking performance and reward	13
3	Two key questions on incentive alignment	28
4	Typical reward packages	43
5	Annual bonus schemes	57
6	Long Term Incentive Plans (LTIPs)	70
7	Fully Invariable Linear Long-term Incentive Plans (FILLIPs)	84
8	Remaining problems and issues with FILLIPs	98
9	Share Option Schemes (SOSs)	113
10	Fixed pay	128
11	Factors influencing executive pay	142
12	The level of executive pay	159
13	The shareholder response	176
14	The future of executive pay	194
	Appendix 1: TSR definition and example	205
	Appendix 2: Layout for executive pay report	208
	Appendix 3: Research on immediate verses deferred rewards	213
	Appendix 4: Modelling the value of Typico's LTIP	217
	Appendix 5: Rules of a FILLIP	228

Appendix 6: Modelling of three kinds of FILLIP   235
Appendix 7: Cost of option and share based remuneration   247

Reference material and further reading   250
Glossary   253
Index   260

Acknowledgements

I would like to thank the many people who have helped me in the writing of this book. I am thankful to the people who responded to the research questionnaire. I am thankful to Edward Hoare for his detailed comments on the ideas and the text. I am thankful to Natania Goldrich for her enthusiastic encouragement. Above all I am thankful to my wife, Elaine, and to my children for giving me the time, space and support necessary to complete the book.

Patrick Gerard
January 2006

About the author

Patrick Gerard has worked in FTSE 100 companies for 16 years with significant exposure to the utilities, regulated networks, commodity markets, and oil and gas. His working experience covers India and Brazil as well as the UK. Throughout his career he has monitored his own pay and reward package, as well as those of his Chief Executives.

His interest in executive pay developed when his own reward package was restructured in the year 2000. The move towards standard industry practices appeared in many ways to be a mysterious backwards step. This motivated Patrick Gerard to research executive pay further and ultimately to write *Performance and Reward*.

A mathematician by background, Patrick Gerard has a profound insight into the incentives and behaviours that arise from different reward structures. He is currently training to become a clergyman in the Church of England so unlike most commentators he has no vested interest in the future of executive pay. His background, experience and independence make him uniquely qualified to write this book.

Introduction

This book is about the way that company executives are paid. It is concerned with finding the best ways of paying executives; the ways that are most likely to lead to successful companies.

Successful companies are the companies that deliver the best returns to their shareholders. This book always considers executive pay from the point of view of shareholders of UK based companies. Many people in the UK today are shareholders. Some people own shares directly, but many more own shares indirectly, through pension schemes or through investment products. The shareholders collectively are the owners of the company and as shareholders they should expect the company to be run in their best interests.

This book is designed to help people who have direct responsibility for setting executive pay in the UK. It will help them to set pay in ways that work in the best interests of shareholders. It should particularly help people who deal with the policy issues associated with executive pay. However the book is also of interest to anyone who wants to see better practice on executive pay. This will include a great many shareholders and managers as well as economists and people who study the objectives and ethics of business.

In chapter 1 of the book we examine company performance. We notice that, for a shareholder, a company that performs well is one that delivers growth in shareholder value on a sustained long term basis. We also look at other, more management orientated views of performance. In chapters 2 and 3 we examine why performance and pay are linked and what can be achieved by doing this. From this analysis it immediately becomes clear that some measures of performance are far better suited for linkage to executive pay than others. What gets highlighted is the importance of incentives, and in this book we examine many of the executive pay issues from the point of view of the incentives arising from the pay.

In chapters 4 to 9 of the book we look at the ways that performance is typically linked to executive pay in FTSE 350 companies today. In the light of what was seen in chapters 2 and 3 it is clear that there is a lot of scope for improvement in the ways that these links are made. The book proposes Fully Invariable Linear Long-term Incentive Plans (FILLIPs) as a way of improving these links.

In chapter 10 of the book we look at the elements of pay that are not usually linked to performance. We notice that the incentives arising from these elements are often very powerful and often badly aligned with shareholder interests. By chapter 11 it is very clear that consideration of incentives has had only limited influence on the way that executive pay has developed in the UK, so we look at some of the other factors that have been more influential. We consider the level of executive pay in chapter 12 and the shareholder response in chapter 13. Finally in chapter 14 we look at things which people who are responsible for executive pay can do to make the pay more effective for shareholders.

1

Different perspectives on performance

In this chapter we look at some different perspectives on what business performance really means. We look at different approaches to performance and consider some of the different ways that performance can be measured.

The shareholder's perspective on performance

What does performance mean for an investor? How does an investor measure the success of an investment? Obviously this depends on what the investor was looking for when the investment was made. So in the case of an investment in company shares, what is it that the investor is looking for?

Compared to other forms of investment, company shares (equities) have very good potential for long term value growth, but can be volatile and carry more risk. Individual companies can do exceptionally well, and can fail completely so the risks are significant. To manage the risk of individual company failures equity investors usually invest in a large number of different companies. This might eliminate most of the risk associated with any one company but it retains the benefit that arises if equities in general do well. Obviously the shareholder is still at risk if equities in general do badly.

Volatility in the share price can distort the value of the shares at the point at which they are bought or sold. If the shares are retained for a long period then this is unlikely to matter because the effect of the volatility is small compared to the long term value growth. Private investors are usually advised that they should plan to keep a portfolio of equity based investments for at least five years, but the longer the investment is held the more confident the investor can be of securing a good rate of return. Investors therefore buy equities for the purposes of long term savings and to cover long term funding requirements such as pensions.

This means that when a shareholder looks at the performance of a particular equity investment the measure of success is the long term growth in value. The value might have come through share price growth, or dividends, but the form of the value is less important. It is the overall growth in value that matters.

It is easy to measure the overall growth in the value of an investment in a particular equity. This is done using a Total Shareholder Return (TSR) index. The index is calculated from the company's share price and dividends such that the percentage change in the index between any two dates is the percentage change in the overall value of an investment in that company. An illustrative example is given in appendix 1.

Because of volatility, it only makes sense to look at the percentage change in a TSR index over a reasonably long period of time. However, over a long period, this percentage change measures precisely and objectively what investors want from an investment in a company's shares. This means that if a company's primary objective is to deliver value to shareholders then long term TSR growth is the performance measure that tells us how successful it has been.

Economic cycles and share price volatility

Share prices tend to move up and down with economic cycles. They also move up and down from day to day in a more random way. Volatility is part of the package for investors who invest in equities. However, other things being equal, volatility in share prices works against the interest of shareholders. If two different companies deliver the same growth in TSR over the same period then the company that has performed best for the shareholders is the one with the less volatile share price. There is a higher cost of risk associated with the more volatile investment, so it needs to achieve a higher rate of return to be as cost effective as the less volatile investment. The value of TSR as a performance measure for shareholders can be undermined by high volatility.

Lower volatility makes it easy for investors to enter and exit the market because the exact timing of when the shares are bought and sold becomes less important. Lower volatility makes it feasible to hold shares for shorter periods, making them accessible to a greater range of investors. In itself, volatility is bad for shareholders. Shareholders should only accept higher volatility if it is genuinely linked to the expectation of higher overall returns in the long term.

At this point it is important to notice that many institutional investors are far more concerned about the short term variations in share prices than they are about long term performance. This is despite the fact that it is the long term performance of the investments that ultimately matters to the people whose money they are investing. This tragic misalignment of interests between institutional investors and their clients is discussed in more detail in chapter 13. As a problem it has been around for many years, but the rapid development of hedge funds during 2003 and 2004 has made the problem much more acute. It creates very difficult situations for companies because their most influential shareholders can be obsessively interested in short term matters that have little importance to the long term performance of the company. Companies sometimes find it very difficult to resist pressure from institutional investors on short term issues. One thing that the company can do is consistently and firmly to give out the message that it is being managed to create long term value rather than to fulfil short term expectations.

Dramatic and unexpected losses in equity value

Long term growth in the TSR index is the performance measure that matters for shareholders. Even if institutional investors look at short term issues it is the long term growth in TSR that matters to their clients. However shareholder confidence in TSR as a performance measure can be undermined if the TSR index can be dramatically and unexpectedly reduced. This can happen for a number of reasons but the worst instances arise when there has been serious mismanagement or significant unethical business behaviour somewhere within the company.

For example accounting fraud was a major factor at Enron, Skandia, WorldCom, and Parmalat. Rogue traders caused the Barings Bank collapse in 1995 and have subsequently caused serious loss of shareholder value at Allfirst Financial and at National Australia Bank.

Business practices that damage other people's legitimate interests can also be thought of as unethical, and also lead to unexpected loss of value. The tobacco companies were sued by their customers. Shell was damaged by environmentalists over the disposal of the Brent Spar North Sea oil platform. Nike and others have been damaged by bad publicity on practices in their supply chains.

For long term shareholders it is essential that companies avoid creating nasty surprises for their shareholders. This makes it important that companies are well managed and behave ethically. Control procedures such as external audit and external reporting on Corporate Social Responsibility (CSR) are designed to ensure sound management and ethical behaviour. Ultimately however sound management and ethical behaviour are matters of company culture. If the company culture is strong, emphasising respect for the legitimate interests of others, trust, integrity and openness then the control procedures will be highly effective. If the company culture is inadequate then the control procedures become a box ticking exercise. They can do no more than constrain and reduce problematical behaviour, and sooner or later difficulties will emerge.

Shareholder value as a business objective

Using long term growth in the TSR index as the critical performance measure for companies is logical if the creation of shareholder value is their primary business objective and this is the case with most large scale listed companies in the UK today.

There are however some dangers with thinking of shareholder value as the primary objective for a business. The desire to create wealth has to be a core value for any successful company, but there are other values that are also very important. For example it is important to provide a good service to customers, to develop and grow employees, to form sound relationships with suppliers and to contribute constructively to the life of communities and nations. Over the long term these other values are closely related to the creation of wealth, but in the short term it is possible to generate wealth at the expense of these other values. Short term wealth generated in this a way carries with it a long term cost. It is therefore very important to measure the creation of shareholder value over the longer term.

In this book I am going to assume that the business objective is the creation of long term shareholder value, and that the success or failure of a company can be measured by the long term growth in its TSR index. In making this assumption however, I am first of all assuming that the company treats its various interest groups properly and that there are no long term debts to wider society that will have to be repaid in the future.

The management's perspective on performance

In this book I use the word "management" to signify all managers at every level in the organisation. I use the term "executive team" to mean the small group of managers at the very top of the organisation who have day to day responsibility for the company. The executive team includes the executive directors, and is likely to include other managers, many of whom will report directly to the chief executive. I use the word "executive" to mean any member of the executive team.

Outlined below are three different techniques that are commonly used by the executive team to manage performance within the company. The techniques operate internally to companies, and are only indirectly relevant to shareholders. However it is important to be aware of these techniques because they are central to way that management thinks about performance and the way that performance targets should be established.

Managing performance through the business plan

The management of performance is about setting demanding targets, and then achieving those targets. Business planning is the activity that makes this possible.

The central part of a business plan is a spreadsheet model that accurately predicts profits, cash flows and balance sheets from projections of sales, prices, operational and capital costs. Assumptions about exchange rates, economic growth and commodity prices are also likely to be required. Obviously there will be some uncertainty about the assumptions and projections, but the model can be used to show how these uncertainties affect the business and to identify the projections and assumptions that really matter.

It is important that the company understands the data items and other factors that have a big impact on the business plan model. These items must be measured and managed. In particular, risks arising from uncontrollable factors like exchange rates need to be understood and managed.

The business planning cycle

Typically a company will have a planning cycle. In stage one of the cycle the central planning co-ordinator creates versions of the business plan model for different scenarios. The scenarios will be defined by different sets of assumptions in respect of any external factors such as exchange rates, or outcome of a court case with important forward looking consequences. The co-ordinator sends the assumptions to the managers responsible for different parts of the business (business units) and asks them to make projections for their business unit each different scenario.

In stage two of the cycle business unit managers complete the projections requested by the central co-ordinator. For each scenario it is likely that two projections will be required; a base case projection, which the manager has a 50% probability of achieving and a stretch case which he or she has a 10% or 20% probability of achieving.

In stage three of the cycle the central co-ordinator collates all the responses from the business unit managers and generates the consolidated company model output for both the base and stretch cases in each scenario. This is then reviewed by the executive team.

Stage four is a dialogue where the executive team say, "We need to do better. Increase your sales and reduce your costs!" and business unit managers respond with amended projections and explanations of things that cannot be changed. At this stage business unit managers should also explain and document clearly any risks or external factors which might undermine their projections. The output of this dialogue is a final set of projections for each year going forward. The projection for year one becomes a performance target for the following year. There will be both a base case target and a stretch target. At the end of the year the performance of each business unit will be measured against these targets. The outcome will affect the reputation of the business unit manager, and may affect his or her pay.

Incentives for business unit managers in the business planning process

It is clear that the executive team want to see bullish projections come in from the different business units, but it remains essential that the probabilities of achievement are realistic.

Business unit managers have to decide how bullish or bearish to be, when they make their projections in the planning process. Managers who are bullish will make their part of the business appear more important, enhance their reputation and will find it easier to secure attention and resources from the executive team. On the other hand they effectively set themselves higher performance targets and potentially make their lives more difficult when performance against target is assessed at the end of the year.

For the executive team to achieve their objective of projections that are bullish but realistic it is essential that they hold business unit managers properly accountable at year end for any gaps between the business unit performance targets and the final results. This is much harder to achieve that it appears at first sight. I have seen accountability break down for many different reasons:

- Change of executive team or business unit managers
- Change of strategy or priorities
- Projections based on unrealistic external factors
- Projections dependent on an action by the executive team
- An external factor described as unexpected or "freak"
- Some problem already informally reported to the executive team

However, if accountability is maintained, then the effect on performance is dramatic. Business unit managers have incentives to set and deliver targets that are both demanding and realistic. Reputations can be built in this way.

Managing performance through a balanced scorecard

The idea of a balanced scorecard is to manage company performance by monitoring a small and manageable number of key performance indicators. An example of a balanced scorecard for a simple business is set out below.

Financial Measures
   Profit before interest and tax
   Cash flow
Revenue Indicators
   Units sold
   Revenue per unit sold
   Units returned under guarantee
   Customer satisfaction index
Cost Indicators
   Supplier costs per unit
   Manufacturing costs per unit
   Sales costs per unit
   Overhead
Other Stakeholder Measures
   Safety and environment index
   Employee satisfaction index

The executive team set targets for each of the twelve identified key performance indicators. Again it is possible to set a base case and stretch case performance target. Each month the key performance indicators are measured and reported. The executive team compare target and actual performance. This ensures that problems and constraints are identified quickly and can be dealt with promptly.

Of course there is great skill in selecting the correct measures for a balanced scorecard. Having too many measures will generate bureaucracy and disperse focus. Having too few will allow important parts of the business go unmonitored. Some measures of performance are particularly useful because they have a predictive effect on future financial performance. For example the Customer Satisfaction Index tells us more about the future financial performance than current performance. Some measures can be cycled into an out of the balanced scorecard, to ensure that they get periodic, rather than continuous top level attention.

Managing performance through Personal Performance Contracts (PPCs)

A Personal Performance Contract (PPC) is a set of between six and 12 performance targets for an individual manager that are documented at the start of the year and signed off by both the individual and his or her line manager. Both base case and stretch case targets can be set.

Because managers tend to delegate tasks and responsibilities to their subordinates, a manager's performance targets will frequently appear on the performance contracts of some of his or her subordinates. In this way, performance targets cascade down the organisation. The setting of the PPC for the chief executive therefore becomes an extremely critical factor affecting the whole company's direction over the year ahead.

The chief executives PPC must be set well before the start of the year in question. This process is likely to involve many of the executive team. The chairman is certain to be a key figure and the remuneration committee may be involved (see chapter 5). Once the chief executive's PPC has been signed by the chairman and the chief executive, the chief executive can start creating PPCs with each of his or her direct reports, which starts the process of performance targets cascading down the organisation.

The targets for financial performance on the chief executives PPC are likely to arise from the business planning process. There should certainly be a target for profit, or earnings, and other financial targets as appropriate.

There will be some targets that originate more from the balanced score approach to performance. Units Sold, Revenue per Unit Sold, Manufacturing Cost per Unit and Safety and Environmental Index could well be key targets on the chief executive's PPC.

There will be some targets that are more personal objectives such as, "Secure board approval for strategy addressing low cost competition emerging in the Far East." There could be base case and stretch case target dates for completion. Another example might be "Sell underperforming operation X" with base and stretch case targets for the value to be realised.

At the end of the year the performance of each executive and each manager is reviewed against his or her PPC. Performance achievements are recognised and celebrated. They should lead to more opportunities for the individuals involved. Performance gaps are evaluated to ensure that the reasons are fully understood. Action plans are created to eliminate barriers to performance and to ensure continuous improvement. The outcome of a performance review also may have an impact on pay. In the case of executives this raises a number of issues that are examined in chapter 5.

Monitoring performance and updating targets

All forms of performance management involve the monitoring of progress towards predefined targets. During monitoring it often happens that a particular performance target starts to look inappropriate. This might be the result of inadequate planning, but it remains a common occurrence, even in the best planning organisations. Perhaps the business requirement has changed. Perhaps expectations are now different. Perhaps it is no longer desirable to "Sell the underperforming operation X".

Coping with changes to requirements is one of the biggest challenges for any performance management system. The problem is that accountability for performance is always reduced, and sometimes lost completely. For example it might be that the inappropriate performance target is dropped and not assessed at the end of the year. In this case all accountability is lost. It might be that the inappropriate target is replaced by a new target. If this is done formally, then it will take time and the period over which performance can be assessed is reduced. If the change is made informally, then accountability at the end of the year is likely to be very low. Sometimes I have seen targets regularly updated over the year to reflect the likely outcome! In these cases it is the performance that is managing the target, rather than the target managing the performance. Very often the targets are not changed, but the change of circumstances is taken into account at the performance assessment stage. Again, this usually amounts to the performance as finally measured having the effect of setting the target.

Performance management is essential to any organisation that wants to perform well. However, the organisation must be realistic about the level of accountability for performance that can be maintained. In particular it must be recognised that it is extremely difficult to maintain accountability through periods of rapid change.

The different perspectives of management and shareholders

For management, performance is mainly about setting and meeting targets. Maintaining accountability and eliminating barriers to performance are also important. Of course it is critically important to set the right targets. The executive team needs to know that the targets cover the issues that really matter, that they are appropriately challenging and that the means used to hit a target will be proportionate to the end. Usually these are very subjective judgements and a detailed knowledge of the company and its environment is required before appropriate targets can be set.

To a shareholder all these targets are simply a means to an end. The end is long term growth in shareholder value and the setting of targets is one of many management tools used to achieve this.

Summary

In this chapter we have seen that, from a shareholder perspective, performance is all about long term growth in shareholder value. This can be measured by the long term growth in the TSR index for the company in question. Shareholder confidence in this measure is reduced if share price volatility is extremely high, or if sudden collapses in the TSR index can occur. However these factors do not usually apply to well run companies, so long term growth in the TSR index is the performance measure that matters.

We have also seen that a company's management has a very different perspective on performance. It uses techniques such as business plans, balanced score cards and PPCs to manage many different aspects of performance. A large number of different performance measures are used, at different levels within the company, to ensure that the company's activities are properly managed and controlled. Such measures are essential tools of management, but from a shareholder perspective they are interesting only as predictors of long term value growth. The performance measure that matters to shareholders is long term growth in shareholder value measured through the TSR index.

2

Linking performance and reward

In the previous chapter we looked at performance from the different perspectives of shareholders and managers. Now let us consider some of the some of the basic questions that arise when we start to link performance to executive pay.

Fixed pay and variable pay

Pay that is directly linked to performance is known as "variable pay" or "performance related pay". Annual bonus and long term incentive schemes are examples of variable pay. Each year variable pay could come out very high or very low depending on the performance measurements at the end of the year. Pay that is not linked to performance is known as "fixed pay". Basic salary and pension entitlement are examples of fixed pay. An executive earns his or her fixed pay each year, irrespective of any performance measurements.

Benefits of variable pay

Let's remind ourselves why it is considered a good idea to have variable pay. Why do we want to link pay to performance?

In the case of executives, the main benefit of variable pay is the motivational effect. Variable pay ensures that executives who want to be well rewarded have concrete incentives to perform well. It is unlikely that many executives actually want to perform badly, but to perform well they need to be continually raising the bar, challenging established norms and dealing with difficult situations that it would be easier to ignore. Incentives can help to make this happen. However it is critically important that the reward package provides incentives that are properly aligned with shareholders interests. Too often the incentives are to make the profit figure appear good, to make the board appear good, or to make the executive team appear good. These are not the right incentives from a shareholder perspective.

A second benefit of variable pay is that the executives who find it most valuable and attractive are the top performers. A good variable reward package will therefore selectively help to recruit and retain a top performing executive team. The big risk to this benefit is individualism. The executives must work together effectively as a team. They must support each other and collaborate effectively. Individual performance is only worthy of credit to the extent that it enhances the overall team performance. Individuals must not be allowed to prioritise their own performance above the performance of the team. For this reason it is important to use common, company wide performance measures as the most significant element of variable pay for all members of the executive team.

A third advantage of variable pay is that it provides a form of recognition when difficult tasks have been accomplished. This usually happens when the performance criteria of an incentive scheme have been met. The company recognises that the performance targets have been met by making the incentive payments that were promised. Recognition is a key factor in motivation, although recognition is obviously about far more that monetary payments. Statements of praise in company news bulletins that are circulated internally or externally also play a big role. In fact other more public forms of recognition are likely to be more important than money in securing the full motivational effects of recognition. Sometimes recognition payments become unlinked from pre-agreed incentive schemes and in these cases they become very problematic. Recognition payments are discussed further in at the end of this chapter.

There are several other benefits of variable pay that relate to the control of costs. These cost control benefits become very significant benefits if they are applied to large numbers of employees in businesses where labour costs are high. They should not however be significant considerations in the case of executive pay, unless executive pay forms a significant part of the company's overall cost structure.

One such benefit is that variable pay reflects what shareholders can afford to pay. When company performance is good, shareholders can afford to pay out, when it is bad they cannot.

Another cost control benefit of variable pay, as opposed to fixed pay, is that increases in fixed pay compound over the years and become a growing ongoing payment liability for shareholders. In contrast, the variable pay can always revert to zero if performance is poor. However, at the executive level this particular advantage of variable pay has been seriously eroded. Annual bonuses and other variable pay have in fact grown steadily year on year. They remain variable, but in general they still have the effect of a compounding annual cost increase for shareholders. Also there have been some unfortunate moves towards "guaranteed bonuses". Clearly a bonus that is guaranteed is not really variable pay at all. It is more like base salary that is not pensionable.

A third cost control benefit of variable pay is that it does not generate future liabilities for pensions or termination payments in the same way that basic salary does. This is very significant where labour costs are high, but in the case of the executive team the value of this advantage can be overstated. Often the forms of variable pay that apply to executives are long term incentive schemes that do themselves generate long term liabilities of different kinds.

It can be seen that, in the case of executives, the advantages of variable pay stem mostly from its motivational effects. The motivational effects are mainly to do with providing incentives and allowing executives to respond to those incentives. This book therefore focuses very rigorously on incentives. It is imperative that shareholder provide the correct incentives to executives when they establish performance related pay schemes. Shareholders also need to consider other incentives that arise for executives from other parts of their reward package which are not variable pay. For example there is a big incentive to stay in post, and a big incentive to secure a higher basic salary.

Problems with variable pay

The disadvantages of variable pay tend to arise from misalignment between the incentives arising from the variable pay scheme, and the behaviours that shareholders would want executives to adopt. For example big rewards for delivering the annual profit target might cause this target to be prioritised over the creation of long term value. Similarly significant rewards determined at the individual level might cause an executive to prioritise his or her own performance over the performance of others, or over the performance of the executive team as a whole.

It is usually possible to eliminate, or substantially eliminate, such problems by considering carefully the incentives that arise from the various different pay schemes. By ensuring the greatest possible alignment of incentives with shareholder interests it is possible to minimise the problems and increase benefits of variable pay.

The implementation of variable pay schemes does usually require shareholders to pay more in total to executives than would be paid if the schemes did not exist. It is these extra payments that provide the incentives. However a well designed variable pay scheme will only provide extra rewards to executives if there has been extra performance that has materially contributed to the value of the shareholders' investment. This should ensure that however much the executive gains from the scheme, the shareholder gains even more. Sadly it is all too common for extra rewards to be paid out for performance which has not added value to the shareholder, and in some cases may even have destroyed it. To defend themselves against these kinds of performance payments shareholders need to insist that the measures of performance used for the variable pay of executives are true measures of shareholder value. Too often the measures used relate to matters that management considers important for its own reasons, and where the link to shareholder value is subjective and unproven.

Variable pay schemes, especially long term schemes, can generate long term liabilities for shareholders as payments become due to executives. Such payments are often made in the form of shares and share options. Once again shareholders should always be able to manage this problem by ensuring proper alignment between what gets paid to executives and increases in shareholder value. The problems only really arise if payments to executives become due without any increase in shareholder value having occurred to fund such payments.

Implementing a variable pay scheme

When a company implements a variable pay scheme for executives it is very important to choose a scheme that secures as many of the benefits of variable pay as possible and avoids as many of the problems as possible. The detailed design of the schemes is therefore very important because benefits and problems can arise very directly from the scheme design.

It is both very important and very obvious that variable pay schemes should be designed to maximise benefits and minimise problems. Unfortunately there is very little evidence that companies give much consideration to the benefits and problems. If they did, the variable pay for executives that we see in FTSE 350 companies would be structured quiet differently from the way it is typically structured at present. There would be far more emphasis on aligning incentives with shareholder value.

What performance measures should be used as a basis for variable pay?

We saw in the previous chapter that there are different perspectives on performance and many different performance measures, each of which gives a different view of how a company or an individual is performing. The question arises about which of these performance measures should be selected as a basis for variable pay.

Conventional wisdom appears to answer, "All of them! Any measure of performance that matters to the company is a potential basis for performance related pay." The trouble with this answer is that it does not take account of the benefits and problems associated with performance related pay. This book is all about finding the forms of variable pay that bring the maximum benefits and cause the minimum problems. When performance measures are looked at in this way then it quickly becomes clear that some performance measures are much better than others as a basis for variable pay.

It is important to realise that the best structures for variable pay are different for different people in the organisation. Clearly "Number of customers added" is more appropriate as a performance measure for a salesman than for a debt collector! This book focuses on variable pay for executives. That is for the small group of very top managers in the company including the executive directors who sit on the company board. The performance measures that are appropriate for executives need to be the performance measures that matter to shareholders. If the executives are not looking after the shareholder interest then who is?

Shareholder measures of performance verses management measures of performance

What is the objective of the company's chief executive? In the previous chapter I suggested that the chief executive should manage the company to maximise long term growth in value for shareholders. The measure of shareholder value is the TSR index. The chief executive's performance over a reasonably long term time period can therefore be measured as the percentage growth in the TSR index for the company. Surely this is the performance measure on which a chief executives variable pay should be based. All other performance measures are subservient to this one. "Number of customers added" matters because of long term shareholder value, "Profit" matters because of long term shareholder value. In the end it is all very simple!

The same is almost certainly true for all other members of the executive team. If they really are the most senior people in the company, with responsibilities that stretch across the whole company then surely it is the long term growth in TSR that measures their performance. This is the measure that is aligned with shareholder interests. Other measures might be important to the management or to the credibility of the company board but these measures only really matter to shareholders to the extent that they affect the long term growth in TSR.

Lower down the organisation there is a good case for basing variable pay on more management focused performance measures. This is because the lower levels of the organisation are accountable to senior management more than they are accountable to shareholders. However the executive team are accountable to shareholders and so at the executive level it is shareholder measures of performance that matter.

Long term performance verses short term performance

Most of the time a chief executive's number one priority is the business of remaining in post. Nobody likes to lose their job. Chief executives are ambitious people who have worked very hard to secure the top jobs; they particularly do not like to lose their jobs. Chief executives also have very strong financial incentives to stay in post. They are extremely well paid, and every year that they can stay in post makes them very significantly wealthier. Whatever incentives might arise through variable pay, the number one incentive for a chief executive is always to stay in post.

This need to stay in post guarantees that a chief executive is always under tremendous pressure to deliver immediate results. A chief executive has to do a great deal of reporting, and this process of reporting goes much, much better when it is good news that is being reported. When quarterly results are published City analysts look at the financial results and the key operating data. If the important figures are perceived as good or encouraging then everyone is happy; the chief executive's credibility is high, proposals get approved easily and problems are not raised. However if the important numbers look poor or disappointing then the chief executive needs to give a convincing explanation. There will be difficult questions about the numbers and about the implications for the future. There is no better time for people to raise other, unrelated, difficult matters that they want the chief executive to address.

To stay in post the chief executive must always have a very close eye on the next financial report. The pressure to deliver good numbers at the end of each quarter or half-year has become disproportionate. The Google IPO documentation of 2004 compared business obsession with quarterly earnings figures to a dieter weighing himself very half hour. Undoubtedly chief executives are very conscious of the importance of short term performance. This can lead to a hand to mouth style of management, where each quarter is addressed as a separate challenge and there is no coherent thought about longer term issues. Hand to mouth management can normally be sustained for between four and eight quarters before serious problems start to emerge. It is often possible to conceal those problems for a bit longer by taking measures that increase short term earnings at the expense of longer term earnings. In the very worst cases hand to mouth management has been extended even further through accounting fraud. In fact most of the really big corporate frauds have been made up of a succession of ever bigger frauds each of which was originated to conceal bad news.

Even the best chief executive, with a genuine focus on long term shareholder value, finds the discipline of quarterly reporting a major challenge. Investors are quite rightly very suspicious of "jam tomorrow" promises. There is a long tradition of earnings growth arriving later and weaker than projected. Above all the chief executive must maintain credibility. The company must set clear targets, and the results that it publishes each quarter must show that the business is on schedule to meet its long term goals. The pressure to report encouraging figures each quarter is therefore very high, even if the chief executive is completely focused on long term shareholder value.

So given that chief executives have huge incentives to focus on the next set of financial results, how should shareholders ensure that the business is really being managed to create long term shareholder value? How can they give incentives which reward long term value creation more than staying in post? Well one way is to make sure that variable pay is totally focused on long term shareholder value. Fixed pay, and the desire to stay in post, already guarantees that the chief executive has very strong incentives to deliver short term goals. As a small step towards redressing the balance, variable pay should be 100% based on long term results. More specifically variable pay should be based on sustained long term growth in the TSR index for the company.

At this point someone might object, and say, "But if 100% of variable pay is linked to long term results isn't there a danger that short term objectives will be neglected?" Absolutely not! Delivering long term value is about having a good strategy, having a step by step plan to deliver the strategy, and then delivering on each step. Short term objectives become both more meaningful and more valuable when they form part of a coherent longer term plan. If variable executive pay is linked 100% to long term value growth then the executives have incentives to set the correct short term targets and to deliver on those targets. A system of PPCs (not linked to pay) might help them to do it. Attainment of short term goals is more directly a service to the company board and management, who grow in credibility, than it is a service to shareholders. Shareholders are interested in the long term growth in value.

In the case of executives, rewarding long term performance is in fact the most appropriate way of rewarding short term performance. A short term initiative that gives rise to a benefit does contribute to long term TSR growth. But by rewarding only long term TSR growth, shareholders can ensure that they do not over reward an increase in earnings that turned out to be only a "blip", and that they don't reward implementation of a new strategy that turned out to be flawed. There is often a trade off between making the most of immediate short term opportunities and maximising the long term value of the company. If variable pay is linked to long term performance, then the incentives to correctly evaluate these trade offs are in place.

Executives are very talented people and usually have a good knowledge of the businesses that they run. No bonus is required to tell them that the annual profit figures are important. They are the best people to judge what the short term targets should be, and to make the trade offs necessary between long term and short term value. Shareholders should not be clouding their judgements by making incentive payments based on short term objectives. Rather, variable rewards should be linked to long term growth in value. This maximises alignment with shareholder interests and gives executives the freedom necessary to manage the short term in the way that creates the highest long term value.

Performance outcomes or performance efforts

Should we reward executives just on the final outcome of what they have achieved, or should we take into account how hard they have tried, the luck they have enjoyed, the misfortunes they have suffered and the external factors beyond their control. Clearly there are arguments both ways.

The arguments in favour of rewarding outcomes only are as follows.

An outcome only assessment is more objective. If factors other than the final outcome are taken into consideration then lots of subjective questions arise. What other factors should be considered? To what extent should they be considered? To what extent had these factors already been taken into consideration when the target was set?

An outcome only assessment is more transparent. If the outcome is measured and directly mapped through to a particular level of variable pay then everybody can understand how different levels of performance are leading to different levels of pay. This is essential to the incentive effect of performance related pay and builds trust and understanding in the organisation. If adjustments to the measured outcome are applied to take account of other factors then the transparency of the process is reduced, dampening the incentive effect and raising questions of fairness for other executives.

An outcome only assessment maximises accountability. A chief executive should not turn round and say, "Our strategy was based on growth, and unfortunately this proved impossible because of the Iraq War and the high oil price." The strategy must be resilient to the world unfolding in different ways. A chief executive must be able to explain how different world outcomes will impact the company. All strategies involve a greater or lesser amount of risk, and the management of that risk is fundamental to the role of the executive team. If luck or misfortune are taken into account when evaluating performance this accountability is undermined.

An outcome only assessment gives incentives to set realistic targets. Executives are likely to think more carefully about the goals and targets that they set if their variable reward will be based solely on achievement of those targets.

An outcome only assessment maximises alignment with shareholders if the performance measure is long term growth in TSR. If, over the long term, the share prices climbs then investors do well and the executive team is rewarded. If the share price falls then investors do badly and rewards for the executive team are reduced.

The arguments above strongly suggest that variable pay should be based solely on outcomes, and take no account of other factors. There are however some arguments that go the other way. Let us examine them now.

It is demotivating to deny reward to an executive who has performed well but missed a target through bad luck. This argument is frequently made, but it is impossible to go along with this without undermining accountability and objectivity. A much better solution to the demotivation problem is to ensure that assessment is on a sliding scale basis with outcomes between 0 and 100%, rather than on a step change basis of "target achieved" or "target not achieved".

Showing "mercy" in performance assessment allows executives to set targets that are more ambitious. The trouble is that the meaningfulness of an ambitious target is undermined if the executive is not fully accountable for meeting the target. Again sliding scales can be useful here. The 100% outcome can be set at an extremely ambitious level such that the 75% outcome still represents a very good outcome with very good reward.

Showing "mercy" in performance assessment allows executives to take legitimate risks. This argument is just too dangerous! Who can possibly be accountable for risks if the executive team are not!

Executives should not lose annual bonus because of PPC targets that have clearly become irrelevant or inappropriate as the year has unfolded. This argument sounds reasonable, but it is equally true that the executive should not be paid bonus in respect of such targets. This is in fact a good reason for not using PPC assessment as a basis for variable pay.

An outcome only assessment can lead to high rewards that are not attributable to the executive performance. This has been a big issue on certain long term incentive schemes where executives are rewarded for increases in the share price. A company's share price may rise because of cyclical movements in the stock market, even though the underlying financial performance is poor. Companies with a highly geared capital structure can experience huge surges in share price because of very small improvements in financial performance. Also an outrageous situation might develop where a very poor executive team is richly rewarded when a takeover bid causes a share price hike. These are very real problems that are all too common in the long term incentive schemes that are typically used by FTSE 350 companies today. Fortunately most of these problems can be eliminated by getting the detail of scheme rules correct. Chapters 6 to 9 of this book consider these issues in detail.

Having looked at the arguments it is clear that it is very desirable to base performance related pay for executives rigorously on outcomes rather than on efforts. This practice maximises accountability, objectivity, transparency and alignment with shareholders interests. The design of a remuneration scheme is much stronger if the performance can be assessed entirely on outcomes. If subjective intervention might be required to avoid an unfair or demotivating outcome then this suggests that the design of the scheme needs to be improved.

Objectively measured performance verses subjectively measured performance

As we saw in the previous section, a badly designed remuneration scheme can easily lead to a situation where intervention is required to avoid a remuneration outcome that is clearly inappropriate, unjust or demotivating. Obviously the objectivity and transparency of remuneration schemes can be increased by avoiding or minimising such situations.

It is always desirable to minimise subjectivity in the determination of executive pay. Subjectivity seriously weakens the incentive effect of variable pay. How can an executive modify behaviour to improve performance, if it is not clear how the performance will be determined? Subjective assessments weaken trust because they are always open to the accusation that they are unfair or discriminatory. It is impossible to keep subjective assessments consistent. Nobody can say if a subjective assessment is right or wrong. Even where reasons are stated, there is no knowing what the real reasons behind a subjective assessment are. Consequently it is possible that a subjective performance assessment is being used to pursue the personal agenda of the person making the determination, rather than to deliver constructive feedback on how performance can be improved in future years.

People sometime argue that subjectivity is required because variable pay is a complicated business and it is possible that any objectively defined scheme will result in unforeseen and undesirable outcomes. This is really an argument for taking great care with variable remuneration schemes and restricting their use to a very small number of well designed and well understood schemes. The argument does not justify subjectivity because subjectivity will seriously undermine the incentive effect of variable pay.

Forward looking or backward looking measures of performance

One of the justifications often given for variable pay is that it recognises and rewards the achievement and contribution of individuals. Recognition is a very important factor in motivation. Recognition has a motivational effect both on the person recognised, and on the people invited to do the recognising. The need for recognition is strongest immediately after some major accomplishment, or when an executive is retiring or leaving the company.

If a company has well organised incentive schemes then the payouts under those incentives schemes should provide sufficient recognition of achievements made against targets. In this case the payments made are associated with the outcome of incentive schemes that were forward looking.

The problems arise when a company attempts to makes backwards looking recognition payments for past performance where the payments are not being made under a pre-agreed incentive plan. In this case the company is retrospectively changing its contract with the employee and this raises many questions. Was the original contract wrong? Were the performance targets wrong? Given that it is all in the past why should it be changed now? Are other historic agreements going to be revised? Companies do not make extra payments to external suppliers who outperform their supply contract. Why should they make extra payments to directors or employees? The suspicion is that it a relationship, rather than performance, that is being recognised and valued. At best the payments appear arbitrary and subjective.

Backwards looking recognition payment do have a motivational effect. However a big part of that motivational effect arises from the expectation of future recognition payments. But what kind of performance will lead to these payments in the future? People should not have to guess about this. It should not be a secret! How can people deliver the required performance if they don't know what it is? Future recognition payments need to be made as part of a forward looking performance incentive scheme. If backward looking payments continue to be made then this will undermine the forward looking schemes that are in place.

Of the all payments made to executives, the ones that cause most controversy are the ones made to executives as they leave the company. Sometimes there is a suspicion that the payments are "rewards for failure", but even when the executive has clearly been successful the payments are problematic. The payments are clearly not being made to recruit, motivate or retain the executive who is leaving and this makes them very hard to justify. Often they have more to do with compensation for loss of office, than to do with recognition of performance. Again the suspicion arises that it is the relationship, rather than the performance that is being recognised and valued.

Companies should always be able to avoid making backward looking recognition payments by ensuring that their forward looking motivational reward schemes are properly aligned with behaviours that they will want to recognise after the event. This is what has happened in sport. The high prize money paid to winners of top competitions in golf and tennis is all about providing an incentive so that the top players will want to compete. Recognition comes when the winner receives the trophy and holds it up high. This is what is celebrated all around the world. The prize money has to be paid, but it works as an incentive payment, not a recognition payment.

Also most companies can make much better use of formal and informal forms of recognition that involve no financial reward. Recognition is really about public proclamation of people and their achievements. There is no need for it to have a financial aspect. There is very little financial reward associated with knighthoods. Some people try to turn public praise and recognition into financial reward by interpreting thanks as the acknowledgement of a debt. This is an unfortunate attitude that makes true and effective recognition much more difficult. However company culture can overcome this problem by openly promoting formal and informal non-financial recognition.

Summary

At the start of this chapter we looked at the benefits and problems associated with variable pay. We noted that, in the case of executives, the benefits of variable pay are concerned with motivation and the provision of incentives. The incentives are all important in driving behaviour. We noted that most of the problems of variable pay arise when the incentives that the pay generates are not properly aligned with what shareholders would want. It is therefore very clear that when designing variable pay schemes the benefits of the scheme can be maximised and the problems minimised by ensuring the greatest possible alignment between the incentives generated within the scheme and the shareholder requirements. The greater the alignment between shareholder interests and executive incentives the more benefits the scheme will produce and the few problems it will create.

The need to maximise alignment has some immediate consequences for the performance measures that are used in variable pay schemes for executives. At the executive level we need to focus on shareholder measures of investment performance rather than on any measures of management performance. We need to focus on long term performance rather than short term performance. We need to focus on measured performance outcomes rather than on how hard the executives have tried. We need to use variable pay schemes where the payments can be safely based on objectively measured outcomes and the need for subjective adjustments is avoided. We need to use forward looking measures of performance not backward looking measures. All of these considerations are important if we are serious about maximising the alignment between the incentives generated by variable pay and shareholder interest.

3

Two key questions on incentive alignment

In the previous chapter we looked at some of the immediate questions that arise when we start to link performance to executive pay. We saw that to secure the benefits of variable pay, and to avoid the pitfalls, it is important to create the greatest possible alignment between the incentives provided by variable pay and shareholder interests. In this chapter we look more carefully at two particular questions about performance measurement that arise when devising variable pay. The first question concerns the respective weightings that should be given to corporate performance and individual performance. The second question is the respective weightings that should be given to absolute measures of performance and to relative measures of performance.

Corporate performance versus individual performance

Should the variable pay of an executive be linked to corporate performance, or to the personal performance of the individual? Remuneration reports suggest that companies seek an appropriate balance between rewarding corporate and individual performance. But what is an appropriate balance? How can it be determined? To help us examine the appropriate balance let us first consider the respective advantages of rewarding corporate and individual performance.

The first big advantage of rewarding corporate performance is that corporate performance is the ultimate goal. An outstanding individual performance is valuable only to the extent that it contributes to better corporate performance. Alignment of executive rewards with shareholder interests are maximised when the executive rewards are based only on the performance of the company as a whole.

The second big advantage of rewarding corporate performance is that it is more objective. The TSR growth of a company over a particular period can be measured and compared with that of another company. Annual bonus schemes attempt to measure and compare individual performance, but the measurement is necessarily affected by perceptions, presentational issues and "spin". Of course share prices can also be manipulated to increase TSR performance, but an artificially high share price will reduce subsequent TSR performance, so the incentive to manipulate is weak (unless the scheme is badly designed!).

The third big advantage of rewarding corporate performance is that it maximises accountability for corporate performance. An executive should not be allowed to say, "The disappointing performance of the company was caused by factors outside the scope of my responsibility. My own personal performance was outstanding and I deserve a big bonus."

A fourth big advantage of rewarding corporate performance is that it gives incentives for the executive team to work together more effectively as a team. It encourages executives to support each other and to constructively correct each other. It allows a diversity of behavioural styles to contribute in different ways and to be rewarded equally. A single, shared objective maximises alignment, understanding and trust. An incentive to address and resolve conflict is created.

So what are the advantages of rewarding individual performances?

The most obvious advantage of rewarding individual performance is that the incentive effect is more direct. An improvement in an executive's performance will lead directly to greater pay, with no dilution effect arising from the performance of other members of the executive team. This argument might be valid for a factory worker who has minimal interaction with his colleagues so can be paid according to the number of widgets he produces. However the argument cannot be applied to an executive in a large organisation, because interaction with the rest of the executive team is central to the executive's role.

In an effective executive team the different team members exercise enormous influence over one another. It is through this process of mutual influencing that the company develops its top level objectives and values. The process necessarily has a tempering effect on some individual aspirations, but this should not be thought of as blunting or diluting, but rather as guaranteeing alignment and giving corporate validity to those aspirations. When an executive team is working well together it becomes extremely difficult to separate the performance of an individual from the performance of the team as a whole. The chief executive cannot claim to have performed better than the company he or she manages any more than a football manager can claim to have performed better than his team. To a very large extent the same is true of the finance director and any other executive whose responsibilities stretch across the whole organisation.

Even executives who have areas of responsibility that are specific to themselves are made significantly less accountable on corporate matters if they have a strong individual incentive. A performance failure in one part of an organisation is often caused by excessive pressure from another part. Excessive selling can cause problems in debt collection. Excessive cost control can damage service to customers. The different performance targets used by the company must be set so as to optimise the performance of the company as a whole. The incentive to get this balance right can be created by only rewarding the ultimate goal; the creation of long term value for shareholders.

An often quoted advantage of rewarding individual performance is that managers are not rewarded for free-riding off the performance of their colleagues. This appears fair and just from the point of view of the managers, but from a shareholders perspective this is actually a big disadvantage if it is applied to the executive team. The true cost to a company of having a poorly performing executive far exceeds the cost of the executive's variable pay. The real cost is in the poor performance of the functions for which the executive is responsible. This is a big problem and other members of the executive team need to take action quickly to improve the individual's performance, or if necessary to replace the individual with someone who will perform. The incentives to make this happen are far stronger when the other executives are rewarded only for corporate performance.

After a football match it is very desirable to analyse the performance of individual players to find ways of improving the performance of the team as a whole. This process requires an honest assessment of strengths and weaknesses. It depends on a certain humility and on trust in the manager and other members of the team. The process would be completely undermined if the outcome was an individual bonus proportionate to individual performance. The process can only work if the focus is on the ultimate goal of team performance.

Some advocates of individual rewards say that they make executives focus on their own specific objectives, avoiding the waste associated with management by committee. But no individual reward is required to encourage executives to work in a focused way. A system of PPCs has this affect, even if the rewards are linked to corporate performance rather than to individual performance. In fact the PPC system works better when the rewards are linked to corporate performance, because the correct incentives are in place to ensure prompt and optimum resolution where personal objectives conflict.

A proponent of individual rewards might argue that an outstanding corporate performance is driven by outstanding individual performances in the executive team. It is therefore necessary to create an environment that recognises and rewards these outstanding individual performances. It is certainly true that the company wants outstanding individuals in its executive team, but this does not mean that they need to have individual financial reward. Public recognition and praise is far more forthcoming from other executive team members if they are working to shared targets rather than competing against each other. The executive's evaluation of his or her financial reward is based on the total remuneration, not on whether it is received for individual or corporate performance. If there is an executive who gives a higher valuation to individual rewards rather than corporate rewards then this strongly suggests that he or she prioritises personal goals over corporate goals, a trait that is unacceptably dangerous for an executive team member.

A more genuine advantage of using variable pay to reward individual performance is that it becomes possible to recognise an outstanding individual performance without increasing the individual's basic pay. This is might be true, but is it really necessary to use variable pay to reward the individual performance? The individual will get financially rewarded through schemes that reward corporate performance, and through enhanced reputation leading to higher basic pay in the longer term. Given the problems that individual variable pay cause to team working it is likely that non financial recognition (public praise, increased responsibility) will be more effective.

Having examined the respective benefits of rewarding corporate and individual performance it is very clear that there are many compelling reasons for linking executive variable pay to corporate performance, and none for linking it to individual performance. It is therefore clear that for executives the appropriate balance of variable reward is 100% corporate, 0% individual.

This same balance is likely to work best for all senior managers whose work has an impact across large parts of the organisation. The case for individually assessed variable pay become more persuasive lower down the organisation where performance is more about the execution of specific tasks and interaction with other parts of the organisation is less of a consideration.

Individual performance culture

The conclusion that variable pay for executive team members should be linked 100% to corporate performance and 0% to individual performance contrasts dramatically with current practice in FTSE 350 companies. People might complain that the conclusion is "unconventional", "unbalanced" or "inappropriate" but it is unlikely that they will be able to produce any hard arguments to support individually assessed variable pay for executives.

Yet the practice of offering rewards for individual performance is so widespread that it is necessary to consider how it might have come about. The presentational issues discussed in chapter 11 are certainly a big factor. There is also a natural, if undesirable, tendency for organisations to drift into individualism. Dominant and ambitious individuals are good at securing important jobs in organisations. Sometimes they favour an individualistic organisational culture because it creates an environment in which their own behaviour style is successful.

Some companies present a strong individual performance culture as an asset to be invested in and developed. But individualism is in fact a terrible liability. Companies with a strong individualistic culture encourage individuals to compete with each other in promoting their ideas and securing the best opportunities. The company will claim that the internal competition process ensures that the organisation selects the best ideas and the best people to move forward with. In practice however it is the strongest, most competitive ideas and people who get selected and these are almost certainly not the ones which add the most value. In particular this competitive process creates a very strong incentive on individuals to promote and drive forward their own programmes even where they have a damaging effect on other parts of the company. For protection individuals form into power blocks behind powerful leaders. Team work and diversity are lost. Shareholder value becomes a card to be played in a game that is really about personal power and rewards.

Companies with this kind of culture continue to succeed to the extent that commitment to shareholder value remains their highest value. The trouble is that if the company continues to promote and reward individual power then "It's alright, if you can get away with it!" starts to emerge as a significant corporate value. This gives licence to vested interest groups to maximise their own interest at the expense of the shareholder. It also creates an environment ripe for fraud. Enron was particularly famous for its individual performance culture.

I once worked for an organisation with a highly individualistic performance culture. Managers competed with one another to secure the best variable pay and the best opportunities for career advancement. The managers were totally focused on their own performance targets, and had no regard for the impact of their behaviour on the organisation as a whole. They did not like to help other managers, because this might help the perceived performance ranking of the other manager at the expense of the helping manager. Managers would only accept performance targets that they could deliver from entirely within their area of control because dependency on an outside department represented an unacceptable risk. Dependencies between departments were surrounded by so many accusations and counter accusations that it was impossible to establish what responsibility lay where. Of course the delivery of any meaningful business objective did require help from many different departments, so an allocation of responsibilities was agreed at a high level. After that departments would not discuss detailed interfaces or requirements between themselves, but rather would rush to finish their own part of the work because the onus would then be on the other departments to fit in with what they had delivered. Departments would deliver what they could rather than what was required. Having direct management control of resources was a vital; the manager who controlled the resources had most control over the task and was most likely to be able to present his own part of the project as successful and to be able to blame other managers for the problems. It was easily the least effective organisation I have ever worked for. Even the simplest of management assignments took weeks to deliver. We also worked longer hours and suffered more stress than I have ever encountered anywhere else.

Probably we can all recognise elements of the individualistic culture in our own organisations. All organisations have to determine basic pay for individuals and have to select managers for promotion, so they must all provide opportunities for individuals to put themselves forward and compete with each other. Indeed well managed internal competition is a very good thing, but critically it must focus people on achieving corporate goals, not individual goals.

There are several ways that companies can protect against individualism. One way is to make sure that the high level corporate goals are very clear and well understood throughout the organisation. For a FTSE 350 company the corporate gaol is likely to be the creation of long term value for shareholders, but this needs to be very clearly stated, and witnessed to by the actions of the executive team.

A second protection is to ensure that all variable pay is heavily weighted towards group, or company wide performance objectives. The wider the scope of influence of a manger, the more important this principle is. The variable pay for members of the executive team should be entirely focused on corporate performance with no individual element. This focus makes a clear statement that it is the corporate goals that matter, and individual performance is only as valuable as its contribution to the attainment of corporate goals.

A third way that companies can protect themselves against individualism is by formally training managers in team working skills. Managers usually seriously underestimate how much they have to learn about team working. Training helps managers to appreciate and use effectively the different personal attributes of different people. It is particularly helpful for dominant and ambitious individuals, who struggle to find the patience necessary to be good team players. It is critically important that the organisation gets these people properly embedded into a team working culture because they are the people who provide the focus and drive that the organisation needs to achieve results.

A fourth protection against individualism is to ensure that feedback from all the manager's "stakeholders" is taken into account when the performance of a manager is being assessed. Too often feedback is only sought from the manager's immediate superiors. The manager's stakeholders include his or her direct reports, peers, and people who provide services to the manager, or receive services from the manager. So called 360 degree surveys of this kind have to be conducted with due care for confidentiality, and without the manager specifying the stakeholder group. The survey feedback can be very useful to the manager, but will also identify areas where the manager has prioritised personal objectives above company objectives.

A fifth protection against individualism is to exercise restraint on executive pay. If the chief executive's pay is perceived as low or firmly linked to shareholder value then this gives out the message that, "Like everything in this company, my personal pay is designed to maximise shareholder value." If the chief executives pay is high then this gives out the message, "I am here to maximise my own personal rewards," which is an invitation to individualism.

Individualism is currently a big problem in the UK and in UK companies in particular. By focusing rewards on corporate objectives we can give our organisations stronger corporate culture and facilitate better team working. This will boost productivity and will make for much better working environments. In particular it will reduce work related stress, which, partly because of individualism, has become a major problem for UK plc.

Absolute performance and relative performance

Some measures of performance are relative. For example, in the design of a Long Term Incentive Plan (LTIP) it is very typical to compare the performance of the company with the performance of a large group of other comparable companies. A ranking of the companies is established, so, for example a company that came out third best out of 28 has clearly performed well, whereas a company that was measured as 26th out of 28 has performed badly. Of course the ranking position tells us nothing about how well a company actually did; if the economic climate is very bad it may be that even the highest ranking company has lost money. The ranking position simply tells us how well the company did relative to other companies that it can be compared to.

Other measures of performance are absolute. That is to say they measure performance against targets that are not affected by the performance of other companies. For example a typical performance condition in a share option scheme might require the company's Earnings Per Share (EPS) to grow by five percent per annum more than inflation for three years. So if, after three years, EPS has grown by 24% and inflation has been 2% per annum then the share options would "vest". That is to say the executives who received the options on a conditional basis would now receive the unconditional right to exercise those options. An absolute performance measure tells us nothing about conditions in the wider economy, or the performance of other companies. It might be that our company achieved 5% EPS growth, but the sector was so buoyant that most companies operating in that sector achieved EPS growth of 10% or more.

The two examples above concern company performance. Absolute and relative performance measures can also be used in the assessment of personal performance. In the early 1990s Andersen Consulting used to use measures of relative performance very aggressively in respect of more junior staff. A composite performance score was determined for all such employees. All employees on the same grade were then ranked in order of score. The top performers were given more money and promoted. The bottom performers were asked to leave. In contrast an assessment of individual performance against a PPC is usually intended to be an absolute measure of performance; the extent to which personal targets have been achieved is not affected by the performance of other people.

Clearly, when assessing personal performance, relative measures can create an undesirable incentive for employees to compete with one another in a value destroying way. The Andersen scheme skilfully addressed this by ensuring that individuals were also assessed by their peers, and the peer assessment was reflected in the final composite performance score. In the first half of this chapter we have seen why assessments of individual performance, although important to improving performance in an executive team, are a very bad basis for executive pay. It therefore seems unnecessary to consider the contrasting benefits of absolute and relative performance measures at the personal level any further. Instead let us focus on the absolute and relative measures of corporate performance.

Absolute company performance versus relative company performance

Should shareholders use relative or absolute measures of performance when they assess the performance of an executive team for remuneration purposes? Should they use a balance of the two, and if so what is the right balance? To address these questions let us first consider some advantages and disadvantages of the two different types of measures.

The big advantage of absolute performance measures is that they are better aligned with what shareholders actually want. Most shares are held by shareholders who own shares in a large number of companies, often through pension funds or unit trusts. If a shareholder owns a wide portfolio of shares then what matters to the shareholder is whether the market as a whole goes up or down. The performance of one share relative to another is far less important; some will always do better than others. It is absolute growth that matters.

For example, if a pension scheme owns shares in all UK retailers then its value increases if the sector as a whole grows. It therefore wants executive teams to make this happen by offering more products, providing better customer access to products, being more cost effective and by attracting foreign customers. It accepts that the companies it invests in compete with one another, and this is necessary to ensure that they remain efficient. However it is not in the pension scheme's interests for them to be overly aggressive in seeking to take market share from each other. If however the executive teams are rewarded on a relative performance basis then the incentive is not to grow the sector, but rather to outperform the other companies. In this respect aggressive campaigns to increase market share are a particularly good idea because they not only benefit the one company but they also have a negative impact on the other companies. Clearly there is an incentive alignment problem here.

For a second example, if a pension scheme owns shares in all North Sea oil producers then it wants them to co-operate effectively to maximise the economic value of the oil remaining in the North Sea. It does not want them blocking each others' development proposals, which is the incentive provided by a relative performance measure.

For a third example, if the pension scheme owns shares in all electricity companies then, when they renegotiate arrangements for trading in wholesale electricity, it wants them to come up with arrangements that maximise economic efficiency across the electricity sector as a whole. It does not want individual companies wasting a lot of time by seeking arrangements that optimise the value of their particular assets compared to other companies'. In fact the pension scheme almost certainly owns more shares in the wider UK economy than in the electricity sector, so it is not in its interests to see electricity over priced, or the electricity sector over valued.

For a fourth example, if the pension scheme owns shares in all fast food providers it is going to be extremely concerned about perceived links between fast food and obesity. It would fear a large loss of value in the sector and it would want the companies concerned to act very responsibly, with a view to retaining as much value as can legitimately be retained. It would for example want them to sponsor objective research to separate fact from fiction. It would want them to properly address legitimate concerns, to formulate industry wide codes of practise, and to focus advertising on improving perceptions and understanding about the industry rather than on maximising sales. However an executive team that is rewarded for relative performance has very little incentive to address industry wide concerns. The incentive is rather to compete with the competition, even if this destroys long term value.

There is also a legitimate concern that relative performance measures lead to copy cat behaviours and reduces diversity which is important to the flexibility and responsiveness of the economy. For example, suppose I am chief executive of a company that sells mortgages. I always limit mortgages to 3.5 times the income of a mortgage applicant, but suddenly I start to lose market share to companies who will lend up to six times income. I might confidently say that such business is high risk because it could fall apart if interests rates rise, but the fact that competitors appear to be doing this successfully will put me under a great deal of competitive pressure. That pressure is intensified very significantly if my remuneration is linked to my performance relative to the competitors. I start to think, "Even if six times income is too risky, I need to go with the industry trend here because I get paid for competing effectively, not for being proved right."

All these factors suggest that it is absolute performance that matters to shareholders. However there is a big problem with using only absolute measures of performance in determining executive pay. High executive salaries are often justified as being required to secure the best executives, but absolute measures of performance provide only a very limited indication of how well the executives of a company are performing. Absolute growth usually tells us much more about trading conditions in the economy in general than about the skills and efforts of executives.

The big advantage of relative performance is that it is not unduly influenced by factors that are beyond the control of the executives. Increasing EPS by 5% per annum might be very easy when the economy is booming, and might be completely impossible if it is weak. It might be easy if the total market size is increasing, but quite impossible if it is shrinking. It might be easy if the oil price is low, but much harder if the oil price is high. It might be easy if sterling is low, but difficult when sterling is high. Very often it is these external factors that have the biggest influence over a business's level of success. Focusing reward on absolute performance therefore risks paying out rewards based more on the external business environment than on the performance of the executive team. By definition, companies that are comparable enjoy broadly the same benefits and experience the same problems in the external environment. Therefore relative performance is usually a much better measure of the effectiveness of the executive team.

The problem with rewarding managers based on their relative performance is that it provides no incentives to try and influence the external environment, even though it is the external environment that has the biggest impact on a company's level of returns. Given that the external environment is so important we should expect executive teams to spend a lot of time trying to influence it. Asking them to influence the rate of economic growth or exchange rates may be rather a long shot! However it is clearly very important, especially for the bigger companies, to expect executive teams to influence matters of direct relevance to their own sector both through trade associations and directly. The legal regime governing a sector, taxation, regulation and codes of practise can almost always be improved to the economic benefit of the whole sector, and even to the benefit of the whole economy. Clearly it is very important that executive teams have the incentive to do this. Relative performance measures do not provide this incentive.

So we have a real problem here. Absolute performance measures tend to reward external factors more than they reward the performance of the executive team. Relative performance measures reward the performance of the executive team, but remove incentives to improve the business environment and create incentives to compete in way that destroys value. Clearly an executive team needs to provide evidence of both absolute and relative performance achievements in order to merit high levels of reward. Payments under incentive schemes need to be conditional on both absolute and relative performance achievements.

This gets us back to the question of balance. How can we know that we have got the right balance of absolute and relative performance measurement when designing a executive incentive scheme?

The main consideration here is how the company board expresses its aspirations for financial performance. Are the aspirations relative or absolute? Does the company aim to be a consistent above median performer, or does it aim to provide investors with a certain rate of return, perhaps adjusted for inflation and the rate of economic growth? If companies made clearer statements about their target financial performance it would be easier for investors to know what they were investing in and for managers to set strategies to achieve the targets. It would also provide clearer performance targets for executive pay. Companies usually shy away from making such clear statements, because of a concern that the statements might start to look inappropriate. This suggests that they are more concerned about relative performance than absolute performance.

In the current environment the levels of executive pay are justified by statements such as, "We need to pay the most to get the best executives" or "top class performance merits top class pay" or "Our executive pay is in line with industry standards established by benchmarking". All of these statements are concerned with the relative position of pay and performance in other companies. In this context it is essential that relative performance measures are used to determine the extent to which the executive team really are "the best executives", "top class performers" and "in line with industry standards", because the pay cannot be justified to the extent that this is not the case. While levels of pay and performance expectations are mainly determined by comparisons with other companies, we have no choice but to accept that relative performance measures are more important than absolute measures in the determination of variable pay.

Personally, I would welcome an environment in which the level of executive pay was determined less by comparison with other companies, and more by considering the requirements of the company in question. Considerations should include the target rate of return to the shareholder, the cost of executive pay to the company, the ratio of highest to average salary in the company and the overall health of the business. If executive pay were to move in this direction then absolute measures of performance would become far more important and relative measures would become less important. This would be a very good thing because there would be much better alignment between the incentives arising from executive pay and shareholder interests. It would also allow for much greater diversity between companies, and this would be a very good for the health of the economy in the longer term.

Summary

In this chapter we have looked at two particular questions about incentive alignment in variable pay schemes for company executives.

On the question of whether variable pay schemes should reward individual performance or corporate performance it is very clear that incentive alignment is far higher if only corporate performance is rewarded. This is particularly important for the most senior executives with company wide responsibilities.

The rather more difficult question is whether variable pay schemes should reward executives for the rate of return achieved by the company in its own right, or for the rate of return achieved relative to other comparable companies. It is very clear that incentive alignment with shareholders is better if rewards are based on the performance of the company itself, with no reference to the performance of other companies. However, current practise in FTSE 350 companies is to determine the overall level of executive pay by comparison with executive pay in other companies. Comparison of performance with other companies is therefore essential because without it the levels of executive pay have no justification. Therefore, while executive pay continues to be set by comparison with other companies, executives must demonstrate performance that is successful in both relative and absolute terms in order to secure high rewards.

4

Typical reward packages

In the last two chapters we have looked at some important considerations about linking performance to executive pay. Now let us look at the way that executives are actually paid in the UK, and consider the strengths and weaknesses of current practice.

Let us base our analysis on the reward package of Joe Figment, chief executive of the imaginary company Typico plc. Typico is one of the bigger companies in the FTSE 100. It has a sophisticated business model with significant international exposure. Joe Figments 2005 reward package is set out below, separated into its fixed and variable components.

Joe Figment's 2005 Reward Package

Element	Estimated Average Annual Value	
Basic Salary	£ 750,000	Fixed
Annual Bonus	£ 525,000	Variable between 0 and 100% of base salary
Option Scheme	£ 375,000	Variable from zero upwards. Hard to value.
LTIP	£ 375,000	Variable from zero upwards
Pension	£ 425,000	Fixed
Other benefits	£ 50,000	Fixed
Total:	£2,500,000	£1,225,000 is fixed and £1,275,000 variable

LTIP stands for Long Term Incentive Plan (as described in chapter 6).

Pension is the increase in the transfer value of Joe's pension, net of his contributions.

Other benefits include a car, private health insurance and life assurance.

The fixed components of Joe Figment's pay are received independent of performance. The variable parts are linked to performance and could in fact be worth anything between zero and about £3 million per annum.

Before analysing Joe Figment's reward package in detail let us first consider some important background information about the way that executive pay is set at large public limited companies in the UK, and at Typico in particular.

Remuneration committees

In the UK the remuneration packages of executive directors and other members of the senior management are determined by a subcommittee of the company board known as the remuneration committee. Remuneration committees became common after a recommendation in the 1992 Cadbury Report[1], and most FTSE 350 companies now have a remuneration committee. Only independent non-executive directors are appointed to the remuneration committee. This ensures that the executive directors have no direct influence over the setting of their own pay.

Regulation and compliance

Remuneration committees never cease to be amazed at the rapid growth in regulation and guidance in the field of executive pay. Before 1992 there was very little external information to take into account, but nowadays new guidance seems to appear all the time. Remuneration committees that are serious about implementing best practice have to work hard to keep up with the latest regulations and guidance.

First of all there is the Combined Code on Corporate Governance[2], published by the Financial Reporting Council. This sets out best practice in the field of corporate governance and can be used by a company chairman as a handbook on how the company board should operate. The Combined Code is derived from two earlier codes of practice; the

Cadbury code[3] about the financial aspects of corporate governance (1992) and the Greenbury code[4] about directors' remuneration (1995). The two codes were combined by the Hampel Committee[5] in 1998. In 2003 the Combined Code was modified to take account of the Higgs recommendations on non-executive directors and the Smith recommendations on audit committees.

Companies whose shares are traded on the London Stock Exchange must also abide by the Financial Services Authority's (FSA) Listing Rules. The Listing Rules require companies to explain in their annual report how they have implemented the Combined Code. At the same time, companies that have not complied with some provision of the Combined Code must explain their reasons for not doing so.

The Directors' Remuneration Report Regulations 2002 require directors to prepare an annual Directors' Remuneration Report setting out the company's policy on directors' remuneration and supplying details of all directors' remuneration. Shareholders must vote on whether or not to accept the report. There is no direct consequence if the company loses the vote, although the loss of face is considerable. These regulations have superseded disclosure requirements on directors' pay in the Listing Rules.

Many shareholder organisations monitor executive pay and provide guidance to companies on what they consider to be acceptable and unacceptable. Probably the most important guidance is provided by the Association of British Insurers (ABI), which publishes Principles and Guidelines on Executive Remuneration[6] and keeps these up to date. This guidance is detailed and gives companies a good indication of what institutional shareholders are likely to support or object to.

It is a huge task for a remuneration committee to ensure that their policies are in conformance with all the latest regulations and guidance. For example, one of the requirements of the Combined Code is that a company should consider its position on director's pay, relative to other companies. To comply with this requirement it is usually necessary to undertake some form of benchmarking project. This in itself is a significant task that usually has to be outsourced. Another major concern for remuneration committees is the external presentation of the remuneration policy. Remuneration is a sensitive issue and inadequate presentation can result in huge problems at annual general meetings and through the annual shareholder vote on the remuneration report.

All these pressing considerations have left remuneration committees with very little time or scope to think about optimising remuneration for their own company. Finding the most effective ways of paying executives has been very low down the agenda. A big gap has appeared between standard industry practice and practices that are likely to be most effective.

Valuation of Variable Pay

According to the table showing Joe Figment's reward package, 51% of Joe Figment's remuneration is variable. That is to say it is linked to performance and could be worth a great deal more or less depending on performance. In this respect his reward package reflects the Combined Code requirement that "A significant proportion of executive directors' remuneration should be structured so as to link rewards to corporate and individual performance."[7]

In real life however it is extremely difficult to determine the estimated annual average value of the different elements of variable pay. Even where all the details of the remuneration schemes are set out in the remuneration reports the valuation is difficult. One problem is that the expected value of a long term incentive scheme changes year by year, and it is not obvious how the total value should be attributed to the different years covered by the scheme. Another problem is that share options are intrinsically difficult to value. With all variable pay it is difficult to know how likely the performance criteria are to be met, or to what extent they will be met. Some companies set demanding performance criteria, others set targets which are easily achievable, but it is not easy to determine which is which.

The difficulty of valuing variable pay presents real problems. Neither executive nor shareholder really knows how much is being paid. The shareholder cannot tell whether the pay represents value for money. The executive cannot tell if the rewards are just. Neither can make meaningful comparisons with other companies or external benchmarks. This is bad for both parties. Commercial contracts, especially engineering contracts, frequently include performance related payments or penalties. Such terms are negotiated with great care such that both parties fully understand their commercial position under all possible performance outcomes. Why is executive pay not like this? Lack of clarity about the value of what is being paid can only mean that there is a large range of values that are acceptable to both executive and shareholder. This suggests that the market for executive talent is actually very uncompetitive, contrary to what we read in remuneration reports. Shareholders are certainly paying far more than they need to.

In its guidelines for share incentive schemes the ABI notes that, "The concept of expected value (EV) should be central to the assessment of share incentive schemes. Essentially, EV will be the present value of the sum of all the various possible outcomes at vesting or exercise of awards This will reflect the probabilities of achieving these outcomes and also the future value explicit in these outcomes."[8] Despite this important advice from a very influential body, few remuneration reports even discuss expected value. Even if they did, it would be very difficult to verify whether any values quoted were realistic. Appendix 2 suggests a layout for reporting an executive's total remuneration over a year such that total amount paid can be identified, and the accuracy of the expected value estimates monitored.

So, why is executive pay structured in a way that makes it so hard to value? One of the main reasons is to do with presentation, and this is discussed in chapter 11.

Complexity

One of the reasons that variable pay is so difficult to value is that the structures for variable remuneration are far more complicated than they need to be. A certain amount of complexity is required to ensure proper alignment of interests between shareholders and executives, but most executive reward packages, like Joe Figment's, are far more complicated than they need to be.

For a start, why do we need so many different categories of variable pay? Joe Figment's package is actually far more straight forward than many because it has only three different variable elements. It is very common for there to be further variable elements arising from deferred bonus, matching share schemes or further long term incentives. For the shareholder, performance is about long term growth in shareholder value. Surely we should have a single performance payment based on long term TSR growth? Anything more is an unnecessary complication.

Remuneration reports sometimes argue that different forms of performance related pay are required to properly reward different forms of performance. But why do we need to reward so many different forms of performance? If we look at the benefits of variable pay set out in chapter 2 it is clear that the benefits depend critically on having a performance measure that is properly aligned with shareholders interests. In chapter 3 we saw that it is important to have a common target for all member of the executive team. Long term TSR growth is the performance measure that properly aligns with shareholder interests. This means we can significantly increase our confidence that we are securing the benefits of performance related pay if we focus performance measurement for executive pay on this one measure.

Remuneration reports also talk about finding the correct balance between rewarding short term and long term performance, individual and team performance, financial and operating performance. But how does anyone determine what the right balance is? Surely the right balance is the balance that will lead to the highest possible growth in long term TSR? Determination of this balance is a job for the executive team. They should be setting targets and priorities to optimise TSR growth. To make sure that they do this optimally they should have no financial incentive associated with any measure other than TSR growth. They should keep the targets under review and decide when they should be changed. Only the executive team has the detailed understanding of the business and the business strategy necessary to do this. The independent non-executive directors should not attempt this; they would be managing the company if they did. Instead the remuneration committee should focus the executive team on the final goal; long term growth in TSR. They should not cloud executive judgements by making payments related to other performance measures.

Incentives

Another problem with complex variable pay is that it creates complex incentives. Under the annual bonus scheme Joe Figment has incentives to increase profit and deliver his personal objectives. He has incentives to increase earnings so that he is awarded options under the option scheme. He has an incentive to increase the share price, increase share price volatility and to remain with the company to increase the value of his options. He has incentives to increase TSR to secure shares under the LTIP. He has incentives to increase the share price so that the value of his shares increases.

Does Typico's remuneration committee really expect Joe Figment to understand and respond to each individual incentive? Clearly they don't! It is more likely that they think, "We can't know the relative importance of all the different types of performance that we are rewarding. This makes it dangerous to focus reward on any particular incentive. It is much safer to spread the incentives around all the different forms of performance because they are all broadly consistent with growth in shareholder value."

This approach is extremely wasteful. If Joe Figment cannot specifically understand and respond to the incentive, then the single most important benefit of performance related pay is seriously compromised.

The approach is also very haphazard. The remuneration committee can not possibly know that optimal weight is being given to each incentive and it is very likely that some of the incentives are value destroying. For example they might give incentives for increasing profit in a year when the priority should be expenditure on future development.

The approach is also dangerous. In the face of a complete muddle of incentives it is likely that Joe Figment will focus on the one or two incentives that appear to deliver the most personal value and seem easiest to achieve. This means that the balance effect of providing lots of different incentives is in fact lost. In Joe's case the more immediately valuable and readily deliverable incentives relate to short term targets. Joe therefore gives much higher priority to hitting short term targets than to building long term value for shareholders.

The core problem here is too many forms of variable pay. Typico's remuneration committee are acting like a farmer trying to shoot a duck by shooting three shot guns simultaneously. It would be far better to use a single gun and aim properly! A single incentive for long term growth in TSR would be far more effective than the cloud of incentives arising from Joe Figment's current reward package.

Some people might argue that using a single incentive payment based on TSR growth puts all the eggs in one basket and could be risky if the incentive scheme worked badly. This is an important point, and it is certainly true that some very badly designed TSR schemes have been used by FTSE 350 companies. However TSR schemes do not have to be badly designed. Chapters 6, 7 and 8 of this book are all about design problems in TSR based remuneration schemes and how they can be eliminated.

My own interest in executive pay started in the year 2000 when my own reward package was changed. Before 2000 I had a single element of variable pay, based on long term growth in TSR. After 2000 I had a more complicated package structured like Joe Figment's. Most of the incentive effect was lost when I moved to the new scheme. It was so complicated that I never had the time to properly understand the variable pay or work out how I should behave under the incentives. I never really got to grips with it until after I left the company! I suspect that I was paid more under the new scheme, but the arrangements were so complicated that I can't be certain.

Transparency

Transparency is very important for variable pay schemes. Firstly, a person working to an incentive has to understand what that incentive is. If it is not transparent to the person how improvements in performance link through into pay then the incentive to improve the performance is reduced. This seriously undermines the benefit of variable pay.

Secondly transparency is important so that other people can see and understand how the incentive scheme is being operated. This gives confidence that the scheme is being operated correctly for the stated reasons and to achieve the stated objectives. It builds understanding of why the scheme is in place. It also allows different employees to know that they are being treated fairly and objectively when compared to their colleagues.

When transparency breaks down then the incentive effects of variable pay are reduced. It also raises a suspicion that something about the scheme is not being run as it should be. For example, I once benefited from an annual bonus scheme that had rules something like this:

1. At the start of the year each business unit would be set a base case and stretch case profit target.
2. At the start of the year each manager in the business unit would agree a PPC with the executive responsible for the business unit.
3. At the end of the year business unit profit was determined and compared with the base and stretch targets set at the start of the year.
4. A "pot" of money for manager bonuses would be allocated to the business unit according to how well the business unit had performed against its profit target. The size of the pot was determined as a percentage of the total annual salary of all managers in the business unit, in accordance with the following table.

Business unit profit outcome	Pot as % of total annual manager salaries
Less than 95% of base target	zero
95% to 100% of base target	Sliding scale from 0 to 10%
100% of base target	10%
Between base and stretch target	Sliding scale from 10 to 20%
100% or more of stretch target	20%

5. At year end each manager in the business unit would have a performance review with the executive responsible for the business unit to determine personal performance against the PPC.
6. Based on the performance reviews, the executive responsible for the business unit would determine a "personal multiplier"

between 0 and 1.5 for each manager in the business unit, such that the average of all personal multipliers was 1.0.

7. Senior management hold a consistency review to check that the proposed personal multipliers were appropriate.

8. Each manager receives a bonus equivalent to the pot percentage of his or her annual salary, adjusted by the personal multiplier.

So, for example, if the business unit profit came out half way between the base case and stretch case profit targets then the business unit pot percentage would be 15%. If, as a result of the performance review, a manager's personal multiplier was determined to be 1.1 then that manager would receive a bonus equivalent to 16.5% of base salary.

The scheme looks reasonably coherent on paper, but its first year of operation was ruined by lack of transparency. My PPC was agreed early in the year, but I did not find out what the business unit profit targets were until November, by which time even the base case target was manifestly unachievable. I therefore assumed that I would get no bonus. In the end however I did receive a bonus. I was told that the executive responsible for the business unit had successfully argued mitigating circumstances on profit and had secured a bonus pot for the business unit managers. I never leant how big the pot was, or what my personal multiplier was. The bonus payment therefore gave me no feedback about either our business unit performance on profit, or my own personal performance against my PPC. The learning points appeared to be "Make sure your business unit has good excuses on profit" and "make sure you keep in the good books of the person who determines your personal multiplier". Sadly the game of securing a bonus was reduced to after the event presentational skills and the focus on performance was lost.

In year two of the scheme a very similar thing happened. Our business unit missed its base case profit target, but I was still paid a bonus. On this occasion I specifically asked my boss what my bonus should tell me about the business unit performance and my own personal performance. I got an evasive answer.

Typico's remuneration committee always works hard to follow best practise, and Joe Figment's reward package is high on transparency. All important aspects are documented in Typico's annual remuneration report and there are only a few places where transparency breaks down. One of these is the performance criteria for long term incentive schemes. At one time Typico's internal web-based Intranet continually displayed the latest measured position of each scheme. This practise stopped because on one occasion the remuneration committee felt it was important to retrospectively adjust the performance data, and this was difficult to do when different performance data had already been publicised.

A second gap in transparency at Typico concerns the performance targets on PPCs. The profit targets are widely publicised, but all other targets are kept confidential, so as not to reveal Typico's commercial strategy. Obviously the targets are known to the people involved, so this particular lack of transparency does not undermine incentives, although full transparency would increase confidence that the scheme was being administered correctly.

So in general the transparency at Typico is high. In fact the biggest problem with transparency at Typico arises because of the number of variable remuneration schemes and their complexity. Although each scheme is highly transparent, Joe Figment's overall position on executive pay is very complicated and unclear. The table presented in at the start of this chapter is actually misleadingly simple in this respect because it contains misleadingly clear estimates of the average annual value of the variable pay schemes.

Objectivity

We looked at the importance of objectivity in the measurement of performance in chapter 2. However it is equally important to be objective about remuneration policy.

The Directors' Remuneration Report Regulations 2002 require companies to publish remuneration policies in their annual remuneration report. The policies show that many of the most critical decisions about executive's variable pay are made "at the discretion of the remuneration committee". Examples often include level of awards under long term incentive schemes, the possibility of retesting long term incentive schemes, the split of awards between different schemes, changes to performance measures and targets, overall level of bonus available. It is very rare for the policies to make any statements about the basis on which the remuneration committee will make these decisions, or even what information they should take into account. Unfortunately this means that even the best remuneration committee using its discretion in the wisest possible way is going to carry with it most of the problems of subjectivity discussed in chapter 2.

It is probable that remuneration committees feel that they need to reserve many powers to themselves so that they can deal with any unexpected situations that might arise. This is understandable, but it would be much better to concentrate on avoiding the unexpected situations. This probably means having less remuneration schemes, avoiding very detailed and complicated performance targets and basing the schemes on externally available performance data. Remuneration committees are probably wise to reserve to themselves powers of intervention, but they should make it clear that such powers will only be used in the most exceptional circumstances, and it is their intention that remuneration should roll forward from year to year in accordance with the remuneration policy.

The ultimate goal should be remuneration policies and schemes that are so transparent and objective that an external analyst can predict the remuneration of the executive directors for a year, based only on the previous year's remuneration report and performance measurement data that is available in the public domain. This ensures a very high level of transparency and objectivity, which in turn guarantees that the incentives associated with the variable pay are real and have the opportunity to be effective.

Accounting for executive pay

In recent years some of the biggest problems in executive pay have arisen because companies have been able to remunerate executives with shares and share options without recording the expense in the accounts. Companies have found this convenient for presentational reasons, but it has had some lead to some serious anomalies.

One important anomaly has been that share options have become a very popular form of remuneration, for all the wrong reasons. Share options are discussed further in chapter 9, but they are in fact a very bad form of executive remuneration.

The other major anomaly is that executive costs have not been properly represented in company accounts. This makes the accounts misleading, and results in understatement of unit costs for activities undertaken by the company. This in turn can lead to the company undertaking activities that appear more economically viable than they really are.

Fortunately the accounting standards bodies are now catching up. In the UK the Accounting Standard Board (ASB) has implemented a new Financial Reporting Standard FRS20 based on the international standard IFRS2. For financial years starting on or after 1st January 2005 quoted companies must use this standard. This ensures that a fair value estimate of share-based payments appears as an expense in the company accounts, and this has already made options far less popular as a form of remuneration.

Summary

In this chapter we have looked at the reward package that Joe Figment receives from his fictional company Typico. We considered the remuneration committees which set executive pay in listed companies in the UK, and some of the rules, regulations and guidelines that influence their work.

Joe Figment's reward package is in fact much simpler than is typical for the chief executive of a large FTSE 100 company. Even so it is surprisingly complicated with six different components three of which are linked to different forms of performance. We saw that this complexity reduces the effectiveness of the variable pay; it makes it difficult to value and the incentives generated are too complicated to be effective. We considered the transparency and objectivity of variable pay schemes and we saw that these qualities are essential to ensure that everyone, and in particular the recipient of the pay, can see how the pay scheme works and understand what the incentives are. Finally we looked briefly at the issue of accounting for variable pay and noted how important it is to reflect the true cost of executive pay in the company accounts.

Notes

1. Cadbury 1992b: paragraph 3.3 and Notes 9
2. Combined Code 2003
3. Cadbury 1992b
4. Greenbury 1995
5. Hampel 1998 and Combined Code 1998
6. ABI 2005
7. Combined Code 2003: Main Principles B.1
8. ABI 2005: Appendix B, Note 2

5

Annual bonus schemes

In this chapter we examine the annual bonus schemes that are operated in almost all large listed companies in the UK. We do this by considering in detail the scheme offered by Typico.

Typico's annual bonus scheme

The biggest element of Joe Figment's variable pay is his annual bonus. Typico have a well developed annual bonus scheme which is based on the system of PPCs described in chapter 1.

The profit targets in Joe Figment's PPC are derived from the business planning process. Some key operational targets are taken from Typico's balanced score card. Some specific personal objectives are also included. The executive team put together a draft PPC. This goes through a formal review and challenge process with the chairman and non-executive directors. It is finally signed off by the remuneration committee.

Half way through the year Joe has an interim review of progress against contract with the chairman. Any guidance provided by the chairman at this stage is documented. At the end of the year there is a formal review with the chairman and the remuneration committee. At the meeting a final score of between 0 and 100 is assigned to each performance measure based on the performance outcome. If the base case performance target was achieved then the score is 50 and if the stretch target was reached then the score is 100. After each performance measure has been scored, the measures are all assigned a weight reflecting their relative importance. Finally a weighted average score is calculated. For the financial year 2004 this weighted average was determined to be 75, so in March 2005 Joe was paid an annual bonus equivalent to 75% of 2004 salary (75% of £700,000 = £525,000).

At Typico all managers within five reports of Joe Figment take part in the annual bonus scheme. The remuneration committee administer the scheme for the executive team. Line management administer the scheme for managers below the executive level. All managers in the annual bonus scheme have PPCs and a formal annual review of their performance. Lower down the organisation the maximum payments are smaller as a percentage of base salary, but the basic structure of the scheme remains the same.

Typico's annual bonus scheme is as well organised and objective as any in a FTSE 350 company. Despite this the scheme still has significant problems. Most of the problems arise because of misalignment between the short term incentives offered by the scheme and the long term interests of shareholders. The problems are discussed in the next sections.

Annual profit targets as a basis for performance related pay

Shareholders want executive teams to focus on the creation of long term value. They want to see credible long term strategies and specific targets and milestones that can be monitored to show that the business is on course to deliver its strategy. For most businesses the annual profit or earnings figures provide the best indicators of future prospects, and these are often the figures that City analysts attribute most importance to.

However the fact that profit is a critical indicator of business performance does not mean that it is a good measure on which to base performance related pay. In fact the opposite is true; profit is such an important performance indicator that it should not be compromise by linking it to pay. If executives are focused on long term value creation then investors can have confidence in the indications they derive from the profit figure. However, if the executive team's goal is to maximise annual profit then long term focus is lost, and much of the meaning of profit as a business indicator is lost.

For example, there are lots of ways of boosting this year's annual profit figure that are harmful to the longer term business. Executives can cut spending on customer service, reduce expenditure on IT systems, market products in an over aggressive way that risks a customer backlash, devalue the brand, reduce assurance checks on quality or supply chains and so on. Of course there are times when it is completely desirable to cutback on development expenditure or engage in some short term marketing, but the really important point is that proposals must be evaluated against long term shareholder value, not against annual profit.

An interesting example occurred over Christmas 2003 when Coors, the owners of Carling lager, started an advertising campaign in Scotland to promote responsible drinking. This clearly did not help short term profits, but was probably important to the longer term business. The government had been expressing concerns about binge drinking and it was a timely moment to promote responsibility.

If an executive team is rewarded for annual profit rather than long term value then it has incentives to maximise short term returns. Future business prospects are damaged and the profit targets for the following year are reduced to reflect a weaker starting point. The executive team can therefore behave in the same way for a second year, earn all their bonuses and face the third year with profit expectations even more depressed after two years of mismanagement.

Clearly this approach is not sustainable. It will eventually lead to a crash in profits. Probably a new executive team will be recruited, but the old team will have already been very well rewarded for their short term behaviour.

Another particular problem with profit and earnings, when used as a basis for executive pay is that the reporting of profit and earning is substantially controlled by the executive team. Clearly they have to follow the accounting rules and get the accounts through audit, but huge discretion exists when defining provisions and exceptional items. Shareholders want to be confident that the discretion is being used to present a true and fair picture of the company. This confidence is significantly reduced if the executive team have a direct and immediate financial interest in a particular outcome.

Balanced scorecard measures as a basis for performance related pay

A PPC will often include targets based on a balanced scorecard approach to performance management. For example, lets consider the fictional case of Typico's marketing director, Pete Cellum, who was given the target, "Increase number of customers by 5%" in his 2005 PPC.

Pete's variable pay was heavily weighted towards annual bonus and delivery of the customer numbers target was central to his PPC. He was very keen to hit the target especially because Joe Figment had recently emphasised the importance of hitting targets. There were two immediately obvious marketing campaigns to set in motion and Pete got these going early in the year. These were expected to increase customer numbers by 3 to 4%, leaving a performance gap of 1 to 2% to be tackled.

Pete examined two proposals to close the gap. One depended on offering expensive benefits to new customers. The other depended on a system of local agents who would need to be identified, recruited and trained. It was clear that the second proposal would take time to implement and could not start to add significant customer numbers until quarter 4, which would be too late. Pete therefore decided to go with the expensive benefit programme.

When Pete reviewed the customer figures for May 2005 the two traditional campaigns looked set to deliver at least 3% growth, and the expensive campaign at least 2%, so performance was on target. However when Pete saw the July figures it became clear that almost a quarter of the new customers signing up under the expensive benefit programme, were in fact existing customers leaving to rejoin and secure the extra benefits!

A quick fix was made to the expensive benefit programme to prevent former customers from rejoining in this way. This lead to a spate of complaints from customers who had already given up the service, intending to rejoin under the new scheme. By September it was clear that the net benefit of the new scheme would be about $1^1/_2$% increase, and the two traditional schemes would add about $3^1/_4$%. There was still a $^1/_4$% performance gap to be closed.

Pete decided to close the gap by reducing the minimum monthly payments required from new customers joining under the two traditional schemes. This made it easier to recruit customers with a very small service take up, and it also made it easier for customers to pass the credit tests. This measure boosted the number of customers added, although the additional customers were, at best, of marginal value to Typico.

At the end of the year Pete was disappointed to discover that the final net increase in customer numbers was 4.9%. He put together a report for the remuneration committee emphasising the 5.4% customers added and acknowledging the 0.5% of customers lost in the small print. The remuneration committee did not miss this point, although they did take the view that the 5% target had been substantively met and decided to pay the bonus. Joe Figment was very pleased that the target had been met, and mentioned the 5.4% customers added in his briefing to the City.

It is very clear that Pete's undue focus on his annual performance target had a negative effect on Typico. If Pete's sole financial incentive had been the creation of long term shareholder value then his behaviour would have been very different. He would have shown more interest in the local agent scheme. He would have checked that costs of the expensive benefit scheme were justified. He would have taken more care to provide a consistent message to customers. He would have made sure that the customers added actually added value to Typico. His communications about customer numbers would have been more focused on building understanding and less focused on securing his bonus.

Specific personal objectives as a basis for performance related pay

When the Typico PPCs are established for the executive team it is usual to include a small number of specific personal objectives as performance targets. In chapter 1 I gave two examples: "Secure board approval for strategy addressing low cost competition emerging in the Far East" and "Sell underperforming operation X".

At the level of the executive team, it is extremely dangerous to base performance related pay on specific objectives like these. The effect of the link to pay is to increase focus on delivering the objective and to take focus off long term shareholder value. No business can afford to do this.

The problem is more obvious with the objective "Sell underperforming operation X". An executive who is assigned this responsibility should always be able to achieve the objective, if necessary by lowering the asking price. Certainly there will be a base case and stretch case target price to be realised, but these can only be numbers plucked from the air unless a great deal of work on the transaction has already been completed. Also the headline transaction value can almost always be manipulated by changing the scope of the transaction, reducing the debt transferred with the sale or giving stronger warranties and indemnities.

In contrast, an executive who is focused on long term shareholder value will first of all determine in detail what the underperforming operation is actually worth to the company, and what it should be worth to other companies. The reasons, risks and benefits of the proposed disposal will be fully understood and documented. The executives will work on strategies to maximise the value likely to be attained, will take account of value considerations arising from the timing, the liabilities, the credit risk and other factors beyond the headline price. When the sale is finally achieved there will be far higher confidence that the company fully understands the issues around the sale and that the sale achieved is in the long term interests of the company.

This problem is well understood by the ABI who state that "Shareholders are not supportive of transaction bonuses which reward directors and other executives for effecting transactions irrespective of their future financial consequences."[9]

The ABI's statement is true even if the word "transaction" is interpreted so broadly as to include any specific personal objective at the level of the executive team. A specific personal objective set at that level is bound to have significant financial consequences either directly or indirectly. If not, it would not be important enough to be set as an objective.

Consider for example the executive charged with "Secure board approval for strategy addressing low cost competition emerging in the Far East". If the executive incentive is to build long term value then the executive will insist that the board focus on the real and difficult questions posed by the competition; "Should we continue with manufacturing in the UK?", "Where can we add value beyond what is produced in the Far East?". If the executive's incentive is to get the new strategy approved then it is much better to produce a bland strategy that challenges no one and does not really address the problem.

In January 2004 the oil and gas group Royal Dutch/Shell shocked the stock market by announcing that it had overbooked its proved oil and gas reserves by a quarter. There were suggestions that the chief executive, Sir Philip Watts, had secured the top job by over booking reserves and so overstating his success in his previous role. Managers always have incentives to overstate their successes to secure better basic salary and promotion. It was therefore very undesirable for Shell to make the incentive even stronger by paying an annual bonus based on reserves bookings. Shell quickly changed its bonus schemes such that the booking of reserves was no longer a performance criteria for anyone involved in the assurance of reserves. Previously reserves bookings constituted up to 15% of possible bonus for some staff.

In February 2004 J Sainsbury, the supermarket chain announced that it had appointed Sir Ian Prosser as deputy chairman and chairman designate. The move outraged shareholders who were taken by surprise and did not think that Sir Ian was the right person for the job. The criticisms lead Sir Ian to withdraw from the appointment within a few days. But how did such an embarrassing mistake ever come about? It emerged that Sir Peter Davies, the chief executive, had an £800,000 performance payment conditional on certain performance objectives of which just one was outstanding; the appointment of a new deputy chairman. This can only have encouraged Sir Peter to focus on completing the objective rather than doing the right thing for shareholders.

Other specific problems with annual bonus

I have shown how large annual bonus payments cause a shift of management focus away from long term shareholder value towards delivery of specific short term targets. However other problems start to emerge when the annual bonus system becomes too important.

Firstly annual bonus encourages executives to set targets that they know they can achieve rather than targets that are right for the business.

This is a very serious problem. If a company sets itself appropriate targets and then struggles to meet those targets then the impact of this difficulty is limited. In fact there may be no difficulty at all if the targets set were challenging. However if the company is not setting itself the right targets and goals then the whole direction of the company starts to go wrong and significant long term value can be lost.

Secondly there is no control that the direct and indirect costs of achieving a short term target are proportionate to the benefit achieved. Executives are the top people in the organisation and they necessarily have a great deal of power. They have the ability to spend a lot of money or do significant damage to a company's reputation with only minimal reference to the other executives. They very often have the ability and incentive to meet a personal performance target even if the cost to the company is excessive.

Thirdly the need to meet annual performance targets can start to confuse the way that performance is measured and reported. We saw a fictional example of this at Typico, where the company understanding of 5.4% more customers became confused. We have seen a real life example at Shell where the definition of proved reserves became confused. Such distortions in measurement and internal communication make it harder for an organisation to understand its own dynamics. The obvious solution to this problem is to separate responsibility for the reporting of a performance measure from responsibility for management of the performance. However such separation leads to bureaucracy and is seldom feasible or desirable. Defining how an activity is measured and reported is often a critical part of the management of that activity.

Fourthly large annual bonus payments completely ruin the PPC method of managing performance. The public celebration of performance achievements can be far more spontaneous when the achievements are not linked to performance payments. Honest assessment of performance failures becomes impossible when there is money at stake. Aspirations to remove barriers to performance turn into aspirations to ensure that barriers are taken into account when targets are set. Forward looking discussions about continuous improvement are replaced by backwards looking discussion of whether or not targets were achieved.

Fifthly bonus payments increase the conflict in the executive team that arise where performance targets compete. Increasing customer satisfaction might compete with higher customer numbers. Lower costs per customer might compete with improved market research. The creative trade offs between these tensions must be made to optimise long term shareholder value. They should not be determined by the risks to individual annual bonus payments.

Why are annual bonus schemes so popular?

So given that annual bonus schemes have so many undesirable consequences, how is it that they have become so popular? Most FTSE 350 companies and almost all FTSE 100 companies now operate an annual bonus scheme and there has been a steady increase in the size of the bonuses available.

Well one reason concerns the presentational issues. Presentation of executive pay is always a critical consideration. Presentational issues are discussed in chapter 11.

A second reason is that most of the alternatives to annual bonus also have undesirable consequences. This is mainly because the UK has not managed to develop a long term incentive scheme that consistently and objectively rewards long term growth in shareholder value. This is a very serious problem that is discussed in detail in chapters 6, 7 and 8 of this book.

A third reason is the herding effect. The annual bonus scheme is justified as "Standard Industry Practice". When it comes to justifying executive pay, remuneration committees find that there is safety in numbers. It therefore pays to stick close to standard industry practice.

A fourth reason is that annual bonus is not covered by the Combined Code requirement for long term incentive schemes to be specifically approved by shareholders.[10] It is therefore easier for a company to increase annual bonus than it is to increase incentives for long term performance.

A fifth reason might be that company chairmen welcome the power that arises from administering an annual bonus scheme. Remuneration committees always need to exercise discretion when evaluating performance at the end of the year. In cases where targets have become inappropriate the level of discretion is very high. Chairmen may not formally sit on remuneration committees, but they are usually extremely influential in the exercising of discretion. This adds to their patronage.

These five reasons might explain why annual bonuses have become popular, but in themselves they are not justifications for annual bonuses. Surely there must be some arguments directly in favour of paying an annual bonus?

Well, one argument that is made is that an annual bonus scheme allows for the recognition of individual performance, whereas a performance measure based on long term growth in shareholder value can only cover corporate performance. However, this argument assumes that it is a good idea to reward individual performance and as we saw in chapter 3, this is not the case at the executive level.

There is an argument that an important, difficult objective will get better focus if it is rewarded promptly and specifically through annual bonus. This argument may be valid lower down the organisation where there are more controls in place to ensure that the right targets are set, and the means used to deliver the target are proportional to the benefits. For executives the incentives to hit PPC targets are already too great, even without an additional bonus being paid. A PPC with no link to variable pay is more than enough to secure the focus required.

The Greenbury report contains an argument in favour of annual bonus. It says that bonuses can be used "to encourage and reward an aspect of performance that is different from that encouraged by long-term incentive schemes, but still relevant and important."[11] But if the long term scheme is properly focused on long term shareholder value, what different aspects of performance should be rewarded? This could possibly mean aspects like safety record, environmental performance or social contribution, but even these, I would argue, are extremely important to long term shareholder value. Certainly annual performance measures such as profit, earnings, cash flow or customer satisfaction are properly captured by the long term scheme to the extent that they contribute to shareholder value, and to the extent that they do not contribute they certainly should not be rewarded! The beauty of rewarding only long term growth in shareholder value is that it ensures that all other aspects of performance are rewarded in their correct balance.

Another argument often quoted to support annual bonuses as

opposed to long term incentive schemes is that the reward is more immediate. The argument goes that by minimising the time delay between the completion of the objective and the bonus being paid the incentive effect is maximised. This argument might have some merit for people low down in an organisational structure, but it cannot be used for senior management. The first problem is that prompt reward encourages short term thinking, and minimises accountability for longer term consequences. Secondly it is unlikely that the incentive effect is actually any greater if reward is immediate. It is simply that the incentive effect is concentrated into a shorter period of time. By offering rewards in three years time the incentive effect is retained for three years. If a bonus is paid immediately then the incentive effect immediately ends, and people start looking for the next incentive.

I have conducted some informal research into managers' desire for immediate rewards and their willingness to see rewards deferred for three years. The results suggest that almost 72% of managers are happy to receive rewards on a deferred basis provided the reward is secure and is growing at a rate of interest comparable with what they could get if they were investing the money themselves. The research is documented in appendix 3. It is clear that the top reasons for rejecting deferral were an immediate need for cash and a suspicion that the money could somehow be lost or withheld if the company performed badly. Most executives are in wealth accumulation mode and it is hard to believe that they suffer much from immediate needs for cash. It also seems appropriate that they should have money at risk if the company faces some catastrophe. The immediate reward argument therefore does not work well for executives.

PPCs and annual bonus lower down the organisation

This chapter has examined arguments in favour of and against using annual bonus as a form of remuneration for executives. It is clear that there is an overwhelming case for not operating annual bonus schemes for executives.

It is however interesting to note that many of the problems

associated with annual bonus schemes are specific to very senior management. Managers who have a few layers of management above them have far less impact on strategy and direction. Their role is more about implementation where a short term focus is more justified. At their level there are more controls in place to ensure that the right targets are set. There are controls to ensure that the means used to hit a target are justified. Payment terms for managers below the executive level are beyond the scope of this book, but there may be situations where annual bonus schemes work well for certain managers, even if they do not work for executives.

Summary

Annual bonus is not a good form of remuneration for executives because the performance targets necessarily have a short term focus which is not aligned with the long term interests of shareholders. Even with no annual bonus the incentives that executives have to deliver on their short term targets can already be excessive.

Annual bonus payments create incentives for executives to distort the normal processes of managing performance so as to increase their bonus. Distortions can occur in the way that targets are set, the way that performance is measured, reported and communicated. Focus is switched from performance to payments.

At the executive level it is not possible to ensure that the means used to achieve an objective are justified. There is a danger that paying annual bonuses creates additional conflict and stress where performance objectives conflict. Bonuses can also promote a more individualistic company culture.

The arguments usually presented to justify annual bonus are very weak from a shareholder perspective. Annual bonus is popular for other reasons, which although understandable, have nothing to do with shareholder value.

Perhaps the most compelling reason for paying large annual bonuses is the lack of high quality alternatives in the way that variable pay is managed. This is why it is now imperative that we consider ways of improving long term incentive plans.

Notes

9. ABI 2005: Page 6, paragraph 7
10. Combined Code 2003: Code Provision B.2.4. See also ABI 2005: Page 9, paragraph 4.1
11. Greenbury 1995: Page 39, paragraph 6.19

6

Long Term Incentive Plans (LTIPs)

In this chapter we look at Long Term Incentive Plans (LTIPs). There are many different kinds of LTIP plan in place in different FTSE 350 companies, some of which provide much better incentive alignment than others. In this respect Typico has one of the best LTIPs operating in the FTSE 350, but even the Typico plan has some serious shortcomings. Let's look in detail at the incentives arising from the Typico LTIP.

Typico's Long Term Incentive Plan

In early October each year Typico's remuneration committee make a conditional award under the Long Term Incentive Plan (LTIP). As chief executive, Joe Figment is conditionally awarded shares in Typico plc which have a value equivalent to 125% of his basic salary. Other executives receive a conditional award equivalent to 100% of base salary. The plan cascades down through all the senior manager grades, with a large number of managers receiving a conditional award of shares equivalent to 30% of their basic salaries.

The share price that is used to determine the number of shares awarded is the average closing share price on each of the last five days of September. For example, Typico's closing share price (in pence) was 628, 638, 637, 630 and 642 respectively on the last five working days of September 2005. The average price was therefore £6.35. Joe Figment's conditional award was worth 125% of his £750,000 salary which is

£937,500. As a share was worth £6.35, his conditional award was 147,637 shares.

The award under the LTIP is conditional, based on Typico's performance relative to its competitors in the three year period starting on 1st October, a few days before the conditional award was made. When the award is made, a list of about 15 competitor companies is published against whom performance will be benchmarked. The companies are those which are most comparable to Typico, so the list does not change much from year to year although some changes are required to reflect mergers and acquisitions that have occurred over the previous year. For each award under the scheme, this list of companies is known as the comparator group.

The idea is that the TSR growth of each company in the comparator group is monitored over the three year performance period. At the end of the performance period the percentage growth (or fall) in TSR for each company is determined and these are ranked in order. The percentage of the conditional award that is transferred to Typico mangers depends Typico's position in this ranked order. If Typico is a top quartile performer then all the conditionally awarded shares are transferred. If Typico is a median performer then 30% of the shares are transferred. For performance between median and top quartile a proportion of the shares between 30% and 100% will be released, determined on a straight line basis. For below median performance no shares will be transferred.

Typico contracts Bonanza, a fictitious firm of remuneration consultants, to administer the LTIP. Bonanza is responsible for calculating the TSR index required for every company in the comparator group. At the end of the performance period Bonanza determines the percentage growth in TSR for each company, ranks the companies, determines their percentile positions and calculates the consequential percentage of shares that is transferred.

For example, the conditional award made in October 2002 had a comparator group of 17 named companies (including Typico) associated with it. The performance period started on 1st October 2002 and finished on 30th September 2005. Bonanza maintained a TSR index for each of the 17 companies over that period, although one company disappeared because of a merger so only 16 remained at the end of the performance period. In fact Typico was the 7th best performing company of the 16 remaining companies. This means that 6/15th (40%) of the other companies performed better than Typico, and 9/15th (60%) performed worse. Typico's 40th percentile position is between top quartile (where 100% shares transfer) and median (where 30% shares transfer). On a straight line basis therefore, the percentage of shares that transfer is 30 + 10/25*70 which is 58%. This meant that 58% of the shares conditionally awarded to Typico managers in October 2002 were transferred to them in October 2005. The other 42% were lost.

There are two other important features of Typico's LTIP. Firstly, shares transferred after the three year performance period are not immediately released to the executives and other managers who participate in the plan. Rather they are held in the name of Bonanza for a further two years and are released into the names of the managers on the fifth anniversary of being conditionally awarded. Bonanza also sells shares to cover the personal tax liabilities of the recipients immediately before release. During the two years that the shares are held by Bonanza, the dividends on the shares are transferred from Bonanza to the managers who will own them. The managers cannot however sell the shares until they are released on the fifth anniversary.

Secondly the remuneration committee have reserved to themselves the right to block the transfer of shares after the three year performance period if they believe that the TSR performance of the company is not representative of its underlying financial performance. For example, if the company's financial performance was poor, but a take-over bid caused a surge in share price and TSR just before the end of the performance period, then the remuneration committee might think it was inappropriate to allow shares to transfer.

Incentives under Typico's LTIP

Typico's LTIP is amongst the best in any FTSE 350 company. It is consistent with the Combined Code and complies with guidance provided by the ABI and other shareholder bodies.

Its main strength is that the incentives provided to executives and other managers under the scheme are aligned with the interests of shareholders. To get a payout under the scheme the executives have to ensure at least median performance growth in TSR, which accurately measures what shareholders want. Beyond TSR growth, there is also an incentive to grow the share price because the value of the shares transferred is increased if the share price grows. This incentive is closely linked to TSR growth and the interests of shareholders. The three year performance period ensures that it is longer term growth in TSR that matters. The subsequent two year retention period ensures that executives cannot afford a share price collapse after the end of the performance period. This gives shareholders further confidence that the TSR growth has a sustained underlying basis. This confidence is reinforced by the fact that a conditional award is made on a regular basis each year. Any share price collapse would therefore have a damaging effect on five years worth of awards under the scheme.

Consistency of performance over time

Many LTIP schemes provide incentives for TSR growth, but do not provide it in a way that is uniform over time. This means that as the months pass by the incentive to grow TSR is sometimes stronger and sometimes weaker, and this introduces an incentive to grow TSR in a volatile way that works against the interests of shareholders. The Typico scheme is very consistent over time and this has successfully eliminated many of the incentives for volatility.

The worst examples of inconsistency over time occur when companies make very large one time conditional awards to newly appointed chief executives, and then plan to make no further awards for three years. This creates a very strong incentive for the chief executive to depress the company share price on appointment and to maximise it in an unsustainable way three years later. Such an approach maximises TSR growth over the performance period, but is likely to damage shareholder interests immediately either side of the performance period.

Typico's use of phased awards ensures that the incentive to grow share price is more consistent, because there are no periods when the share price can fall without adversely affecting the TSR growth associated with a conditional award. Also if, at the start or end of a performance period, the share price is unrepresentative of underlying value for some reason, then the adverse effect of this is confined to only a proportion of the benefits available through the scheme.

Typico's conditional awards are not just phased; they are phased on a totally regular basis. This is a further strength because it ensures that the incentive to grow TSR is completely consistent over time. At any one point in time precisely three separate performance periods are in progress. There is never an incentive to defer or bring forward TSR movements so that they can be captured in more or fewer performance periods. Typico's remuneration committee also dogmatically insist that the share price used to determine the final TSR index for a performance period is also used to determine the starting TSR index for the new performance period. This makes executives indifferent to the share price used to measure performance. A higher share price is better for the performance period just ending, but worse for the one just starting and visa versa.

Retesting of LTIP schemes

Another strength of the Typico LTIP is that it does not allow any retesting. In fact when the plan first started it used to allow executives to extend the performance period from three years to four years, if the percentile position was disappointing after three years. This retest facility after four years made it easy for executives to secure payouts from the LTIP, and the retest was eventually withdrawn following suggestions from institutional shareholders. Retesting allows executives to count periods of good performance in an additional phased performance period. This double counting destroys the consistency and uniformity of necessary if an incentive to generate volatility is to be avoided. An example is illustrated in appendix 4 by comparing scenario 5 and scenario 7. A company who steadily grows TSR by 9% per annum can significantly increase its performance in a LTIP scheme with retesting by understating and overstating its performance in alternate years. The share price and TSR index show greater volatility, which allows the executives to display better LTIP performance because of retesting. The increase in volatility works against the interest of shareholders and it is quite wrong that executives should have this incentive.

A well designed LTIP will always ensure that all periods of time are covered by the same number of performance periods. It should never be possible to exclude a period of poor performance, or to double count a period of good performance, through retesting. Using the same share price at the change over of performance periods is also important because it ensures that a drop in share price performance cannot escape measurement in a performance period. In this book I will describe an LTIP as "fully invariable over time" if the number of phased performance periods that are affected by any change in the share price is always the same. The Typico scheme is fully invariable and clearly this is a very good quality. Most FTSE 350 schemes are not fully invariable.

Consistency of incentives over different performance outcomes

The Typico scheme, in common with even the best LTIP schemes in the FTSE 350, suffers from a lack on consistency between incentives and performance outcomes. This creates a number of problems.

For example, in April 2003 the executives at Typico received a report on their comparator group position for the LTIP conditional award made in October 2000. The report showed that with five months of the performance period still to run, Typico was in 14th position out of the 16 companies in the comparator group. Under the rules of the scheme Typico needed to achieve median position before any shares were transferred. The executives realised that they had no chance of receiving any shares in respect of the October 2000 conditional allocation. Even if they performed exceptionally well during the last five month and raised their position from 14th to 9th they would still get no shares because even in 9th position they come out below median.

Once this realisation had been made, the October 2000 allocation ceased to have any incentive effect for them. In fact the real incentive for them at that point was to appear to perform as badly as possible. Joe Figment realised that summer 2003 was an excellent time get all his bad news out in public, while good news could afford to be held beck until the last quarter. This approach ensured the lowest possible share price at the end of September, which ensured the best possible starting position for the TSR index in respect of the LTIP conditional allocation for October 2003.

It is not just at the bottom of the comparator group that there is a motivational dead zone. Had the April 2003 report shown Typico in first place then the incentive effect would also have been weakened. Why bust a gut to come out first, if you get just as well paid for coming out fourth, and in fourth position you would have the added benefit of commencing the next performance period from a lower starting point?

By contrast, if the April 2003 report had shown Typico in 9th position then the incentive effect to move upwards would have been overwhelming. In Joe Figments case the difference between 9th position and 8th position was worth roughly £350,000 with a further £150,000 for each subsequent position gained. This huge step change in the level of reward is completely out of proportion with the very small benefit to the shareholder if the company came out in 8th place rather than 9th. There is a danger that this extremely powerful incentive would result in extreme short term measures to temporarily boost the share price at the end of performance period. At best it will create unnecessary volatility. At worst, long term value will be sacrificed to achieve a short term blip in the share price.

The problem here is that under the rules of Typico's LTIP there are some potential outcomes where reward is extremely sensitive to small changes in performance, and other potential outcomes where there is no sensitivity at all. The table opposite summarises the level of reward for each outcome position in the comparator group.

It is clear that moving from position 1 to position 4 results in no change to reward. It is a motivational dead zone. Each step from position 4 to position 8 results in big change in reward. The step from 8th position to 9th position is exceptionally big, but any changes involving 9th position and below fall into another motivational dead zone.

This is a problem area, but Typico's scheme is still far superior to the average FTSE 350 LTIP on this point. Many FTSE 350 companies use smaller comparator groups and use bigger step changes in reward at median performance level. This results in even greater disparity between changes in performance and changes in reward.

This lack of consistency creates several problems. First of all there is the volatility problem. The lack of consistency creates an incentive to

Reward for each Position after Ranking Performance
(16 companies in the Comparator Group)
(100% at top quartile, 30% at median)

Position in Group	Percentile Position	Transferred Shares (%)
1st, 2nd, 3rd or 4th	20 or above	100
5th	26.7	95.3
6th	33.3	76.7
7th	40.0	58.0
8th	46.7	39.3
9th to 16th	53.3 or below	Zero

make the share price volatile. If Typico was a steady, average performing company the executives might expect to come out near to median position every year. Sometimes they would come out just above median and receive 30 to 40% of the conditionally allocated shares, sometimes they would come out just below median and receive nothing. On average they might expect to get 15 to 20% of the conditionally allocated shares. By contrast, if the executive team can achieve the same underlying performance in a more volatile way then they will be much better rewarded. If in alternate years they were to come out in the top and bottom quartile, their reward would be alternately 100% and 0% of the conditionally allocated shares. The average reward would be 50%, about three times higher than on the steadily performing basis.

The way that increased volatility increases rewards can be seen modelled out in detail in appendix 4. A comparison of scenarios 1 and 2 or scenarios 5 and 6 shows that increased volatility pays big rewards, even if underlying performance is constant. The problem is that this increase in volatility works against the interest of shareholders. It is quite wrong that LTIPs should provide this incentive.

The second and third big problems arise from the large step changes in reward that can occur for very small changes in performance. This is particularly an issue where performance is coming out near to median in a comparator group. Statistically we should expect the companies' performance outcomes to be most tightly bunched around the median position. That means that only a very small increase (or decrease) in TSR growth is required to lift a company several places up (or down) the ranking. This is in sharp contrast to the change in rewards. Most LTIP schemes offer no rewards for below median performance, but very high rewards at median or above.

This creates the disproportionate incentive problem. There is a very strong incentive to come out above median position. This incentive is completely out of proportion with the value of the objective, and it invites short term action to manipulate the share price. It also creates a situation in which disputes are very likely. The difference between 8th and 9th position may be of minimal importance to the shareholder, but a management team who come out just below median have very strong incentives to spend time arguing that in fact they were just above median.

A disproportionate incentive also creates a demotivation problem. This hurts companies whose performance comes out just below median. Under most LTIP schemes managers and executives receive no rewards at all in this circumstance, but would receive very significant rewards if their performance had been just a fraction better. This feels very unfair and has the potential to be extremely demotivating. It is a situation that companies have to avoid.

Remuneration committees and consultancies like Bonanza have come up with several different tricks and techniques for dealing with the demotivation problem. Some of these are listed below:

Trick 1

Find some justifiable reason for excluding some of the best performing companies in the comparator group. Perhaps they have been involved in a merger, demerger, acquisition or disposal? Perhaps they have made a rights issue? Excluding them might push our company's performance above median.

Trick 2

Find some way of not excluding from the comparator group a poor performer who was previously excluded.

Trick 3

Use some form of weighting system such that by increasing the weighting attributable to poor performing companies and decreasing the weighting of high performing companies it is possible to move our company above median position.

Trick 4

Re-determine the way that share prices are determined to calculate TSR growth. Is it the share price on the last day that matters, or the average over the last week, month or year? Surely there is some way of determining it for which we come out just above rather than just below median?

Trick 5

Determine the percentage TSR growth of foreign companies using local currency or in sterling according to which gives the lower outcome.

Trick 6

Can we retrospectively redefine the comparator group?

Trick 7

Can we redefine the performance period? Perhaps by making small changes to the start and end date we can find a performance period for which we come out just above rather than just below median.

Trick 8

Can we allow retesting next year?

Tricks and techniques such as the above are deemed necessary to avoid unfair or demotivating outcomes. This is why Bonanza advises its clients to avoid maximum transparency and to leave some hidden discretion, so that there is scope to use tricks if this becomes necessary. However this approach is very damaging to the credibility and transparency of the scheme. It weakens the incentive effect for managers and destroys trust with the investor community. By definition, only half of all performance determinations should come out above median, but investors always suspect that far more than half of them do. The fact that it is so difficult to verify this makes the suspicion even greater.

Usually consultancies like Bonanza can be counted upon to do the dirty work. It is particularly unfortunate when it is the remuneration committee who come under pressure to manipulate the outcomes of LTIP performance conditions. As independent non-executive directors they are precisely the people that shareholders look to, to uphold the rules and promote transparency and consistency. Remuneration committees would do much better to avoid LTIP schemes where the demotivation problem might require them to intervene. If LTIPs were designed such that changes in reward were proportional to changes in performance at any point on the performance scale, then the need for tricks would disappear. It would be possible to make schemes far more transparent, and completely remove the requirement for discretion. This would build trust and confidence, and would maximise the incentive effects for managers and executives.

Sliding scales

I am sure that many people reading the last section have been wanting to shout at me, "but LTIP plans must use sliding scales!" Of course, these people are absolutely right. The ABI guidelines state, "Sliding scales that correlate the rewards potential with a performance scale...are a useful way of ensuring that performance conditions are genuinely stretching. They generally provide a better motivator for improving corporate performance than a "single hurdle".[12]

Thanks to the ABI "single hurdle" incentive schemes are now well on the decline. It used to be very common for share option schemes to pay out massively for top quartile performance, and not pay out anything below that level. It is clear that these schemes caused huge problems. Imagine coming out on the 26th percentile! One of the inevitable, if negative, consequences was that re-testing become common.

The Typico LTIP scheme made a 100% pay out for top quartile performance and a 30% pay out for median performance, with a sliding scale operating in between. The arrangement can be represented graphically like this:

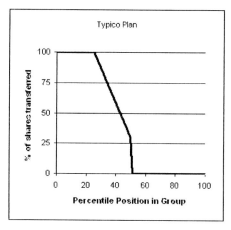

It is clear from the graph that although Typico do use a sliding scale it is still the case that rewards grow very rapidly over some percentile outcomes, and there are some flat areas which represent motivational dead zones. It is also important to note that what is represented in the graph as a smooth diagonal line, is in fact a series of small steps. If the comparator group is small then these steps can become quite big. In Typico's case moving just one place up the comparator group ranking causes a jump of 6.7 percentiles on the horizontal scale.

It is clear that Typico's LTIP would work much better if it was a half linear plan and the rewards to performance graph looked like this:

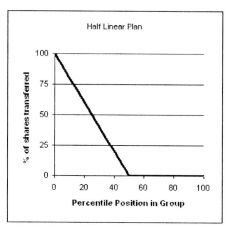

There are less motivational dead zones and the rise in rewards is less rapid. The disproportionate incentive problem is substantially eliminated, as is the demotivation problem. Unfortunately the volatility problem has got worse. The incentive to cycle performance is even stronger than before. Managers of a company with steady median performance would see almost no reward from this LTIP, whereas managers in a company that alternates between top quartile and bottom quartile performance might expect about 80% or 90% of conditionally allocated shares to be transferred every second year.

At this point some readers are probably mystified. Why consider a graph for a half linear plan, when you could consider one for a fully linear plan? A fully linear plan would look like this:

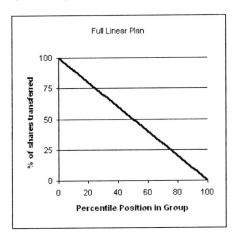

A fully linear LTIP is superior to a half linear LTIP in every respect that we have considered in this chapter. There are no motivational dead zones. There is no disproportional incentive problem. There is no demotivation problem. Best of all there is no incentive to create volatility. If the LTIP scheme is fully invariable over time and fully linear over outcomes then the timing of a rise or fall in the share price ceases to have any material effect on remuneration. Rather the only way to grow remuneration is to grow the TSR index in a way that is sustainable into the longer term. This is precisely the incentive that shareholders want to give executives! Surely this means that a fully invariable, fully linear LTIP is the holy grail of executive remuneration?

Well unfortunately it is not as simple as that! Fully invariable, fully linear LTIPs have significant advantages over the LTIPs that are used by FTSE 350 companies today. However they still have some very significant problems, which are examined in detail in the next chapters. The good news is that the problems with these special LTIPs can be overcome by making changes to other parts of the remuneration package, and by inserting some additional special rules.

Summary

In this chapter we have looked at LTIPs. We have seen how a well designed LTIP does provide incentives for executives and managers that are normally well aligned with shareholders interests. We saw how it was important to make regular phased conditional awards under an LTIP, and to eliminate re-testing, so that all periods of time are equally covered by performance periods. We described such LTIPs fully invariable. We have also looked at the problems that arise if the LTIP allows small changes in performance create large changes in reward, or large changes in performance to generate no change in reward. We noted that such situations could cause a volatility problem, a demotivation problem or a disproportionate incentive problem. We saw that all three problems could be substantially eliminated by linking rewards to performance outcomes in a way that is completely linear, across all possible performance outcomes. We described LTIPs with this design feature as fully linear. We noted that fully invariable, fully linear LTIPs have many advantages, but still suffer from some problems that we will look at in the next chapters.

Notes

12.   ABI 2005: Page 11, paragraph 6.5

7

Fully Invariable, Linear Long term Incentive Plans (FILLIPs)

In this book I am going to use the acronym FILLIP for an LTIP which is both fully invariable and fully linear, as described in the previous chapter. The rules of a FILLIP have been documented in appendix 5. These rules aim to maximise transparency and to ensure that payments are based solely on objectively determined outcomes. The incentives created are therefore very clear and much better aligned to shareholders interests than is the case with a normal LTIP.

Despite the better alignment of incentives, there are still some problems with FILLIPs. There are also some reasons why a FILLIP does not sit comfortably with traditional thinking on executive pay. In this chapter we look at some of the areas where we need to change our way of thinking if we want to implement share based incentive schemes that are well aligned with shareholder interests. In chapter 8 we deal with the other outstanding problems.

First of all, let us examine the mismatch between FILLIPs and traditional thinking on share incentive schemes.

The traditional thinking behind share based incentive schemes

When remuneration consultancies first started promoting share based incentive schemes in the 1980s one of the slogans used was "exceptional reward for exceptional performance". The argument was that an extra tier of exceptional rewards should be provided for executives who delivered the most exceptional performance for their shareholders. This extra tier of rewards would only kick in if performance truly was exceptional, so most of the time the schemes would cost shareholders nothing. However, if shareholders did benefit from some truly outstanding performance then the schemes would pay out and both shareholders and executives would be winners.

It was a compelling argument and many schemes were introduced. Many schemes depended on large, one time only, conditional awards that paid out on an all or nothing basis if performance was top quartile. Naturally the schemes suffered, in very extreme ways, from the problems still seen in the Typico LTIP. The disproportionate incentive problem and the demotivation problem were particularly acute.

As the 1990s progressed, shareholders developed a better understanding of the adverse consequences of these schemes. They started to promote the regular phasing of awards and the use of sliding scales. The design of share based incentive schemes gradually improved but one principle remained firm. These long term incentive schemes represented extra reward for exceptional performance. The schemes therefore made no sense if they paid out for below average performance. This understanding of share based incentive schemes remains to this day. The ABI guidelines are very clear that, "Awards should not be made for less than median performance."[13] This means that the half linear plan described at the end of the previous chapter is compatible with ABI guidelines, but the fully linear plan is not.

Under the Combined Code, shareholders must specifically approve significant changes to long term incentive schemes.[14] The support of investor groups like the ABI is therefore very important to any remuneration committee seeking to implement a FILLIP. The remuneration committee would need to discuss its proposals with the ABI. Given that the fully linear plan removes the incentive to create volatility, my guess is that the ABI would have some sympathy for the proposal. The big issue is likely to be the extra remuneration received for below median performance. It would be necessary to adjust for this by making a reduction in other parts of the remuneration package such as basic pay or annual bonus. These are all matters that remuneration committees can debate with the ABI and other shareholder organisations.

The thinking behind incentives and variable pay

The traditional thinking behind variable pay for executives emphasises the importance of a strong link between performance and reward. By measuring executive performance, and adjusting rewards according to the performance measured, we create a strong incentive to maximise performance.

The problem with this thinking is that it is extremely difficult to quantify executive performance in a complete and objective way. PPCs attempt to do this, but they measure management performance rather than performance from a shareholder perspective. It is impossible to be confident that the PPC that was agreed was actually optimal. The assessment at the end of the year can never be completely objective, and can be influenced by internal politics as much as by performance. From a shareholder perspective, measures such as earnings per share and TSR are clearly highly relevant to an assessment of executive performance, but they certainly do not give the full picture. In particular, under these measures it is impossible to distinguish individual performance from the team performance.

The problem of accurately quantifying executive performance becomes even more difficult as soon as executive performance is linked to pay. Suddenly executives have strong incentives to make sure their performance looks good on the different performance measures that are used. This alters behaviours, but it will only have a positive impact if the performance measures are very accurately aligned with what shareholders actually want.

This traditional thinking needs to give way to some new thinking that originates more directly from the desire to safeguard and increase returns to shareholders. Traditionally shareholders have wanted to measure executive performance so that they can set the incentive to perform. But they don't need a complicated assessment of executive performance in order to set the right incentive. They already know what the incentive they should set is. They want companies to focus on long term growth in TSR, while reducing volatility and ensuring the shareholder value is secure. They should give executives incentives to grow TSR in a long term and secure way, and leave the whole business of management performance to management.

In the context of setting the correct incentive, a FILLIP is easily the best form of executive remuneration. The incentives it provides are far closer to what the shareholder actually wants then those offered by any other form of remuneration.

Executives might be concerned that if variable pay schemes are focused solely on the TSR growth incentive then some unfair outcomes might occur. An executive who has performed very well might, through bad luck, be worse rewarded than a poorly performing executive who has been lucky. It is true that this might sometimes happen, but good executives, like good golfers, have to create their own luck. In the long term real luck evens out. Actually, executive pay has very little to do with fairness. Executives are not paid 100 times more than ordinary people because it is fair; they are paid it because it helps to generate shareholder value.

Similarly shareholders have to live with the fact that an incentive based scheme might occasionally provide reward to executives whose achievements arise more from good fortune, or other peoples efforts than through their own good management. Shareholders should certainly protest if the remuneration schemes give the wrong incentives, and most of the current FTSE 350 remuneration schemes are very poor in this respect. However, if the incentives are correct then shareholders should not complain about favourable outcomes. If the incentives are correct and an unmerited payout does occur, then at least the shareholders know that they are the biggest net winners.

The thinking behind FILLIP based remuneration

The thinking behind FILLIP based remuneration is quite different from the thinking behind a normal share based incentive scheme. A FILLIP is not some extra tier of remuneration, adding to the many remuneration schemes already in place. Rather it is a replacement for those other schemes, and becomes a central component of an executive's basic remuneration.

The thinking behind a FILLIP accepts that it is impossible to quantify the performance of an executive in a complete and objective way. Rather the FILLIP seeks to ensure that executives face the correct incentives. It is therefore critically important that the incentives that arise from FILLIP based remuneration are very, very closely aligned to the interests of shareholders.

Under a FILLIP conditional share awards are made on a regular basis, once a year, or even better once a quarter. Let us suppose that a conditional award is being made at the start of every quarter with each conditional award linked to a three year performance period starting on the first day of the new quarter. Unlike a traditional LTIP, the conditional award should be thought of as remuneration for work completed during the quarter just finished. The expected present value of the conditional award should be determined assuming the company achieves median performance. This value should be shown as an expense in the accounts for the quarter in which the work was done. The executive's entitlement to receive a payout of shares from the conditional award has already been earned and should not usually normally be lost in the future, although both the number of shares received, and their value will be heavily dependent on the performance of the company over the three year performance period and two year retention period.

The idea here is that it takes time for the true value of the work completed by the executive in the quarter to become fully apparent. At least three years must go by before we can determine the extent to which the executive team had it right, and the extent to which they were leading the company up a dead end street. After three years the performance is assessed and a proportion of the conditionally allocated shares are transferred, but a further two years must pass before they are actually released to the executive.

In effect the variable pay of executives is paid five years in arrears. The level of their variable pay is determined by the amount of shareholder value (relative to other companies) that has been created over the period. The scheme is all about providing the correct incentive. It should be extremely difficult to get well rewarded without having delivered good long term performance for shareholders.

Critics might point out that the value of the variable pay for a particular quarter depends on the increase in TSR over the subsequent performance period, which is effected more by work completed during that performance period than by work completed during the quarter in question. This may be true, but it is not the important point. The idea is to make sure that the executives have an interest in the long term performance of the company that extends well beyond their current activities. This creates a strong incentive to maximise future value. This strong incentive is required to counterbalance the very strong incentive that executives have to maximise current performance figures so as to stay in post, increase basic salary and increase annual bonus.

The arrival of a new chief executive

In the previous chapter we have seen that a FILLIP can provide incentives that are very closely aligned to the interests of shareholders. Certainly they are far better aligned than even the best variable reward schemes that we see in place today. So far the analysis of FILLIPs has assumed that the executive has been in post for some time, and expects to be in post for some time to come. However many of the biggest problems in executive pay occur when executives, particularly chief executives, are first recruited into a company or when they leave the company. Let us start by considering the issues arising from recruitment.

First of all it is important to remember that in roughly three cases out of four new chief executives of FTSE 100 companies are appointed from within the company. This is exactly what we might expect. People inside the company usually have huge advantages over external candidates. They have a working knowledge of the company and its business. They already have established relationships with many of the key people they would need to relate to as chief executive. They have proven track records inside the company, and are known to work effectively within the company culture. The presence of suitable, potential chief executives within the company may well be sign that the company has good processes for career development, succession planning, training and the recruitment of external experience lower down the hierarchy. By appointing an internal candidate the company is saying that it believes in and will reward its own people. This helps it to retain and motivate other senior managers, who might otherwise feel they need to look outside the company for their next career step. There is far less risk associated with an internal appointment, both for the company and for the candidate. Research also suggests that chief executives appointed internally are on average more successful than chief executives appointed from outside.[15]

Normally a company will only want to recruit a new chief executive from outside if it has really difficulties which its own business model or company culture is struggling to adequately address. Appointment of an external chief executive usually means that some major change is required. It might also mean that the company's processes for developing its own executive talent are lacking in some way. Sometimes it is important for companies to recruit from outside to increase the breadth of experience within the company. Appointments like these are usually made below chief executive level where the risks are lower. After a few years inside the company people appointed in this way might well become good candidates for the top job.

Where a new chief executive is recruited internally the problems for executive remuneration are not significant. The structure of the individual's remuneration is unlikely to change very much; it is just that some of the numbers might get bigger.

When a new chief executive is appointed from outside, or indeed when any senior figure is appointed from outside, there are a number of additional issues. If the new chief executive is leaving an existing job then he or she faces some significant risks. Once an executive has quit a senior position he or she is always likely to be seen as an outsider. Insider status takes years to build. There is almost certainly a big financial cost to leaving. Remuneration that has been deferred or is tied up in share incentive schemes is very often lost. These promises of financial rewards that are lost to managers who leave the company are known as "golden handcuffs", and they can be very significant. The leaving executive may also be saying good-buy to some exciting career opportunities in the old company. Even when the new chief executive is not leaving a job there are big risks to be faced. Can the hiring company actually be turned around? Will the chairman and board support big changes? Are there powerful vested interest groups who could make the chief executives job impossible? Could reputations be ruined here?

Chief executives' pay is usually pitched at a high level that already reflects a high degree of risk. Despite that, remuneration committees sometimes feel the need to make extra allowances for these one time transition risks. They sometimes allow a two or three year initial contract as guaranteed, before the more normal one year rolling contract commences, and this often seems justified. Sometimes, however, some form of "golden hello" payment is also made. These may be justified as compensation for breaking the golden handcuffs of the chief executive's former company, but even in these cases golden hellos tend to suggest a lack of confidence in the long term success of the appointment. If the new chief executive was confident of long term success then golden hellos would not be required. Rather than pay golden hellos the hiring board should focus on taking the non financial actions necessary to support the newcomer in his or her new position. This maximises the likelihood that the appointment will prove to be successful for both the company and the new chief executive. There is also a big danger that, if things go badly for the new chief executive then a golden hello will be seen as a reward for failure.

New chief executives arriving in post usually have very strong incentives to overstate the company's problems and difficulties. Doing this ensures that their personal performance is measured from a low starting position. It helps to build the case for change within the company and above all it ensures that share option schemes and LTIPs conditionally awarded to the chief executive are based on very low initial share prices. This ensures that even a modest improvement in performance will yield significant rewards.

The conditional award of large blocks of share based incentive schemes to new chief executives creates incentives that are not well aligned to the shareholders interest. Firstly the new chief executive has big incentives to drive down the company share price when he or she is newly arrived in the company. This causes conflict with existing executives who see the recognition of their previous work undermined and the value of their existing LTIPs compromised. Secondly the chief executive's new drive for performance is likely to focus on share price optimisation in three to five year's time when the rewards under these schemes come through. The focus on sustained long term performance beyond the optimisation point is lost, and a big incentive to create volatility is introduced.

If a new chief executive were to join a FILLIP scheme that makes regular phased awards then the incentive to focus on real long term value growth is ensured. The strong incentive to depress share value for the first two years in post would however remain. A remuneration committee can mitigate this problem by making back dated conditional awards to the new chief executive, similar to what he or she would have received had he or she been working for the company for the last three years. This would reduce the chief executive's incentives to depress the share price, and would ensure that all incentives were well aligned with the interests of shareholders and the other executives. The back dated awards could be funded by a reduced level of FILLIP reward in the first three years of service. Also, if any golden hello payments have been determined necessary, then backdated conditional FILLIP awards would be a good way of making them.

The departure of a chief executive

Often public outcry against executive remuneration is at its strongest when it concerns a departing chief executive, especially when the departure is caused by poor performance. In 2003 the UK government used the catch phrase "Rewards for Failure" as the basis for a public consultation on this matter. In February 2004 the government concluded that, at least in the short term, it was better to encourage the market to move voluntarily towards best practice rather than to attempt any direct intervention through legislation.

Payments to departing executives are very difficult to justify. The main principle of the Combined Code on executive directors' remuneration is that "remuneration should be sufficient to attract, retain and motivate directors of the quality required to run the company, but a company should avoid paying more than is necessary for the purpose."[16] As there is no requirement to attract, retain or motivate a departing executive there appears to be no justification for a payment.

Some institutional shareholders have published excellent guidance on executive contracts and severance.[17] This makes several important points and includes good suggestions not included here. The guidance emphasises the importance of taking into account the possibility of executive failure when executive contacts are negotiated and drafted. The remuneration committee should be in a position where, if an executive is pushed out, then the contractual payments due to him or her will appear reasonable and no further payments will need to be made.

The FILLIP structure for variable pay is potentially very helpful in this respect. Because FILLIP shares are effectively received five years after they are earned then significant benefits are still due to be received by a chief executive for several years after he or she leaves a company. Psychologically this mitigates the need for extra payments, but in fact the FILLIP benefits to be paid are not new benefits; they were all earned while the chief executive was working for the company. There is no additional cost to shareholders. The FILLIP also ensures that the departing chief executive continues to have very strong incentives to see the company succeed, even after he or she has left.

Current remuneration schemes frequently overlook the importance of incentives for ensuring continuing success after a chief executive leaves. Often there is a desire to make a clean break and this means that incentive schemes are wrapped up as quickly as possible after departure. However an important opportunity is missed in this way. Shareholders want the chief executive to develop the company on a sound long term basis such that it will continue to succeed after he or she has left. In particular shareholders want the chief executive to have a succession plan and to develop people who could become future chief executives. They also want to see the executive team operating with sound processes and good relationships that remain resilient to a change at the top. These shareholder aspirations are not naturally aligned with the personal interests of the chief executive. A chief executive who is allowed to run a company in a way that is heavily dependent on his or her own personality and with no obvious successors in waiting clearly builds a position of great personal power. This can undermine the role of the company board and can be leveraged in negotiations on salary. FILLIP style incentives ensure that a chief executive has incentives to build for the future which continues, even after he or she leaves the company.

Many of the share based incentive plans in place in FTSE 350 companies today contain clauses that that are inexplicably favourable to the executives when they depart. For example there is sometimes a "change of control" clause that deems all performance targets to have been met if the company is taken over. This can result in huge payouts that are completely unjustified. A particularly bad example of this occurred at the end of 2003 when Carlton Communications merged with Granada to form ITV. Shareholders had little faith in Carlton's chairman, Michael Green because of a disastrous loss of shareholder value at Carlton in the three years leading up to the merger. A dramatic shareholder revolt prevented Mr Green from becoming chairman of ITV, but it later emerged that his payments on leaving the company were worth more than £15 million. One of the most important factors behind these excessive payments was a weak change of control clause in a share incentive scheme.

The performance conditions in a well designed FILLIP continue to track the returns from investing in a company, even after the company has been taken over. This allows the scheme to carry on unchanged through major restructures ensuring that the incentive effects remain consistent. It also completely removes the need for special change of control rules.

Of course sometimes executives leave companies by their own volition. Sometimes they get poached by other companies. To protect the company in these cases it can help to draft golden handcuff clauses into a FILLIP. Rewards from a FILLIP normally continue to be paid out for five years after the executive leaves a company. However a remuneration committee may wish to restrict these payments if the executive's departure is damaging to the company. This issue is not straight forward and is discussed in more detail in appendix 5. It is important to realise that golden handcuff have certain disadvantages and cannot be used in an overpowering way.

If an executive leaves one company and joins another he or she might continue to benefit from a FILLIP in the old company for up to five years after changing job. This might be a legitimate matter of concern to the new company who might see a conflict of interests, particularly if the old company is a competitor. In such cases the new company would need to insist that all benefits from the FILLIP are transferred directly to the company and, in exchange, they pay a fixed amount to the new executive. The size of the fixed amount would obviously reflect the expected value of the FILLIP benefits, but once determined this amount must remain fixed. The payments could be phased to match the expected payments under the FILLIP.

Dilution through the issuing of new shares

Share based remuneration always raises the question of how the company should obtain the shares used for remuneration. This question does not affect the incentives faced by the manager, and makes little difference to the real cost of the scheme to shareholders. Since the Finance Act 2003 it has also lost its taxation significance, so the question is really not all that important from a remuneration perspective.

To me it usually makes sense for a new and developing company to issues new shares. The company effectively attracts new shareholder funds for investment in this way. The new shareholders are the employees who receive the shares and the new funds are the payments that would otherwise have been made to them in cash. Trading in a new company's shares can also suffer from low market liquidity. Illiquidity does not stop new shares from being issued, and the new shares can only help the liquidity problem.

Similarly it seems to me that a mature company which is returning cash to shareholders through dividends should aim to obtain shares for remuneration from the normal traded market for those shares, unless a liquidity problem prevents this. The clarity and transparency necessary to make a valuation of a company's shares is much increased if the number of shares in circulation is constant. Other things being equal companies should therefore seek this kind of stability.

Sadly presentational concerns about executive pay have often made companies reluctant to reveal its true level in a clear and direct way. The issue of new shares was often preferred because the true cost to shareholders was less clear in the company accounts. Understanding the dilution effect of new shares being issued became a big problem for shareholders and the reduced transparency of accounting statements eroded trust between shareholders and executive teams. Fortunately accounting standards are now addressing this, as described towards the end of chapter 4.

Summary

In this chapter we have seen that a change of thinking is required if variable pay for executives is to achieve what it sets out to do. Rather than attempt to quantify the subjective concept of executive performance it would be much better to directly provide executives with incentives to increase long term shareholder value. This means that incentives must be focused much more totally and much more accurately on long term growth in the TSR index for the company. This can be achieved if a FILLIP incentive scheme is used to replace all variable pay schemes and a proportion of fixed pay as well. Fixed pay needs to be reduced to take account of the fact that FILLIP based remuneration continues to arise, albeit in a proportionately reduced way, for performance that is below median level in a comparator group.

We have also looked in detail at the incentives that arise when new executives, particularly new chief executives, are appointed into companies from outside. We have see that benefits arise if the new executives immediately participate in FILLIP style remuneration schemes because this ensures that the correct long term incentives are in place. We noted that special back dated FILLIP awards might be needed to maintain consistent short term incentives, but that any backdated award should be funded by reduced future awards. In contrast we also saw that non-FILLIP style incentives such as golden hellos or large scale one time conditional awards of shares or options can have a very damaging effect on the incentive regime for a new executive.

We looked at the incentive regime that exists when an executive leaves a company. We noted that the desire to make a clean break with the executive can lead companies to make very poor arrangements in LTIPs and these can create huge, undesirable incentives. In contrast we saw that a FILLIP which continues to operate for five years after an executive leaves ensures that the incentives faced by the executive are consistent, and that the executive really does have an interest in the long term future of the company. This encourages an incumbent chief executive to make proper provisions for his or her own future departure. Such incentives are important because they mitigate the natural incentives that exist for a chief executive to develop a position of indispensability and strong personal power.

Notes

13. ABI 2005: Page 11, paragraph 7.2

14. Combined Code 2003: Code Provision B.2.4. See also ABI 2005: Page 9, paragraph 4.1
15. See work on succession planning such as Cohn 2003
16. Combined Code 2003: Main Principles B.1
17. ABI 2005: Page 22

8

Remaining problems and issues with FILLIPs

In chapter 6 we have seen how the incentives arising from a FILLIP are much better aligned with shareholders interests than those arising from a typical LTIP. In chapter 7 we have seen how a FILLIP is not a simple replacement for an LTIP, but must also replace a proportion of basic salary and annual bonus because of the rewards it provides for below median performance. We also saw how it provides much better incentives for arriving and departing chief executives than the arrangements currently in place in a typical FTSE 350 company.

It remains the case however that a number of problems typically associated with LTIP style remuneration are still present in FILLIP style remuneration. In this chapter we look at these issues in more detail. We will see that two serious problems with FILLIPs can be properly addressed by making small changes to the plan rules. We will also see that some of the other typical criticisms of LTIPs are much less important once the problems in the plan designs have been addressed.

Let us start of by looking at the two serious problems.

FILLIPs and poor performance

One of the very unfortunate aspects of a typical FTSE 350 LTIP is that it can sometimes provide very rich rewards to executive teams that have destroyed shareholder value on a grand scale. Clearly this is an absolutely disastrous incentive to give to executive teams and a design fix to remove this problem is absolutely essential.

The problem arises because an LTIP is typically more generous in rewarding value growth than it is in punishing value destruction. It therefore pays for an executive team to temporarily destroy a lot of value, because the personal rewards for partially restoring that value will far exceed the loses associated with destroying it. The way this could work for the Typico LTIP is illustrated in appendix 4, scenario 9. Joe Figment and his team would get no payment from the LTIP for three years while value was destroyed, but would then see huge payouts over the next three years as the value is partially recovered. On average their rewards are the same as those for an executive team who have consistently delivered consistent TSR growth at the 33rd percentile (so performance in the top third) for seven years. Clearly this is quite wrong from a shareholder perspective.

This problem was another major factor that lay behind Michael Green's excessive reward, discussed in the last chapter. The share price doubled from around £1.40 to around £2.80 during Michael Green's last year at Carlton Communications and because of this the share based incentive schemes paid out on a grand scale. The trouble was that this achievement should have been seen in the context of some terrible value destruction that had occurred earlier. The share price had been steady in a range around £5.00 from 1997 to 1999. It rose to over £8.00 in early 2000 before problems with advertising revenue and the ITV Digital joint venture came home to roost. In this context £2.80 still appeared a very poor result from a shareholders perspective.

So what can be done to address this problem? I have modelled a number of different changes to the FILLIP rules that might help. On the basis of this modelling it seems to me that the most practical rule change is to insert a "pro rata rule". A pro rata rule actively punishes value destruction by reducing the size of a conditional award in proportion to the size of any loses in the TSR index over the last three years. The drafting of the rule is included in appendix 5.

Appendix 6 shows the rewards provided in different scenarios by a FILLIP both with and without a pro rata rule. It can be seen that the pro rata rule reduces incentives to create volatility and significantly reduces the incentive to destroy value. In scenario 9 the effect of the pro rata rule is to reduce the average rewards by 55%. This substantially eliminates the incentive to destroy value. Some shareholders may think that, even at this much lower level, the executive rewards in scenario 9 are still rather high. However it is very important that a value destroying chief executive retains strong incentives to restore the value destroyed, even if this is done by accepting a takeover bid. Reasonable payments for the value restored are therefore necessary, even if they feel rather galling.

The modelling in appendix 6 shows that the pro rata rule is a sensible addition to a FILLIP. This rule should always be included to eliminate the problem of big payouts for poor performance.

FILLIPs and absolute value growth

In the second half of chapter 3 we considered the respective merits of rewarding relative and absolute corporate financial performance. A FILLIP rewards relative performance more than absolute performance. On the whole this is a good thing because the current high levels of executive pay are usually justified by considerations relative to other companies. However shareholders have a legitimate concern that rewarding relative performance gives incentives to compete aggressively rather than to create shareholder value. Over aggressive competition is not aligned with shareholders interests because shareholders usually own shares in many companies. They benefit more when companies focus on growing the value of their market, than when companies focus on market share.

I have investigated various ways to provide greater incentives to create shareholder value, without compromising the importance of performance relative to other companies. The best solution that I have found is to add an "Enhanced Return" rule. The enhanced return rule provides extra incentives to grow the TSR index during the two year share retention period between transfer and release of shares under a FILLIP. The number of shares released is increased twice over in proportion to the growth in the TSR index during this period. For example if the TSR index grew by 20% over this two year period then the number of shares transferred would be increased by 44% (from 1.2*1.2 − 1) when the shares are released. Obviously this increases the overall expected value of a conditional award (unless TSR is falling!), so it is necessary to reduce the number of shares conditionally awarded to ensure that the expected value remains unchanged.

Under an enhanced return FILLIP the final value of a conditional award is determined by relative performance during years one to three and by absolute performance over years four and five. This increases the alignment with shareholders interests without compromising the importance of relative performance. The drafting of an enhanced return rule is included in appendix 5. Appendix 6 shows spreadsheet modelling of the value of a pro rata enhanced return (PRER) FILLIP. In conjunction with a pro rata rule the enhanced return rule increases rewards for good performance and reduces rewards for bad performance. It also has the desirable effect of reducing the returns associated with volatile performance and price spikes.

Other criticisms of LTIPs and TSR

A FILLIP with a pro rata rule and an enhanced return rule (a PRER FILLIP) is a very good form of variable pay. It aligns executives' incentives far more closely to shareholders' interests than any variable pay scheme currently used in the UK. It is simpler, more transparent, more objective and provides clearer incentives than other schemes. Used in place of these other schemes, and in place of a proportion of base salary, FILLIPs could help overcome many of the problems seen in UK executive pay today. A well designed FILLIP scheme is suitable for any company with liquid share trading whose primary objective is to deliver value to shareholders.

There are, however, some important figures in the investment community who have a great distrust of LTIP style remuneration schemes and of the TSR performance measure in particular. This distrust arises from some bad experiences, where poorly designed LTIP schemes have resulted in some very inappropriate remuneration outcomes. The important point is that a PRER FILLIP as set out in appendix 5 is a very well designed LTIP. It does not suffer from the problems associated with other LTIP schemes. Financial modelling of the PRER FILLIPs behaviour is included in appendix 6, and shows that it delivers appropriate outcomes in a wide variety of circumstances. In the next paragraphs we look at some of the common criticisms of LTIPs and TSR and see how they have been addressed in the design of the PRER FILLIP.

Share price and the underlying value of a company

The most common criticism of TSR as a performance measure is that it is critically based on share price, and share price is not always a reliable indictor of the underlying value of a company.

In theory, if a share price is too low compared to the value of a company then investors will buy that share because it is good value. Similarly investors will sell a share that is over priced, so that they can lock in the benefit of the over valuation. This behaviour ensures that unrealistic share prices are quickly corrected. The share price is therefore good indicator of company value, even though it suffers from volatility in the short term.

However, in March 2001 Paul Myners published a report about institutional investment in the UK, requested by the Chancellor of the Exchequer. The report revealed that there are a great many reasons why institutional investors buy and sell shares that have nothing to do with value. Often they buy and sell to ensure that a fund conforms to certain indexing requirements, and this is becoming more and more common with the increasing popularity of index tracking style investments. Sometimes buying and selling occurs to adjust risk profiles or to boost the short term performance of a fund. Reward decisions for fund managers are usually based on the short term performance of their funds, so the short term performance of an investment matters far more to a fund manager than it does to the underlying owners of the fund. These and several other factors mean that the stock market is much less focused on value than an ordinary investor might expect. The market is therefore less than perfectly efficient and, at least in the short term, share price is less good as an indicator of company value than it should be. This in turn should create opportunities for value orientated investors to make money on the stock market, and in doing so correct the problem.

The question of stock market efficiency is a question of how fast unrealistic share prices correct. From the Myners report, it seems that they may correct within weeks or months, rather than within minutes or hours as we might have expected. However, it remains true that if TSR is measured over any reasonable period of time, say three years, then changes in the TSR index do still provide a reliable indicator of company performance. Also it is important to note that under a quarterly phased FILLIP the damage caused by an unrealistic share prices is far less than in a normal LTIP. The share price at any one quarter end affects only one twelfth of the live performance periods. Also by using the same share price to start and end performance periods the FILLIP ensures that any share price "error" has an equal and opposite effect on two different performance periods.

The concerns about unrealistic share prices are not reasons to move away from TSR as a performance measure for executive pay. They are reasons to make LTIPs fully invariable and to make other design improvements such that they become FILLIPs. They are also reasons to ensure that the institutional investment industry moves in the direction suggested by Paul Myners such that the stock market becomes more efficient.

Take-over speculation

It is sometimes said that LTIPs make inappropriate payments when a company's share price is affected by takeover speculation. Takeover speculation can cause a surge in share price, which does not reflect any effort or skill on the part of the executive team. In fact the most dramatic share price surges often occur when the executive team is performing badly. This is because the City hopes that a new management will unlock value in the company in a way that the present executive team is not able to.

Badly designed LTIP schemes can easily pay huge rewards because of takeover speculation. The higher share price causes rapid growth in TSR resulting in performance conditions being met and all conditionally allocated shares transferring.

It is very important to notice however that if an LTIP or FILLIP is well designed then a share price spike does not increase overall rewards to the executive team, unless there is a lasting increase in shareholder value. If a takeover bid does lead to a lasting increase in shareholder value then it is necessary to reward the executive team for this. This is discussed further below.

When designing an LTIP to be resilient to price spikes the most important design defence is to ensure that conditional awards are made on a regular phased basis. This ensures that the share price spike only affects a proportion of the conditional awards that are currently within their performance periods. The second most important design defence is to ensure that the share price used to close one performance period is also used to open the next performance period. This ensures that if the executive team make unmerited gains because a performance period closes while the share price is spiking then they will make equivalent unmerited loses on the performance period just starting. If these two defences are in place and there is no retesting, then the scheme is fully invariable ensuring that rewards attributable to the price spike will be much reduced. Although most FTSE 350 LTIPs are not fully invariable the Typico scheme is. By comparing scenario 5 and scenario 8 of appendix 4 it is clear that the price spike has increased average rewards over seven years by 8%.

It is clear that a fully invariable LTIP can be further improved by making it fully linear such that it becomes a FILLIP. Comparing scenarios 5 and 8 again, this time in appendix 6 shows that in the case of a FILLIP the average rewards are actually slightly decreased by the price spike. The decrease becomes more pronounced if pro rata rule is included. It is therefore clear that design improvements can eliminate problems arising from share price spikes.

The thinking behind FILLIPs is more concerned with giving an executive team the correct incentives, than with making assessments of their performance. It is very important that executive teams have a strong incentive to accept an attractive takeover offer. Takeovers are almost always a good result for the shareholders of the entity being taken over. By contrast takeovers are usually a very bad result for executives of the entity taken over because they may well lose their jobs, and will certainly lose much of their power and influence. If incentives are to be properly aligned in this situation then shareholders have to accept that even a poorly performing executive team should be rewarded for selling out to better management who will add value to the company. The FILLIP rules in appendix 5 do provide this incentive in a consistent way. It might sometimes grate to pay a poor management team to sell out, but it is unquestionably in the shareholders interests to do this.

Share price and underlying financial performance

Periodically the financial press reports that some badly designed LTIP has made a big and clearly inappropriate payout. When this happens shareholders sometimes respond by saying that incentive payments should be based on the underlying financial performance of the company, rather than on share price. This reaction appears to place the blame for the inappropriate payout on TSR as a performance measure. In fact the problems are not with TSR, but rather with the design of the LTIP.

The modelling in appendix 4, particularly scenarios 2, 6, 7, 8 and 9 show how an LTIP, which by current standards is quite well designed, can easily deliver inappropriate remuneration outcomes. In particular it rewards volatility, price spikes and can even reward value destruction. Appendix 6 shows that a pro rata FILLIP and a PRER FILLIP provide far better remuneration outcomes in these same circumstances. When making the comparison it is important to remember that implementation of a FILLIP requires lower base salaries because a FILLIP does provide some reward for below median performance.

It is of course very possible to base the performance conditions for long term incentive schemes on underlying financial measures such as profit, earnings or earnings per share (EPS) in stead of on TSR. Such performance measures are common, particularly in share option schemes. In a typical share option scheme the EPS figure for a financial year is compared to the corresponding figure three years earlier. This longer term view of EPS growth as a performance measure has many advantages. In particular it does not generate the same incentives for short term behaviour as profit does when it is used as a basis for annual bonus. The effectiveness of three year EPS growth as a performance measure is often undermined by a failure to phase the awards, by retesting and, most outrageously of all, allowing the start date of a performance period to be flexible. Good scheme design however can quickly sort out these problems.

There are however other problems with EPS growth as a performance measure, and some of these are much harder to sort out. For example, exceptional items cause real difficulty. A one off cost or benefit arising from a disposal, a discontinued business activity, a lawsuit, an asset impairment, or any form of restructuring can easily have a significant impact on EPS growth. Typically such costs or benefits are excluded from the EPS growth performance measures so that the underlying financial performance can be compared from one year to the next. However exceptional items do represent real and material costs or benefits to shareholders and to exclude them from a performance measure is dangerous. The desire to achieve EPS growth performance targets could easily start to affect accounting policies on exceptional items. Worse still it might start to affect strategy. A strategy where the costs or risks would materialise as exceptional items might appear more attractive to management than a strategy where they clearly affect the bottom line profit and EPS figures.

Another problem is that EPS growth tells us very little about the quality of capital investment. If a growth in EPS was caused by an investment then the question of whether or not the investment represented good value for money is very important to shareholders. It is not however captured by the EPS growth performance measure. Similarly an executive team might show good EPS growth, but then squander the earnings on an ill-advised foreign acquisition rather than returning them to shareholders.

EPS growth tells us very little about long term issues. An oil company might show excellent EPS growth, but fail to replace its reserves. A pharmaceutical company might show good EPS growth but fail to develop new products. The long term sustainability of earnings is a key issue for shareholders and it is not captured by the EPS growth measure.

City analysts take great interest in a company's figures for profit and earnings. Usually, higher earnings are a sign that the company is worth more and so the share price increases. However the City also makes very sophisticated judgements about the quality and sustainability of earnings, and the confidence that the earnings will in due course be returned to shareholders. Companies who perform well on these counts get a higher share price to earnings ratio than companies who don't. In other words the company's share price contains a great deal of information about the quality of earnings that is not captured by a simple earnings growth measure. This is why TSR growth measured over the long term, is far superior to EPS growth as a performance measure.

Long term TSR growth is a measure of precisely what shareholders want. It is an objective measure, determined independently of the company management. In the short term a TSR index can be distorted by volatility but long term TSR growth is the thing that matters. Remuneration committees should not allow some bad experiences with inadequate LTIPs to put them off TSR growth as a performance measure. Rather the focus should move to resolving the design problems in LTIPs, for example by migrating towards PRER FILLIPs.

Advantages and dangers of assessing variable pay using a single performance measure

After a large, unmerited LTIP payout shareholders sometimes comment, "It is dangerous to base a large proportion of variable pay on a single performance measure such as TSR". This comment is very valid when we consider the low quality of the incentive schemes typically in use in FTSE 350 companies today. However, the more confident we become that we have devised a reward scheme that gives the right incentives and pays appropriate rewards then the more we should focus our available remuneration on to that scheme.

The way to get confident about a reward scheme is to use spreadsheet models to investigate the payouts that the scheme makes in a variety of different performance outcomes. Appendix 4 contains such models for the Typico LTIP scheme. Appendix 6 contains the equivalent models for three different kinds of FILLIP. It is very clear from scenarios 2 and 9 in particular that it would be dangerous to put to much faith in the Typico LTIP. However the models in appendix 6 demonstrate that a FILLIP with a pro rata rule and enhanced return rule gives very appropriate remuneration outcomes in a wide variety of performance outcomes. It is therefore very appropriate to focus available remuneration onto a FILLIP such as this.

It is also important to remember that significant difficulties arise when remuneration is spread over a large number of small schemes. These difficulties were discussed in under the headings of complexity, incentives and transparency in chapter 4.

Problem of deferred payment

One genuine problem with the FILLIP form of remuneration is that executives have to wait five years before they actually receive their variable pay. This would be a major issue for staff lower down the organisation, but for senior management and executives it is often less of a problem than it might appear at first sight. Some informal research on this issue is included in appendix 3.

First of all it is important to remember that, even without their variable pay, executives are in general very well paid. Base salaries provide them with significant amounts of cash and it is very rare for their personal activities to be hampered by the kind of cash constraints that affect most of us from time to time.

Secondly the uncertain nature of variable income makes it unsuitable for funding ongoing financial commitments. Executives always have to plan their personal expenditure at a level which does not depend on variable income and this means that a delay to the arrival of the income is less serious.

Thirdly the problem is much reduced where conditional awards are made on a regular phased basis. It is therefore very likely that every year, or every quarter, a batch of shares is released to the executive from the FILLIP scheme. This creates a continuous flow of income which slowly grows as the executive moves up the organisation. Obviously the value of this income stream depends on performance, but that is precisely the point. The fact that the income stream arrives five years in arrears can almost be forgotten, but it becomes a positive benefit in the five years after the executive leaves the company. The only executives who might have difficulties are those who are new to the company, having recently joined from outside. The situation of executives who are new to a company is discussed in chapter 7.

Fourthly the proceeds of share based incentive schemes are very typically put into savings or some form of investment. Provided that what is saved within the FILLIP is secure and earning a reasonable return, it is of little consequence to an executive whether the money is saved inside the company or in other forms of personal investment outside of the company. Of course, one of the whole points of the design of FILLIPs is to ensure that executives have incentives to make sure that shares in the company represent secure investment providing a reasonable rate of return.

If there is an executive who desperately needs cash then I can see no problem with him or her using a FILLIP as security to borrow money. If the borrowing is done on strictly commercial basis then the rate of interest charged will reflect the perceived risks to the value in the FILLIP. This is entirely appropriate because it further aligns shareholder and executive interests. Companies should not however get involved in the organisation of schemes for employees and directors to borrow money against FILLIPs. Any such involvement would undermine confidence that the borrowing was being done on a strictly commercial basis, accurately reflecting the risks to the value of the FILLIPs.

Difference in reward between good and bad performance

Typical share based incentive schemes pay very high rewards to top performers and nothing for below median performance. In contrast a FILLIP makes rather more consistent payments, even though the size of these can still vary very significantly. Some remuneration experts might be concerned that a FILLIP does not adequately differentiate exceptional performance from moderate performance.

This difficulty is partially addressed by the enhanced return rule. The modelling in appendix 6 shows how the enhanced return rule increases rewards for good performers and reduces rewards for poor performers.

In general however it is difficult to devise remuneration schemes that create a big differential between exceptional and moderate performance without creating a very strong and undesirable incentive to create volatility. This is discussed in detail in chapter 6. Usually schemes that purport to reward exceptional performance actually reward increased volatility. Appendix 4 shows how this works for the Typico LTIP. Many FTSE 350 schemes reward volatility even more than the Typico scheme does.

The problem with exceptional performance is that it cannot usually be sustained over time. In the long term the rate of growth in shareholder value usually reverts to mean. This has been well illustrated by index tracking investment methodologies. The methodologies make no attempt to distinguish good and bad performance but consistently deliver an investment performance that is well above median level after costs have been taken into account.

In the same way the investment community need to be much more realistic about what an executive team can hope to achieve in terms of exceptional performance. There is no point in setting top quartile performance as a target. A better target is long term consistency in beating median performance. Institutional investors feel naturally sympathetic to the "exceptional reward for exception performance" argument because it is an argument that fund managers like to use in respect of their own remuneration. However the argument only works for the underlying investor in the fund if above average performance can be sustained in the long term.

In this respect a FILLIP is far more realistic than the share based incentive schemes that we see in use in FTSE 350 companies today. Rather than experiment with highly geared remuneration schemes the way to increase the differentiation between good and bad performers is to reduce the level of fixed pay and divert the equivalent value into the FILLIP.

Restructure of Joe Figment's reward package

Let us remember Joe Figment's reward package set out at the start of chapter 4 and consider what it might look like if reorganised into a FILLIP based approach to remuneration. Taking care not to not change the estimated average present annual value the reworked package might look like this:

Element	Estimated Average	Present Annual Value
Basic Salary	£ 337,500	Fixed
PRER FILLIP	£2,000,000	Variable from zero to £4,000,000
Pension	£ 112,500	Fixed
Other benefits	£ 50,000	Fixed
Total:	£2,500,000	£500,000 is fixed and £2,000,000 variable

FILLIP stands for Fully Invariable Linear Long term Incentive Plan.

Pension is the increase in the transfer value of Joe's pension, net of his contributions.

Other benefits include a car, private health insurance and life assurance.

Let us assume that this restructure has no net effect on the actual amount of remuneration that Joe Figment will on average receive. The package therefore does not cost the Typico shareholder any more or less than the package set out in chapter 4. The change does however provide some very significant benefits to the Typico shareholder. First of all it is far clearer how much Joe Figment is actually being paid, and how that moves with performance. Secondly the incentives are far clearer. Joe has a very strong and clear incentive to grow shareholder value in a way that is consistent, secure and that can be sustained into the longer term. This will increase trust between shareholders and executives. Thirdly the undesirable incentive to create volatility has been eliminated. Fourthly Typico's process for PPCs can be freed from remuneration implications such that its focus can really be on performance. Fifthly the executive team will find it far easier to agree common goals and build trust now that they all have the same remuneration incentive. Sixthly the modelling in appendix 6 gives shareholders high confidence that the remuneration outcome will be appropriate throughout a wide range of different performance outcomes. Seventhly the fixed component of the salary is lower, so in lean times the package will be more cost effective. Eighthly the much simpler structure will cost less to administer.

So, what is the downside? From a shareholders perspective I really can't see one.

Summary

In this chapter we have examined two serious problems associated with LTIPs and FILLIPs. We have seen that the problem of potentially rewarding value destruction can be appropriately addressed by introducing a pro rata rule into the design of the FILLIP. We have seen that the shareholder requirement for absolute performance can be addressed by introducing an enhanced return rule into a FILLIP. A FILLIP which includes both a pro rata rule and an enhanced return rule is called a PRER FILLIP and provides far better alignment of incentives than any form of remuneration currently used in FTSE 350 companies. The resilience of the incentives under a PRER FILLIP in many different performance situations is demonstrated by the spreadsheet models in appendix 6.

We also examined the various criticisms that commentators sometimes make about LTIP style remuneration and about TSR as a performance measure. It was very clear that all these problems arose from bad design of the LTIP rather than from the use of TSR as a performance measure. A PRER FILLIP properly addresses all these design concerns and shareholders can be very confident that a PRER FILLIP provides extremely good alignment between executive incentives and shareholder aspirations.

At the end of the chapter we considered what Joe Figment's reward package might look like if it was restructured using a PRER FILLIP. We showed that although the cost of the revised reward package to shareholders was unchanged, the benefits of improved incentive alignment, higher transparency, simplicity and increased trust would be extremely significant.

9

Share Option Schemes (SOSs)

Share Options Schemes (SOSs) are amongst the most common and most valuable forms of remuneration provided to company executives. We therefore need to look carefully at the advantages and disadvantages of such schemes.

What is a share option?

A share option is an entitlement to buy a particular share, at a particular price, known as the exercise price. For example, as part of his remuneration in 2002, Joe Figment was awarded 175,000 options to buy shares in Typico at £5.51 each. The Typico share price is now around £6.25 so Joe's options are "in the money". He could exercise the options today, buying 175,000 Typico shares at £5.51 each (total cost £964,250) and immediately sell those shares for £6.25 each (total benefit £1,093,750) making a net benefit of £129,500. If he were to exercise them today, Joe's options would be worth 74 pence each. In fact Joe will wait before exercising the options. They do not expire until 2012 and the Typico share price is likely to rise very significantly before that time. Joe wants the share price to grow as much as possible before he exercises the options, because in this way the value he derives from the options is maximised.

When remuneration is paid in the form of share options it is likely to be subject to income tax (and possibly capital gains tax) when the options are exercised. The tax rules are complicated and beyond the scope of this book. The tax treatment is different depending on whether or not the options were "approved" in accordance with Inland Revenue rules.

Sometimes options are "out of the money" or "underwater" because the exercise price is higher that the current share price. Nobody would exercise a share option while it was underwater because they would be paying more for the share than it was worth. An underwater option might therefore appear to have no value, but this is far from the case. The option could still prove to be very valuable, because the share price might rise high above the exercise price at some point in the future, before the option expires.

Typico's Share Option Scheme

Like almost all companies in the FTSE 100, Typico operates a Share Option Scheme (SOS). This provides extra remuneration to managers in the form of share options and gives them incentives to improve the financial performance of the company. The way that the Typico SOS works is set out below.

In early September each year the company makes a conditional award of share options to each member of the scheme. The options are awarded with an exercise price equal to the average closing share price for the five business days before the day of the conditional award. Provided that the performance conditions have been met, the options can be exercised at any time between three and ten years after the award was made. Unexercised options lapse after ten years or after five years if the performance condition has not been met.

All members of the executive team are members of the SOS and each is awarded options over a number of shares, such that the value of those shares at the exercise price is equal to twice basic salary. The size of conditional award was reduced from four times salary to two times salary when the LTIP was introduced in 1998. The SOS extends to all management grades, although the size of the awards relative to basic salary gets much smaller lower down the organisation.

All the options awarded are conditional, based on performance conditions, which are tested at the end of each financial year when the Earnings Per Share (EPS) for the year are published. Under the performance condition options become unconditional (they "vest") if the company's Earnings Per Share (EPS) grows by at least 5% per annum more than inflation, over a three year performance period. The performance period for each conditional award of options starts on 1st January of the year in which the award was made, and finishes at financial year end three years later. If options do not vest after three years then the scheme allows for a retest of the 5% per annum more than inflation condition after four years and again after five years.

For example, if inflation was steady at 2% then for all options to vest the EPS growth must be 21.88% (calculated from 1.05^3-1 + 1.02^3-1) after three years, or 29.79% (calculated from 1.05^4-1 + 1.02^4-1) after four years, or 38.04% (calculated from 1.05^5-1 + 1.02^5-1) after five years.

The performance test also includes a sliding scale such that if EPS growth is $2\frac{1}{2}$% per annum more than inflation over the performance period then half of the conditional options would vest. If EPS growth exceeded inflation by between $2\frac{1}{2}$% and 5% per annum then a proportion between half and all of the options vest, determined on a straight line basis. If EPS growth does not exceed inflation by at least $2\frac{1}{2}$% per annum, over the three, four or five year performance periods then all of the options lapse.

Like the LTIP, Typico's SOS is administered by Bonanza, the remuneration consultancy.

Incentives under the Typico Share Option Scheme

The Typico SOS has a number of strengths and provides significantly better incentives then many of the SOSs currently used by FTSE 350 companies. For example it makes awards on a regular phased basis, and uses a sliding scale. One of its particular strengths is that performance condition requiring 5% EPS growth over inflation is set at a reasonably challenging level. It is very common for full vesting to occur if EPS growth exceeds inflation by 3%, and in some cases the performance conditions are even weaker than that, or even none existent.

Another strong point is that the base year for the performance period is fixed when the options are conditionally awarded. Some option schemes allow the performance period to start at any financial year end after the option has been conditionally awarded. This makes it extremely easy to satisfy the performance condition because it provides a ten year window in which to look for a three year period of good earnings growth.

Despite these strengths, from a shareholder perspective there are still several serious weaknesses with the Typico SOS as a form of remuneration. Some of these weaknesses arise from the use of EPS growth as a performance measure. The issues with EPS growth as a performance measure are discussed in chapter 8. There are also weaknesses arising from the scheme design and from the nature of the share options themselves, which we look at in this chapter.

Problems of scheme design

The first and most obvious scheme design problem is that retesting of the performance condition is allowed. This effectively allows periods of good performance to be double counted, so that more conditional awards vest than would otherwise be the case. Institutional investors are very sensitive to the problem of retesting and increasingly SOSs do not allow it. Having said that, it is important to note that the specific type of retest allowed in the Typico scheme is far less damaging to the incentive regime than many other kinds of retest provisions. Financial modelling shows that, even with the retest, sustained growth in earnings is required to get the best rewards from the scheme.

The second big weakness in the scheme is a disproportionate incentive problem. The executive team have huge incentives to show that EPS growth has been fractionally over, rather than fractionally below $2^1/_2\%$ per annum. As discussed in chapter 6, a disproportionate incentive problem encourages executives to manipulate outcomes and frequently leads to disputes. It can also cause serious problems of demotivation if critical reward thresholds are narrowly missed. When EPS growth is the performance measure then manipulation of outcomes becomes an issue of particular concern. Accounting rules give the directors some discretion on how provisions, accruals and exceptional items are shown in the accounts. This discretion should be used to ensure that the accounts present a picture of the company's finances that is as true and fair as possible. It should not be used to maximise the rewards paid under the SOS.

A third problem with the scheme is motivational dead zones where EPS growth is in excess of 5% or below $2^1/_2$% per annum, after subtracting inflation. Executives have incentives not to post EPS results significantly above the 5% level because in doing so they unnecessarily make future performance conditions harder to achieve. Similarly if EPS growth rate is below $2^1/_2$% then the incentive is to post EPS as low as possible, because this will make future performance conditions easier to achieve.

Typico's share option scheme could be significantly improved from a shareholder perspective if EPS growth over inflation was linked to reward by a linear sliding scale that covered the full range of likely outcomes, say 0 to 10% per annum growth, with no retesting. This would ensure that consistent incentives to grow EPS were always in place. It would avoid the disproportionate incentive problem, motivational dead zones and the possible demotivation problem that can all arise under the current scheme design.

The valuation of share options

The biggest problem with share options as a form of remuneration is that they are extremely difficult to value. It was not until the 1970's that credible mathematical valuations became possible with the development of the Black Scholes Model. Even this model makes assumptions about volatility that cannot always be depended upon, and which famously led to the collapse of the Long Term Capital Management Hedge Fund in 1998.

I once tried to value the options that I had received through a SOS. I quickly found an internet site that provided a software tool for me to do this, but I found it difficult to know how to input the data into the tool. I then had to make bold assumptions about how likely the performance conditions were to be fulfilled, and about how long I would continue to work for the company. I finally generated a valuation, although I had little confidence that it was "correct". Experimenting further with the internet tool I realised that the valuation was extremely sensitive to small changes in input parameters such as share price. I came to the conclusion that the valuation had the potential to change so rapidly that whatever valuation I put on my options today, it would tell me very little about what they would be worth in three months time. For me this rather undermined the point of trying to generate a valuation. Even if I got a valuation and was certain it was correct I would not be able to count on it in any meaningful way, because it was likely to change so very quickly.

For me, this seriously undermined share options as a component of my remuneration. When evaluating my total remuneration I could not assign any value to the option scheme, but at the same time I knew it had the potential to be very valuable.

The difficulty of valuation makes share options a hugely inefficient form of remuneration. Options are sophisticated financial instruments designed for offsetting specific risks rather than for transferring value. The fact that the value of an option is so haphazard suggests that a wide range of remuneration outcomes is satisfactory to both the employing company and to the executive. As we noticed in chapter 4, this suggests that the market for executive talent is actually far less competitive than remuneration reports might lead us to believe.

As we also noted in chapter 4, contracts for commercial services often envisage variable payments depending on performance. In these cases all parties to the contract take great care to analyse their contractual position under the different performance outcomes. They want to ensure that they do not have financial exposure for matters that are beyond their control, and they want to know that the payment appears reasonable, whatever the performance outcome. Should we not expect performance related remuneration contracts to also work in this way? They clearly don't in cases where share options are used as remuneration. The value of such remuneration is so uncertain that neither party can possibly have confidence that it represents "good value" in all performance outcomes.

The tendency to undervalue share options

Share options are a very inefficient form of remuneration because they are very difficult to value. From a shareholder perspective this problem is further aggregated because people tend to undervalue rather than overvalue share options.

Instinctively people think of the value of an option as being the difference between the current share price and the exercise price. For example, if a share is worth £4.50, then an option that to buy that share for £4.20 is, at first sight, worth 30 pence. However this massively undervalues the option. Under the Typico SOS there is normally a seven year window during which an option can be exercised. The holder of the option is therefore able to delay exercise and gain seven years worth of share price growth without tying up any capital or putting capital at risk. Further, if the share price is very volatile, the option holder can choose to exercise the option at a time during the seven-year window when the share price appears unusually high. The option is certainly worth far, far more than 30 pence.

The tendency to undervalue options means that a remuneration committee which makes payments in options is probably paying more than it realises, and so getting a worse deal than it realises. Executives who are paid in options are probably being paid more than they think and so are less likely to be recruited, motivated or retained by the option package than by a package of equal, but more transparent value. From a shareholder perspective therefore payment in options is extremely wasteful.

The incentives that arise from option ownership

When companies introduce new share option schemes they frequently justify them as increasing the alignment of interests between executives and shareholders. This always seems strange to me because it is obvious that alignment would be far better served if the payments of the same market value were made in shares, rather than being made in options. Obviously to have the same market value fewer shares are needed than options, because each share is worth more than each option.

The big advantage of payment in shares is that it very naturally leads to executives holding much of their personal wealth in the form of company shares. This very clearly does increase the alignment of interest with shareholders. In contrast, payment in options often does not increase an executive's shareholding in the company. When an option is exercised, the executive needs capital to pay the exercise price. The natural and obvious way of raising this capital is by selling the shares secured when the option is exercised. Companies often provide bridging loans to make this process quick and easy. The result is that most shares obtained by exercising options are immediately sold for cash, with a proportion of the cash being used to cover the exercise price. The executive's long term shareholding in the company is very often not increased at all.

There are also many situations in which the interests of an option holder are not aligned with the interests of a shareholder. Clearly both benefit if the price of the share rises, but their common interest does not stretch far beyond this.

For example dividend policy is an area where the interests of option owners and shareholders are not aligned. Shareholders like dividends because they provide confidence that invested money is being returned. Also the value that they receive as dividends is being given specifically to shareholders and is not received by option holders. Option holders prefer to see dividends minimised so that the value of the company's past earnings is stored up in the share price. This allows them to receive the benefit of past earnings when an option is exercised.

Another misalignment is that executives who own options have much stronger incentives to take risks than they would have if they owned only shares. The option holder has no downside risk once the share price sinks below the exercise price, but has more upside risk because a small increase in share price leads to a larger proportional increase in the value of the option.

This can be illustrated by a rather crude example. Suppose the share price is £4.50, the option exercise price is £4.25, and the option must be exercised soon. Suppose the executive team can take a gamble, which is 50% likely to add £1 to the share price and 50% likely to remove £1 from the share price. The owner of a share is equally likely to end up with a share worth £3.50 or a share worth £5.50, so would probably prefer not to take the risk, and would stick with a share worth £4.50. The owner of an option is equally likely to end up with an option worth nothing or an option worth £1.25. This bet is clearly more attractive than sticking with an option worth 25p, so the option holder would probably take the gamble.

Risk is more attractive to the holder of an option than to the holder of a share. An executive team who own options therefore have incentives to take risks and create volatility in the share price. If a share price becomes more volatile without any change to underlying financial performance then the risk to reward trade off position gets worse for shareholders. By contrast an option to buy the share becomes more valuable.

Suppose you are chief executive of a start up technology company which has been very successful, but which now needs to find new opportunities for rapid growth. You have examined various possible opportunities for growth, some of which look more promising than others. If you own options but not shares you have strong incentives to invest in the new opportunities, make very bullish statements about the prospects and then exercise your options while they are at their most valuable. If you own shares but not options your incentive is to be prudent about new investments because you have a great deal of value at stake in the shares that you own.

If the option exercising chief executive's new investments perform badly and the share price crashes, there is a problem. The chief executive's behaviour in hiking the share price, exercising options and walking away with cash appears to be a cynical, if not criminal, trick to steal value from shareholders. Nobody wants chief executives to behave in this way. At the same time remuneration committees approve share option schemes precisely because they want chief executives to work to the incentives given and so they can hardly complain if chief executives do just that. The really, really important point is that share based incentive plans must always give incentives that have the closest possible alignment with shareholders interests. It is clear that interests would be far more closely aligned if remuneration was paid in shares rather than in share options.

Someone might doubt this conclusion by arguing that the chief executive who owns shares has the same incentive to create a share price peak and then sell up, as the chief executive who owns options. This is not true. First of all the number of shares that could be sold is much smaller, because the fair market value of each share is far higher than the fair market value of each option. Secondly it is much easier for chief executives to exercise options than it is for them to sell shares. Investors know that options have to be exercised sooner or later, so they can never read very much into a chief executive's decision to exercise options and turn the proceeds into cash. By contrast it is very difficult for chief executives to sell large numbers of shares without sending alarm bells ringing in the City. There is no good reason why the chief executive should need to sell a large numbers of shares. Also many companies have share retention rules, which limit or prevent such sales.

Option incentives and capital restructures

Any long term incentive scheme depends critically on maintaining the incentives for the executives in a consistent way over the long term duration of the scheme. This is very difficult to achieve with a SOS because it is almost impossible to preserve the consistency of the scheme if the company undergoes any form of capital restructuring. For example a special dividend, a merger or an acquisition is almost certain to have a significant effect on the value and even on the continued existence of the underlying share for which the option can be exercised. This has a huge impact on the value of the option and to avoid outcomes that are extremely unfair and inappropriate it is almost always necessary to buy out the options or to replace them with new options that hopefully have a similar value and provide similar incentives to the old ones. In practice it is very difficult for a remuneration committee to do this in a way that is both fair and not excessively generous to the option holders. There is also a danger that executives will start to take into account the treatment of their own personal share options as they try to determine the desirability or otherwise of the proposed capital restructure.

If remuneration is paid in shares rather than in options it is far easier to maintain consistency because the shares in the FILLIP and the TSR indexes can be restructured following the same rules that apply to any other ordinary share. This ensures that the incentive regime is not damaged by the capital restructure.

Why did share option schemes become so widely used?

Given that there are so many problems with options as a form of remuneration, and given that remuneration in shares clearly aligns executives' interests with shareholders' far more closely it is worth asking why options ever became a common form of executive remuneration. Well, some of the reasons normally given to support share option schemes are discussed below.

To get value from share options executives must invest their own money in the company.

This is not true for the Typico scheme, or indeed for most SOSs used in the UK. In the Typico scheme executives do not put their own money at risk until the time comes to exercise the option. Normally executives sell shares immediately after exercise to pay the exercise price, which ensures that their own money is never put at risk. Only where executives choose to put in their own capital and retain the shares post exercise does real executive investment occur.

The value of option based remuneration is at risk with the share price.

This argument is true, but the risks would be better aligned with shareholders risks if remuneration was made in shares.

Remuneration through share options does not reduce profit or earnings.

This argument assumes that new shares are being issued when options are exercised. The value passed to the executive therefore comes from the dilution of future earnings amongst more shares rather than by a simple reduction in current company earnings. The remuneration still constitutes value passing from shareholders to executives; it is just that the transfer cannot be seen in the accounts. This is in fact a problem with the accounts and a reason to support of Financial Reporting Standard FRS20, which requires the fair market value of share options to be shown as an expense in the accounts.

If the exercise price is set at the current share price then the option has no value.

If this was really true executives would not be interested in share option schemes! A 10-year option clearly has significant value even if the exercise price is the same as the current share price because the share price should rise significantly over 10 years.

Remuneration in share options is more tax efficient that remuneration in shares.

This may have been true at one time, but it is not true anymore. Even if it was true it would not justify giving executives the wrong incentives. Tax efficiency is far less important than getting executive incentives correct. This is because executive pay usually forms only a very small proportion of the company's total costs, so the tax considerations are not significant.

Awards made in options provide stronger incentives to grow the share price than awards made in shares, because their value appreciates faster as the share price grows.

The value of options appreciates faster because the fair market value of an option is far less than the fair market value of a share. This means that an award made in options contains more options than an award of equal value made in shares. For example if the fair market value of the share is £2.50 and the fair market value of the option is £0.50 then a £10,000 award would contain 4,000 shares or 20,000 options. In the case of the share award, a 1p rise in the share price is worth £40, but in the case of the option award it is worth £200. However this is not a good reason for using options as remuneration. Shareholder should aim to provide incentives that are closely aligned with shareholder interests, not stronger than the shareholder interest. An excessive executive incentive to grow the share price creates incentives to take risks to generate share price peaks and volatility rather than consistent and sustainable value growth. It also reduces the incentives to pay dividends. If the company is very successful then option based remuneration costs shareholders far more than necessary.

A share option has value only to the extent that the executive team can increase the share price over the 10 years following award.
Certainly shareholders are reassured by the idea that if the share price does not rise then remuneration paid in the form of options has no value. If the remuneration was paid in shares the shares would continue to have value even if there was no rise in the share price. This, on the face of it, is an advantage of options as a form of remuneration. However there are two other considerations here. Firstly, if the share price has not risen at all then it is unlikely that the performance conditions will have been met. This means that the conditional awards will be lost to the executive, so it makes no difference whether those conditional awards were made in shares or options. Secondly, if share price growth is rapid then payments made in options will become much more expensive to shareholders than payments made in shares. The cost to shareholders in the upside case is very large and certainly can not justify the possible benefit in the downside case. This point is examined in more detail in the section on shareholder hedges at the end of this chapter.

From the above it is clear that the arguments usually used to support options as a form of remuneration are very weak and executive incentives would be much better aligned with shareholder interests if remuneration was paid in shares rather than in options. Obviously fewer shares would be paid because the fair market value of an option is less than the value of a share.

Variable pay as a shareholder hedge

One of the advantages of performance related pay that we examined in chapter 2 was that shareholders would need to pay more to executives when financial performance was good and they could afford it, but would need to pay less when financial performance was bad and they could not afford it. In other words variable pay has a hedging effect that partially offsets the risks that a shareholder faces through owning shares.

This hedging effect is desirable, but is usually too small to have significant value because the cost of executive pay is usually very small compared to a company's total income and costs. The hedging effect can become much more significant if all employees are paid on a variable basis. This is especially true if manpower is one of the company's major costs.

Appendix 7 examines the different hedging benefits to shareholders arising from option based remuneration and shares based remuneration. The modelling assumes that no dividends are paid and that share price volatility can be ignored. Scenario 1 concerns a well-established company, with a share price growth target of 8% per annum. In this scenario shares provide a better hedge than options, because the options become very expensive if the company is successful and offer only modest savings if the company performs badly. Scenario 2 concerns a rapidly developing company, which targets a 25% annual growth in share prices. In this case the hedging effects of share and options appear very similar. Options are slightly more expensive in successful outcomes, but slightly cheaper in unsuccessful outcomes. It is also important to remember that in poor performance situations it is likely that neither shares nor options would vest because performance conditions would not be met. This further undermines any advantage that might arise from option based remuneration.

We can conclude that option based remuneration is far less cost effective than share based remuneration as a shareholder hedge.

Summary

From a shareholder perspective a SOS is a very poor form of executive remuneration. SOSs are usually badly designed such that there is a serious disproportionate incentive problem and a big problem with motivational dead zones. They typically use long term EPS growth rather than TSR growth as a performance measure and this encourages the manipulation of outcomes and creates undesirable incentives in the definition of accounting policies. These problems of scheme design could be fixed by making improvements to the scheme rules. However there are other serious problems associated with the share options themselves and these are much harder to fix.

Share options are difficult to value effectively and even when valued correctly their value can be extremely volatile. This reduces the transparency of remuneration and its effectiveness in recruiting, motivating and retaining executive talent. Further, people tend to undervalue share options so the incentives provided are very bad value for money from a shareholder perspective. If remuneration committees really are competing hard to attract and retain the best executive talent then we would expect them to use reward packages where it is easier to overestimate rather than to underestimate the value of the package. With share options the real value of the reward package is usually underestimated.

The alignment of executive incentives with shareholder interests would be far better served if payments where made in shares rather than in share options. In particular the incentives to pay dividends and evaluate risks responsibly would be far stronger. The risks to shareholders are much greater when an executive realises cash by exercising options rather than by selling shares. Capital restructures would also be far easier to handle.

The arguments usually made to justify SOSs are very weak. The use of options rather than shares for executive remuneration does not save shareholders any money if company performance turns out to be poor and performance conditions are not met. However, if performance is good then share options are far more expensive to shareholders than shares based remuneration would be. It seems likely that share options are only popular as a form of remuneration because they do not reduce the profit or earnings numbers reported in company accounts. The new accounting standard FRS20 has improved the accounting treatment of options so that their costs are more transparent. This may lead to reduced use of options in executive pay.

10

Fixed pay

Fixed pay is pay that an executive receives irrespective of any personal or company performance considerations. It includes basic salary and other rewards such as company car and pension which may not be exactly "pay", but which the executive continues to benefit from, irrespective of company performance.

Components of fixed pay

At the start of chapter 4 we looked at Joe Figments reward package. His fixed pay consists of his basic salary, his pension entitlement, a company car, private health insurance and life assurance provided by the company.

In general shareholders like to see fixed pay set at a low level, and prefer to see the larger part of a reward package as variable pay that is linked to performance. The Combined Code says, "A significant proportion of executive directors' remuneration should be structured so as to link rewards to corporate and individual performance."[18] It also says, "The performance-related elements of remuneration should form a significant proportion of the total remuneration package of executive directors and should be designed to align their interests with those of shareholders and to give these directors keen incentives to perform at the highest levels."[19]

Clearly the incentives to perform are central to any variable pay scheme, and a large part of this book has been devoted to examining those incentives in detail and showing how they can be brought into better alignment with shareholders interests. However consideration of incentives is also important when thinking about fixed pay. Fixed pay may not be designed to deliver incentives but its existence has a very strong incentive effect and this needs to be taken into account.

Importance of basic salary

When I worked in management, there was absolutely no doubt in my mind that the most important financial incentive that I faced (apart from keeping my job!) was the incentive to enhance my basic salary. In the long term this was by far and away the most important thing financially. Admittedly I was not senior enough to secure the most lucrative variable pay arrangements but I know that even for managers a great deal more senior than myself, basic pay remained the most important factor. I suspect that even in the biggest companies in the UK the very top managers care more about their basic salaries than about their variable pay, even though the variable pay might be worth several times more than basic salary. Why is this?

Well the first big advantage of basic salary is that it is dependable. You can count on it arriving month in, month out. An individual can take on financial commitments in a very secure way if they are paid out of basic salary. Commitments paid out of variable pay look far more risky. It is more natural to use variable pay against one time costs, or to put it to savings or investment, than to use it against ongoing financial commitments.

The second big advantage of basic salary is that it is pensionable. This becomes more and more important as you get older. For a mature chief executive approaching the end of his or her career this becomes extremely significant. If a full final salary pension has been earned then every £1000 rise in basic salary guarantees an extra £666 of pension for every year for life after retirement.

The third big advantage of basic salary is that usually all variable pay schemes are indexed off the base salary. A 5% rise in base salary therefore means an expected 5% rise in annual bonus, a 5% rise in LTIP awards, and a 5% rise in SOS awards. Pensions, cars, insurance and other benefits also go up with basic salary.

A fourth big advantage of basic salary is security. Companies find it extremely difficult, if not impossible, to reduce basic salary once it has been increased. Further if a job is lost for any reason outside the direct control of the executive then there is likely to be some kind of pay off or benefit that is almost certain to be proportionate with basic salary.

A fifth big advantage of basic salary is that increases usually compound. An increase in basic salary is usually permanent and it increases the effect of subsequent increases.

Basic salary is also the most easily benchmarked part of a reward package. There is a tendency, probably an undesirable one, to measure overall levels of accomplishment in business in terms of basic salary. When investigating new job opportunities in new companies, basic salary in the last company is likely to set the starting point for any reward negotiation.

So basic salary is very, very important. It is much more important than variable pay schemes, even where the variable pay schemes are significantly more valuable. The strongest financial incentive faced by an executive is to stay in post (unless moving to a better post!). The second strongest financial incentive is likely to be enhancement of basic salary.

The incentives arising from basic salary

So, suppose you are a chief executive of a large company and you want to enhance your basic salary. How do you go about it?

Well, unfortunately from the shareholders perspective, you probably want to focus on areas other than company performance. The problem with company performance is that it is specifically rewarded through the variable pay incentive schemes. This seriously blunts the argument that good performance justifies higher basic pay. There are other ways of justifying increased basic salary that are likely to work better for you.

First of all there are some cheap tricks that you might try. You could insist on hiring the most expensive finance director possible. This might have the effect of pushing up the chief executives salary, because the chief executive is usually paid more than the finance director. In the same vein you could hire some executives from the US on US level salaries. Taking over a US operation would be a good tactic, especially if it allows you to base yourself in the US.

There are also more serious ways of justifying higher basic salary. When the Typico remuneration committee consults Bonanza about basic salary for chief executives, Bonanza says that the two most important factors in the determination of basic pay are the size and the complexity of the company. Bonanza has a composite measure of company size, which is derived from market capitalisation, turnover and number of employees. It also has a composite measure of complexity derived from extent of international operations and technological innovation, the complexity of the regulatory regime and average salaries within the company. Bonanza plots the positions of different companies on a scatter graph with these two composite measures as axes. They then show that there is a high correlation between the company's distance from origin on the scatter graph and basic salary of its chief executive.

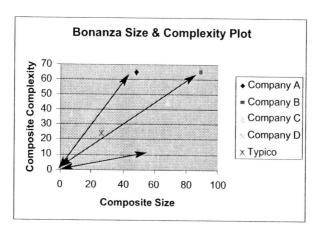

So to increase your basic salary what you really need are ways of increasing the size and complexity of the company. Acquisitions look like a good idea. Foreign acquisitions look even better. A rites issue would increase the market capitalisation. Increasing manpower and salaries within the company would certainly help. A dispute with the regulator might aid the complexity rating.

From a shareholders perspective it is rather depressing to read this list of suggestions for increasing basic salary. It reads very like a list of the most common ways that companies destroy shareholder value on a grand scale. This may, or may not be a coincidence, but one thing is very clear. The incentives that arise from a desire to increase basic salary generally work against the interests of shareholders.

Clearly this is a problem, particularly as even the executives with the most valuable performance based incentive schemes are likely to regard basic salary as more important than variable pay. This problem has no easy solutions, but the way for remuneration committees to address it is to make basic salary less interesting to executives and to make variable pay more interesting to executives. In this way executives will become more interested in the incentives arising from variable pay, which are performance based, and less interested in the incentives arising from fixed pay, which have a tendency to work against shareholder interests. The next section suggests ways of doing this.

Shifting the balance in the total reward package

The balance of the total reward package should be shifted so that variable pay becomes more important. This suggestion is a very well established theme of shareholder guidance on executive remuneration. Unfortunately remuneration committees have focused far more on increasing the variable pay then on reducing or even constraining growth in basic salary. As executives tend to see basic salary as more important, it is more important for remuneration committees to focus on constraining or reducing the importance of basic salary. Here are some suggestions on how basic salary can be made less important and variable pay made more important.

Break the link between basic salary and pension

As we will see later in this chapter, pensions are very often one of the primary reasons that executives consider basic salary to be so important. If pension entitlements were determined independently of basic salary, such that changes in basic salary had no impact on pension then much of the pressure to increase basic salaries would disappear. The way to break the link is to move from defined benefit pension schemes to defined contribution pension schemes. This is explained later in the chapter.

Break the link between basic salary and variable pay schemes

An increase in basic salary will normally feed through to an automatic increase in the expected benefits from annual bonus schemes, SOSs and LTIPs. Instead the benefits received under these schemes could be determined independently of basic salary such that a change to basic salary has no automatic consequence to the variable pay schemes. This would make basic salary appear much less important.

When awards under variable schemes are benchmarked between companies it is very useful to express those awards as percentages or multiples of basic salary. Breaking the link between basic salary and the variable schemes does not stop the company from publishing the value of awards as percentages of basic salary. It simply means that the percentages and multiples will change slightly from year to year rather than appearing fixed.

Make variable pay more dependable

The variable pay schemes that are currently in place in FTSE 350 companies in the UK reflect the "exceptional rewards for exceptional performance" philosophy that is discussed in the earlier part of chapter 7. This means that the final value of awards can be extremely high, but can easily have no value at all. This makes it difficult for executives to count on scheme payments when they assess the value of their reward package. The schemes therefore appear less important, and as such they are rather inefficient as a form of motivation.

Variable pay schemes such as FILLIPs that provide more predictable and consistent rewards for performance in the second and third quartiles will appear far more tangible to executives who will take them much more seriously when they assess the total value of their reward package. This will help to increase the relative importance of variable pay.

Pensions

Pensions are usually one of the most valuable, if not the most valuable component of an executive reward package. Despite this they seem to attract far less attention than basic salary, annual bonus or long term incentive plans. Since the Directors' Remuneration Report Regulations 2002, the true cost and value of executive pensions has become more apparent and this will hopefully lead to greater consideration of the role of pensions in executive remuneration.

Pension entitlements are part of fixed pay. The entitlements continue to grow while an executive is in post, with no reference to personal or corporate performance measurements. The Combined Code says that, "In general, only basic salary should be pensionable"[20] so performance does not usually affect pensions even indirectly through changes in variable pay.

As with basic salary, the fact that there is no performance measurement associated with pensions does not mean that pensions do not provide incentives to executives. In the next sections we look at how those incentives arise, and the behaviours that they encourage.

Pension schemes - defined contribution or defined benefits

Pension arrangements are very technical and generate lots of specialised work for accountants, lawyers and actuaries. These technicalities are beyond the scope of this book. However in this book we do need to be clear about the difference between a "defined contribution" pension scheme and a "defined benefit" pension scheme because the incentives that arise from the two different types of scheme are quite different.

A defined contribution pension scheme is a scheme where the employee and employer pay into a scheme at a set rate. When the employee retires the total value that the individual has accumulated in the fund is used to buy a pension. The size of the pension will depend on the value accumulated in the fund at retirement. This is very dependent on the market value of shares, bonds and other investments at the point of retirement. The size of the final pension cannot therefore be predicted in advance with very much certainty.

A defined benefit scheme is a scheme where the employee steadily earns pension entitlement as he or she continues to work for the company. Typically the employee is entitled to an annual pension of $n/60*$(final salary), where n is the number of years that the employee has worked for the company up to a maximum limit of 40. This means that if the employee works for the company for 40 years then on retirement he or she will be entitled to a pension that is two thirds (from 40/60) of the salary that the employee held at retirement.

Defined benefit schemes normally require employees to pay into the pension fund at a fixed rate, perhaps 6% of salary. The employer will also contribute to the fund, but the rate of employer's contributions can vary very significantly. The cost of pensions can change with changing perceptions about life expectancy. The value of the pension fund's assets changes with share prices and value of other investments. This means that estimates of how fast the employer needs to pay into the fund change all the time. The employer's contributions are reviewed regularly to reflect this.

A defined contribution scheme leaves uncertainty and risk with the employee, who does not know how big his or her pension will be. A defined benefit scheme gives a clear picture of the size of pension, but leaves uncertainty and risk with the employer, who does not know what size of employer contribution will be required in the future, in order to pay for the defined benefit.

The Typico Executive Pension Scheme

Typico runs a defined benefit staff pension scheme, which all company employees are entitled to join. The scheme is approved by the Inland Revenue so it enjoys certain tax benefits. However Inland Revenue approval also carries with it limits on the funds in support of each pension that restrict the size of pension payable to somewhere in the region of £60,000 to £70,000 per annum, which is significantly less than two thirds of salary for many of Typico's more senior management. Typico therefore runs a parallel, unapproved pension scheme that tops up the pensions of more senior staff to the levels that would be enjoyed if the Inland Revenue limits did not apply. The top-up pension scheme is less tax efficient than the main scheme, but it covers a relatively small number of people.

Incentives arising from the Typico Pension Scheme

Joe Figment has worked for Typico all his working life. He joined as a graduate trainee in at the age of 21 and is now 49. He has 28 years of pensionable service and this is already enough to make Joe think of pension as a key component of his remuneration package. Joe Figment's current basic salary is £750,000. Each year that he continues to work for Typico he adds a further $1/60^{th}$ of this to his pension. That is worth £12,500 for every year of his life after retirement, which is very significant. It provides a very strong incentive for Joe to continue working in his current post.

The other big incentive arising from the Typico pension scheme is the incentive to increase basic salary. Last year Joe Figment's basic salary was increased by 7.1% from £700,000 to £750,000. Assuming that this 7.1% increase will affect Joe Figments final salary then it is equivalent to a 7.1% increase in his pension, which is £22,365 (calculated as 7.1% of 27/60*700,000) for every year of retirement.

Overall, by working the year 2005 Joe Figment increased his pension entitlement from £315,000 per annum (calculated as 27/60*700,000) to £350,000 per annum (calculated as 28/60*750,000), which is an increase of £35,000 per annum for every year of retirement. In accordance with actuarial standards an increase in pension entitlement of £35,000 per year for Joe Figment has the effect of increasing the transfer value of his pension by £425,000 more than the value of the contributions that Joe himself made. This makes it clear that increased pension entitlement was one of the biggest elements of Joe Figment's remuneration during 2005.

The two big incentives arising from pension are to keep working (adding pensionable service) and to keep basic salary increasing. This often works in a very extreme way, particularly for executives who are approaching retirement. Let us consider the case of Pete Cellum, who joined Typico as a board level marketing director in 2001 at the age of 56.

When he joined, he transferred his pension entitlement from his previous job into the Typico pension scheme. Although Pete had 34 years of pensionable service in the pension scheme at his previous job, his salary at Typico was higher, and the pension scheme benefits at Typico were better. The transfer value of his old pension therefore bought him only 28 years of pensionable service at Typico.

The benefits Pete was entitled to on 28 years of pensionable service at Typico were very comparable with the benefits he would have received with 34 years worth of pensionable service in the pension scheme at his old job. However, Pete repeatedly expressed concern about the "loss" of pensionable service that he "suffered" as a result of changing companies. He succeeded in persuading the Typico remuneration committee that each year of service he contributed to Typico should add not one but rather two years of pensionable service to his pension entitlement! This would allow Pete to attain a full pension ($40/60^{th}$ of final salary) by the age of 62, if he continued to work for Typico.

As the years of pensionable service grow, the benefit to pension entitlement of growth in basic salary increases. By the start of 2005 Pete Cellum had earned 35 years of pensionable service. At this point he was awarded an increase in basic salary from £320,000 to £365,000 (14%). Consequently by working the year 2005 Pete Cellum increased his annual pension entitlement from £186,667 (calculated as 35/60*320,000) to £225,083 (calculated as 37/60*365,000). This increase in pension entitlement of £38,416 per annum is equivalent to an increase in the transfer value of Pete's pension of £541,000. It was worth more to Pete Cellum that the combined value of his basic salary and annual bonus in that year! Pete Cellum's 2005 experience may sound rather extreme, but such situations are in fact very common. Any executive approaching retirement on a defined benefit pension scheme will see very valuable increases in pension entitlement arising from even small increases in basic salary.

It is clear that a defined benefit pension scheme is extremely sensitive to final salary. It therefore creates very strong incentives to force basic salaries higher. It also makes it almost impossible for a company to ever reduce basic salaries. The prospect of a basic salary reduction would be so damaging to the pension entitlement of an executive with a large number of pensionable years service that the executive might well be better off leaving the company than accepting the lower salary.

The defined benefit pension scheme creates rigidity in basic salary and contributes significantly to the incentive effects arising from basic salary that are discussed earlier in this chapter. These incentives generally work against the more desirable incentives associated with variable pay, and significantly undermine the incentive effect of the total reward package.

Incentives arising from a defined contribution pension scheme

Under a defined contribution pension scheme both employer and executive will contribute to a pension scheme at a fixed rate. For example in any one year they might both contribute 6% of gross salary. Let us see how Joe Figment and Pete Cellum's pensions would have increased during 2005 had the Typico pension scheme worked on this basis.

The transfer value of Joe Figment's pension scheme would have increased by 12% of £750,000 which is £90,000 (plus or minus any change in value of the fund accumulated to date). In Joe's case £90,000 of pension fund is equivalent to about £7,400 per annum of pension, which is very modest compared to £35,000 under the defined benefit scheme.

The transfer value of Pete Cellum's scheme would have increased by 12% of £365,000 (net of changes in fund value), which is £43,800, equivalent to about £3,100 per annum of pension. Again this is very modest compared to the £38,416 see under the defined benefit scheme.

It appears that the pensions generated by a defined contribution pension scheme are likely to be much lower than those generated by a defined benefit scheme. This tends to be the case where large increases in basic salary occur in the years leading up to retirement. However, in general it need not be the case and companies can always make defined contribution pensions bigger by increasing the size of their contribution.

However it is also clear that, even if companies significantly increase their contributions under defined contribution schemes, the undesirable incentive link between basic salary and pension is very small compared to the link that exists for a defined benefit scheme. In particular where defined contribution pension schemes are used basic salaries can be increased and decreased without having an impact on the pension entitlement earned to date. This very significantly increases the flexibility associated with basic salaries, and enables the incentives arising from variable pay to have a more direct and compelling effect on executive behaviour.

From a shareholder perspective another big advantage of defined contribution pension schemes for executives is that the value of the executive's own pension will fluctuate with the values of the equities and other assets owned by the executive's pension scheme. This gives the executive direct financial exposure to the same overall investment conditions that are of common concern to all long term investors. In particular the executive has strong incentives to see long term sustainable gains in the whole UK equity sector. This creates very real incentive alignment between the executive and other typical UK investors. The executive gets strong incentives to act very responsibly towards the investment community and to play a full part in ensuring a safe and healthy investment environment for all. In contrast, defined benefit pension schemes allow executives to use company balance sheets to insulate themselves from problems in the investment world, which they themselves might be partly responsible for. Investors should therefore always insist on defined contribution pension schemes for executives. Remuneration committees should likewise favour defined contribution schemes.

From an incentives perspective it is clear that there are several reasons why it is far better if executives have defined contribution rather than defined benefit pension schemes. This remains true even if the defined contributions appear to be very large.

Other benefits

It is very typical for an executive reward package to include a number of benefits such as entitlement to a company car, life assurance, health insurance, club membership or financial advice. These benefits are not usually linked to performance so are effectively part of fixed pay. The value of such benefits is usually relatively small compared to the total size of an executive reward package. The lack of size and performance link ensures that the incentive effect of these other benefits is usually quite small and they do not need to be considered in detail in this book.

There are, however two very concrete advantages of keeping these other benefits as restricted as possible such that the highest possible proportion of total remuneration is paid in cash or shares. The first benefit of this approach is that it maximises the executive's flexibility in how his or her remuneration is spent. He or she might not be interested in financial advice or club membership and to pay remuneration in this way might just be inefficient. The second benefit of this approach is that simple payments in cash and shares will appear far more transparent in the remuneration report, such that it is much easier to make an assessment of what is being paid and what the incentive effect of such payments really are.

There are some good and obvious arguments that go the other way. There may be clear benefits of cost or administration arising from the company offering benefits like company cars rather than individuals all making their own arrangements. Sometimes executives give disproportionate value to benefits like company cars or club membership, such that they represent very good value for money to shareholders as a form of remuneration. Similarly the company might have its own reasons why it wants all executives to belong to a particular club or have a particular level of life assurance. However it remains the case that the more fragmented and dispersed the remuneration benefits become, the more difficult it is for shareholders to feel confident that they are properly understood, controlled and justified.

There are some benefits associated with status that are not always remuneration, but which can be powerful sources of motivation. Issues such as size and location of office, quality of office artwork and private access to company jet can have a very significant incentive effect. From a shareholder perspective heavy use of such incentives is almost certainly undesirable. It can never be transparent, and a working culture that puts a high value on personal status is usually lacking in flexibility and team working skills.

Summary

Remuneration committees go to a great deal of trouble and expense to create powerful and well aligned incentives for executives through variable pay schemes. Often however executives give much more attention to their basic salary than to the variable pay schemes, despite the higher value of the latter. This is very unfortunate because the incentives that arise through basic salary usually work against shareholder interests. This means that if a remuneration committee is serious about creating an incentive regime for the executives, which is well aligned with shareholder interests then the committee must find ways of shifting the balance of importance away from basic salary and towards the variable pay schemes.

The reason why executives are so interested in basic salary is that most of the financial benefits that they ever hope to receive through their reward packages are linked directly or indirectly to their basic salary. An increase in basic salary therefore results in an immediate increase in all other components of the reward package. Remuneration committees therefore need to start breaking these links.

The most important link to break is the link between basic salary and pension. This can be achieved by switching from defined benefit pension schemes to defined contribution schemes. The incentives generated by a defined contribution scheme are far better than those generated by a defined benefit scheme and this remains true even if the defined contribution is very large.

It is also important to break the link between basic salary and variable pay schemes such that a change in basic salary has no immediate consequences for the benefits received under the variable pay schemes.

Remuneration committees can also make variable pay schemes appear more important by making the variable benefits more predictable and consistent. FILLIP style remuneration is much better than traditional variable pay schemes in this respect.

Notes

18. Combined Code 2003: Main Principles B.1
19. Combined Code 2003: Code Provisions B.1.1
20. Combined Code 2003: Schedule A, paragraph 6

11

Factors influencing executive pay

In chapter 2 of this book we looked at the potential benefits associated with variable pay. It was clear that, in the case of executives, easily the most important benefit of variable pay was the motivational effect arising from the incentives associated with variable pay. Since chapter 2 we have looked in detail at various forms of pay commonly used by FTSE 350 companies today and considered the incentives that arise from those forms of pay.

In most cases it has been very clear that there is a significant gap between the behaviours encouraged by the incentives and the behaviours that shareholders would want to see adopted by executives and managers. For example, in chapter 5 we saw how annual bonus generates incentives to maximise short term performance, especially annual earnings, at the expense of long term performance. In chapter 6 we saw that the incentives arising from a typical LTIP are very inconsistent, and in many cases promote volatility or share price manipulation rather than long term growth in shareholder value. In chapter 7 and 8 we saw how it is relatively easy to improve the design of an LTIP such that incentives are far better aligned with shareholder interests. In chapter 9 we saw how the incentives arising from the ownership of options are often quite different from the incentives arising from share ownership. We saw how alignment could be immediately improved by paying remuneration in shares rather than options, assuming that the fair market value of the payment remains the same. In chapter 10 we saw how basic salary, where linked to defined benefit pension schemes and the size of payments under variable pay schemes, generates incentives that are very contrary to shareholder interests. We saw that the situation could be quickly made much better by breaking these links and using defined contribution pension schemes, even if the overall size of payment was not changed.

It is, to say the least, very disappointing to realise that companies which spend so much money on variable pay appear to have made so little effort to secure the benefits of variable pay, by properly aligning the incentives given with shareholder interests. If these were normal commercial contracts then huge efforts would have gone into the contract design, and designs would have undergone a process of continual improvement as experience was accumulated. We would have expected to see the emergence of industry standards for executive pay in which the incentives are very closely aligned with shareholder interests, as they are for example in the PREP FILLIP.

From the above it is clear that maximising the benefits associated with variable pay has not been the main driving force behind the implementation of variable pay schemes in FTSE 350 companies during the 1990s or in the early years of the new millennium. So, if remuneration committees have not been primarily influenced by the desire to secure the benefits of executive pay, what have they been driven by? In this chapter we consider three of the most important factors influencing executive pay over this period. They are presentational considerations, comparative pay positioning and remuneration consultancies.

The importance of presentational issues when determining executive pay

Since the late 1980s discussions about executive pay have been characterised by controversy. The controversy has arisen because of a need or desire on the part of remuneration committees to increase the levels of executive pay, and a need or desire on the part of shareholders, the public and politicians to prevent to such increases. The determination of appropriate levels for executive pay is examined further in chapter 12, but a consequence of this conflict is that changes to executive pay have to be handled with great sensitivity. This has lead to an environment in which remuneration committees need to take extreme care about the way that increases in executive benefits are presented to the outside world. Presentational considerations have become a major driver on the way that executive pay is structured.

The Greenbury Report

In the UK a big breakthrough in the external presentation of executive remuneration came with the Greenbury Report of 1995. The Greenbury Report included an authoritative code of best practice for directors' remuneration. The code made statements about several different forms of remuneration and gave clear guidance on what was, and what was not acceptable in each case. Remuneration committees, advised by their consultants, soon realised that each such statement could be used as a "hook" from which an acceptable piece of executive remuneration could be hung.

The code said, "Remuneration committees should consider whether their Directors should be eligible for annual bonuses."[21] This meant that it was OK to introduce annual bonus schemes, providing that the code's guidance was followed.

The code said, "Remuneration committees should consider whether their Directors should be eligible for benefits under long-term incentive schemes. Traditional share option schemes should be weighed against other kinds of long-term incentive scheme."[22] This meant that it was OK to introduce share option schemes and the new LTIPs style schemes, provided that the code's guidance was followed.

Elsewhere the Greenbury Report stated that, "In many companies [...] there will be a case for high gearing of performance-related to fixed pay."[23] This meant that it was OK to increase the levels of variable pay such that fixed pay was small by comparison.

The aspiration to hang elements of remuneration from every available hook provided by best practise guidance is one of the reasons why remuneration packages have become very fragmented, being made up of a large number of different elements. The negative consequences of this complexity were discussed in chapter 4.

Obviously the reading of the Greenbury Report presented above is grossly unfair and one sided. However selective reading of the Greenbury Report did allow remuneration committees to present significant increases in executive rewards as in conformance with best practice. This in turn made it much harder for shareholders, the public and politicians to challenge such increases.

The fragmentation and complexity of remuneration schemes

The need or desire of remuneration committees to use every hook provided by best practice guidance has been one reason why executive remuneration schemes have become fragmented and complex. However there are other reasons too.

Often, for good reasons or bad, a remuneration committee might want to increase executive rewards without creating unnecessary controversy. In such circumstances there is a big presentational advantage in using remuneration built up in a complex way over several different remuneration schemes delivering rewards over different periods of time. The Directors' Remuneration Report Regulations 2002 require full disclosure of all remuneration for directors. However if the remuneration is built up in a complex way over many schemes then even with full disclosure it becomes extremely difficult for anyone to work out the actual value of what is being paid. This in turn makes it much harder for shareholders, the public and politicians to challenge payments made as part of executive pay.

Share options are particularly effective at concealing the value that is being paid. As we saw in Chapter 9 it is very difficult to value a share option, and most people seriously underestimate what an option is really worth. Further, even where a fair market value for the option has been disclosed, its meaning is undermined by the very high volatility of the option valuation. The valuation is also affected by the toughness of the performance conditions. Also, if consistent comparisons of executive pay are to be made then it is necessary to define the point in time that the value inherent in the option is actually earned. Is it earned when the conditional option is awarded? Is it earned uniformly over the performance period? Is it earned at vesting? Is it earned when the option is exercised?

In the US, fierce battles have been fought over accounting standards for share options, which are known as stock options in America. Many companies stated that they would be forced to stop using stock options as remuneration, if the fair market value of the stock option had to be shown as an expense in the company accounts. This is despite the fact that the accounting treatment of the option has no real impact on underlying shareholder value; it is only the perceptions gained by looking at the accounts that are affected. This demonstrates that for many companies the decisive factor in deciding to use stock options was the presentational "benefit" of the costs not appearing in the accounts.

Many companies offer schemes for deferring annual bonus payments to their executives. These schemes usually have the effect of clouding the question of when remuneration has been earned, making it harder to get a clear picture of what has been earned in any particular year. One of the arguments used to defend the $187.5 million remuneration of Richard Grasso as Chairman of the New York Stock Exchange in September 2003 was that the remuneration included deferred earnings over several years. Mr Grasso's total reward package was also a case study in complexity, being composed of more than a dozen different components.

It can also be very difficult to attribute clear valuations to LTIP schemes. The problems arise from the performance conditions and uncertainty about precisely when the shares are actually earned. The FILLIP scheme documented in Appendix 5 is easier to value because of the consistent linear relationship between performance and reward. This means that an assumption of median performance can be used to generate a meaningful estimate of present value.

The effect of presentational considerations on transparency

The presentational advantage of complicated remuneration schemes comes at the expense of transparency. Even with full disclosure it is very difficult to see the actual value that is being earned and how that relates to performance. As the Hampel report noted in 1998, "Remuneration disclosures are often excessively detailed, to the point where the essential features of remuneration packages have been rendered obscure to all but the expert reader..."[24] In fact the reader needs not only to be expert, but also needs to have plenty of time to devote to the task of understanding a remuneration report.

The requirement for transparency has been a consistent theme of all best practice guidance and regulation of executive pay since the Cadbury report of 1992.[25] Remuneration committees understand its importance, and would argue that remuneration reports are as transparent as they possibility can be when the complexity of pay and reporting constraints are taken into account. However this position further highlights the concern that the complexity has arisen precisely to reduce transparency and despite the negative consequences of complexity discussed in chapter 4. Transparency could be much increased if remuneration reports provided a single number to best represent the total expected present value across all remuneration schemes that was transferred to an executive director during the year. Appendix 2 illustrates how this could be done. Remuneration reports don't usually do this. Probably remuneration committees feel that such a number could easily be misunderstood and become very emotive, particularly in a year when variable pay is very high. It might lead to great controversy, just as the $187.5 million figure caused the downfall of Richard Grasso.

It is clear that presentation issues will continue to be an extremely important feature of all executive pay proposals until the controversies surrounding executive pay have been reduced. While controversies rage it will be difficult for remuneration committees to be as enthusiastic about full transparency as they should be.

Comparative pay positioning

The 1995 Greenbury code of best practise included recommendation C2. "Remuneration committees should judge where to position their company relative to other companies. They should be aware what other comparable companies are paying and should take account of relative performance"[26]

To comply with recommendation C2 a remuneration committee

needed to compile a large amount of detailed information about the pay and performance of other comparable companies. The required data about what other companies were paying was just becoming available because Greenbury also recommended increased disclosure of executive pay. Remuneration committees therefore started to make much greater use of remuneration consultancies which were well place to gather all the necessary data and to advise remuneration committees on what can be deduced from it.

The effect of comparative positioning of pay levels

However, right from the beginning there were concerns about recommendation C2. The Greenbury report itself includes several cautions about the practice of positioning pay relative to other companies. It states, "Companies should not pay above average regardless of performance. They should also beware of basing remuneration levels on a skewed comparator group so as to justify higher remuneration levels. If companies generally pursue such policies, the effect will simply be to ratchet up the general level of executive remuneration. Remuneration committees' annual reports should disclose and justify any deliberate policy of paying above average."[27]

These warnings appear to have turned into self fulfilling prophecies! Companies paying below average found that they could move up to average levels very easily and quickly by paying more, whereas companies that were above average did not generally want to move downwards so also paid more. Almost all companies aimed to pitch pay at average levels or above. Many companies aimed to pitch pay at top quartile levels. This ensured that the average level always moved upwards. Similarly the choice of comparator group, and the choice of which components of executive remuneration to include in the benchmark, gave companies plenty of scope to demonstrate that they needed to move pay upwards to achieve average position. The result was indeed a powerful upward ratchet on the general level of executive remuneration.

This quickly became a matter of concern. When the Hampel Committee produced its report in January 1998 it urged caution about the use of comparative pay surveys in setting executive pay because it suggested that few remuneration committees would want to recommend lower than average salaries.[28] When the first version of the Combined Code was finalised in June 1998, it included the original wording of recommendation C2 from Greenbury, but added to it, "But they [remuneration committees] should use such comparisons with caution, in view of the risk that they can result in an upward ratchet in remuneration levels with no corresponding improvement in performance."[29]

Executive pay continued to ratchet upwards quite rapidly after 1998, and even continued to ratchet upwards though the bear stock market from January 2000 to March 2003. From the policies described in remuneration reports it is clear that benchmarking performed for comparative pay positioning is usually the main reason why increases in executive remuneration are deemed necessary. Despite the endless upward ratchet the principle of comparative pay was included in the revised version of the Combined Code finalised in July 2003. This requires that, "The remuneration committee should judge where to position their company relative to other companies. But they should use such comparisons with caution, in view of the risk of an upward ratchet of remuneration levels with no corresponding improvement in performance."[30]

The origins of comparative pay positioning

Most shareholders invest across all UK equities, usually as part of a pension scheme or investment product. To such shareholders comparative pay positioning, as currently practised, makes no sense at all. It forces executive pay relentlessly upwards irrespective of performance considerations. So why is comparative pay positioning considered a good thing? Why is it included in the Combined Code as good practice? It is very clear why executives like it but from a shareholder perspective the logic is far less clear. Should remuneration committees support it?

The mainstream interest in comparative pay positioning arose with the widespread public outrage at substantial increases in pay awarded to the directors of newly privatised utilities in the late 1980s and early

1990s. The Greenbury committee was concerned that the companies in question were paying more than was required to recruit, retain and motivate quality managers. It affirmed that companies should "take a rounded view of the markets in which they operate and the marketability of their Directors"[31] when setting executive pay.

Shareholders were certainly prepared to support this comparative reasoning when it was very clear that certain directors were being paid too much. However this rather obvious "sense check" is very different from the approach to comparative pay positioning that we see today. Pay positioning today has become a science. The consultants produce very detailed reports that systematically consider each different element of the reward package and the total reward position. The result is a pool of data and information that is both extensive and deep. Depending on how the data is selected and presented, a wide range of possible conclusions on executive pay can be justified.

Advantages and disadvantages of comparative positioning on pay

The big argument used by remuneration consultants to justify comparative pay positioning to shareholders is that if a company falls seriously out of line with industry practise then its reward package may fail to recruit, motivate and retain executives of the required calibre. This is a powerful argument that has been used very effectively, but on close examination the argument has many weaknesses.

Firstly the augment does not work for investors who invest in a wide range of UK equities, as almost all investors do either directly or indirectly. Increasing executive pay to keep up with the market only forces the same problem onto other companies, who the investor also has shares in. If the other companies respond in the same way then executive pay ratchets upwards across the board without shareholders seeing any benefit at all.

Secondly the argument depends on a very competitive and liquid market in executive talent. It is doubtful whether the market really behaves in this way, and these market based considerations are discussed in the next chapter.

Thirdly the falling out of line has to become very significant before it becomes noticeable and starts to have an effect. The very detailed surveys produced by the consultancies pick up discrepancies that are far more subtle than executives themselves could ever hope to notice, never mind act upon. The complexities of reward packages today mean that, without expert help, it is very difficult to compare overall levels of executive pay in different organisations.

Fourthly the argument assumes that pay is the all important factor in recruiting, motivating and retaining executives. In fact, it is far from the most important factor. When Gerard Roche, the head hunter, was asked how he persuades the people he finds to change company he replied "Oddly enough, it's not compensation. How much they earn is important, but it is not their main reason for moving. They can only eat two eggs a day, drive one car at a time. What they really want is, number one, to run their own show. After that they want to be sure that they will enjoy working with their new colleagues, that the job is in an industry that they like and in a part of the world they would be happy to live in. Compensation could not get Jim Kilts to go to Coke."[32] These other factors beyond remuneration actually have far more impact on an executive's quality of life than pay does, but they have become seriously overlooked because of excessive interest in pay.

Fifthly even if a company is demonstrably paying market rates, or even top quartile rates, this does not necessarily protect it from a competitor who wants to poach executive talent. For very senior executives the competitor can always offer more money, although in practice the quality of the role offered may well be a more decisive factor than the money.

In addition, from a shareholder perspective, there are serious disadvantages with using comparative pay positioning for senior executives.

Firstly there is the upward ratchet problem, caused by the average company seeking to remunerate its executives in an above average way. This ensures that average remuneration either steps or nudges upwards each year.

Secondly comparative pay positioning reflects what other companies are paying rather than the needs and aspirations of the company in question. Can the company afford it? Is it in the best interests of the company? If executive pay goes up, does pay increase for those people just below executive level? How far do the effects of executive pay cascade down the organisation? Is the company still competitive on this basis? Will other people in the organisation resent the higher executive pay? How does the executive pay fit with the culture and values of the company? Does the level of executive pay make the leadership of the company more or less credible? Are executives reaping rewards for sacrifices made by others? What does the executive pay say about the company's commitment to shareholder value? These more internal company considerations are extremely important. They are part of what makes each company unique and ensures a healthy diversity in our economy. Unfortunately such internal considerations are seldom discussed in remuneration reports. It would appear that remuneration committees are usually more influenced by the need to keep executive pay in line with the market.

Thirdly comparative pay positioning is concerned solely with relative considerations and has no points of reference in more absolute considerations. If the overall level of executive pay in industry and commerce rose to such a high level that companies could not flourish and the stock market could only stagnate, then this problem would never be identified by comparative pay positioning. Is it possible that we reached this point a few years ago and still have not realised it?

The role of remuneration consultancies

Remuneration committees are made up of part time independent non-executive directors, who usually have very limited time available to devote to their duties. It is also difficult for them to use company employees to work on executive remuneration issues because of concerns about conflicts of interest. This means that it is very common for almost all hands on work on the development, implementation and presentation of executive remuneration policies to be done by remuneration consultancies. This approach is strongly endorsed by the Combined Code which states, "The remuneration committee should also be responsible for appointing any consultants in respect of executive director remuneration. Where executive directors or senior management are involved in advising or supporting the remuneration committee, care should be taken to recognise and avoid conflicts of interest."[33]

This role of remuneration consultancies really took off with the inclusion of recommendation C2 in the Greenbury code of best practise in 1995. Collecting the large amount of data needed for comparative pay positioning was a natural task to outsource to a consultancy, and certainly one that a remuneration committee would struggle to do itself. Recommendation C2 appears to have been a massive scoop on the part of Towers Perrin, the remuneration consultancy who acted as professional advisors to the Greenbury study group. It guaranteed them, and many consultancies like them, a huge new market with excellent possibilities for further expansion.

The large and important role of remuneration consultancies has made them extremely influential in executive pay matters ever since Greenbury. It has also ensured that a very large part of all expertise on executive remuneration resides inside the remuneration consultancies. A big proportion of all serious public comment on executive pay, be it in government consultations, books, newspaper articles or TV interviews, originates either directly or indirectly from remuneration consultancies. Remuneration committees need to be aware of the huge influence that the consultants therefore have.

The business model of the remuneration consultancies

Just like any other consultancy a remuneration consultancy's main business objective is to sell consultancy services. They get paid for the consultancy that they provide, and the more consultancy they can provide the more they get paid. In support of this objective the remuneration consultancies offer an ever increasing range of services.

The corner stone service offered by remuneration consultancies is the detailed survey of executive remuneration practices in other companies, suitable for comparative pay positioning. This service has had a guaranteed market ever since recommendation C2 appeared in the Greenbury report. There is no doubt that one of the reasons that comparative pay positioning is considered so important and has survived in the Combined Code is that it is always very strongly supported by remuneration consultancies. Whether they are engaged by government, shareholders or executives the remuneration consultancies are always going to strongly support comparative pay positioning.

A second key service offered by remuneration consultancies is the administration of company remuneration schemes. This is a significant task, particularly with LTIPs or SOSs where options and shares have to be handled. It is a good source of steady revenue, and provides important ongoing business relationships from which the consultancies can leverage future business.

Another key service offered by the consultancies is the Strategic Review of Executive Remuneration. The consultants, being good business people, are always delighted to recommend changes and new developments that allow them to offer further services helping the company to implement the changes.

In addition to these services the consultancies offer a great deal of practical help and advice to remuneration committees. They can, with supervision, compile remuneration reports. They can advise on all the various codes of practice and guidance, and what the current hot issues are in the investor community. They can help with presentation issues and advise on forms of remuneration that currently appear the least controversial.

The incentives on remuneration consultancies

Given that remuneration consultancies are so influential it is important that remuneration committees are aware of and understand the incentives to which the consultants are operating. In doing this I do not wish to suggest that remuneration consultancies operate with anything other than the greatest professionalism and integrity. However the fact remains that the remuneration consultancies that grow and develop and become most influential are the ones that sell the most consultancy services. They are in the business of selling consultancy services.

Given this, remuneration consultancies tend to welcome any developments in executive pay that will help them to sell more services. In practice most developments in executive pay will help consultants to offer more services. New regulations, new guidance from shareholders, new definitions of best practise and new research all help to move industry practice forward and all create opportunities to sell services.

There are some potential developments in industry practice that would work against the interests of the consultants. For example a move away from comparative pay positioning would seriously undermine the remuneration consultancy business. Any such proposal can expect to meet fierce opposition from the consultancies.

Remuneration consultancies stand to benefit from the growing complexity of executive remuneration packages. Complexity increases the dependency of remuneration committees on consultancies. They need someone to keep track of what is happening and to advise them. This increases the influence of the consultancies and creates new opportunities for them to sell services. In itself higher complexity generates additional work that the consultancies can charge for, increasing the size of their market. Complexity also makes it more difficult for non-specialists to provide the services required, improving the consultancies competitive position.

Remuneration consultancies usually benefit from controversy and shareholder rows associated with executive pay. There is a good chance that a remuneration committee engaged in a row will hire a remuneration consultancy to develop its case and find a way forward. Perceptions about good practice are very likely to move on as a result of the controversy and it may lead to additional guidance or regulation in the longer term. All these things create opportunities for remuneration consultancies.

To keep executive remuneration practice moving along it is firmly in the interests of remuneration consultancies to recommend increases in executive pay. Justified proposals to increase executive pay are likely to lead to further work for consultancies. A new incentive scheme might be required to make the payments. Explanation and justification of the higher pay will be required, especially if shareholders are uncomfortable. The bigger executive remuneration becomes as a financial cost and as a business issue then the more work there is for remuneration consultancies.

At first sight the remuneration consultancies might be able to build their business just as effectively by recommending reductions in executive pay. However in practice this just does not work. It is far easier to sell the idea of higher executive pay to a remuneration committee than the idea of lower executive pay. Most remuneration committee members have been executive directors at other companies and they naturally identify with suggestions that good executives are a scarce commodity, under paid and under appreciated who really deserve more. In contrast it is extremely difficult to attract attention with a message about reducing executive pay. It is difficult enough for a remuneration committee to make a reduced payment under an annual bonus scheme. To actually reduce the expected value of remuneration is extremely difficult and could easily cause serious rifts at board level.

Remuneration committees therefore need to take notice of the fact that most of the incentives that are faced by remuneration consultancies actually work against the shareholder interest. Shareholders want to see stable long term incentives in place whereas remuneration consultancies always want remuneration practice to move forward. Shareholders are suspicious of the upward ratchet arising from comparative pay positioning, but remuneration consultancies firmly support this practice. Shareholders want simple and transparent remuneration schemes. Remuneration consultancies benefit from complexity. Shareholders want remuneration committees who they can trust, but consultancies benefit from rows and controversy. Shareholders want to see the average level of executive pay constrained or reduced whereas remuneration consultancies have a strong interest in seeing it rise.

Summary

It is clear that the serious consideration of incentives has had very little effect on the development of executive pay in recent years. In this chapter we have therefore looked at three factors that have been far more influential.

Presentation issues have been extremely important because of the controversy that has generally surrounded the subject of executive pay since the late 1980s. Only skilful presentation has allowed remuneration committees to increase executive pay without causing excessive public outcry or conflict with shareholders. Sadly the skilful presentation has often had the effect of increasing the complexity and reducing the transparency of executive pay. Remuneration reports may present all the relevant information but it is usually very difficult to get a meaningful view of how much in total a particular director has earned.

The comparative pay positioning technique advocated by remuneration consultants and enshrined in the Combined Code has become the most important method of establishing appropriate overall levels of executive remuneration within a company. This approach generally forces the levels of executive remuneration upwards because it is difficult for remuneration committees to deliberately pay below median level. However there is no link to performance or the internal needs of the company so comparative pay positioning remains very problematic from a shareholder perspective.

Remuneration consultancies have become extremely influential in the development of remuneration policy for executives. It is now almost impossible for a remuneration committee to fulfil its obligations without using such a consultancy. Comparative pay positioning is an excellent business opportunity for remuneration consultancies. Further business opportunities arise from any difficult issues, particularly high executive remuneration, that forces remuneration policy to move forward. Remuneration committees need to be aware that the incentives faced by remuneration consultants as they seek to develop their own businesses are, in most cases, incentives that work directly against the shareholder interest.

Notes

21. Greenbury 1995: Code of Best Practice, C5
22. Greenbury 1995: Code of Best Practice, C6
23. Greenbury 1995: Page 38, paragraph 6.16
24. Hampel 1998: Page 37, paragraph 4.16
25. Cadbury 1992a: Paragraph 4.40
26. Greenbury 1995: Code of Best Practice, C2
27. Greenbury 1995: Page 37, paragraph 6.12
28. Hampel 1998: Page 33, paragraph 4.4
29. Combined Code 1998: B.1.2

30. Combined Code 2003: Supporting Principle B.1
31. Greenbury 1995: Page 50, paragraph 8.6
32. Financial Times 29/07/04: Page 10
33. Combined Code 2003: Supporting Principles B.2

12

The level of executive pay

Most of this book has been about the way that executive pay is structured, and how important it is to ensure that the incentives generated by the various pay schemes are in fact the incentives that shareholders would want to give to executives. We have seen that, sadly, there is often a very big gap between the actual and desired incentives.

However, beyond the way that pay packages are structured, the overall level of executive pay is also an important consideration for remuneration committees. High levels of pay give rise to different business environments from low levels of pay. The two lead to different incentives, different business values and different executive behaviours. This chapter is about finding the optimum overall level of executive pay for a company. It examines the way that companies currently determine their overall level of executive pay, and it looks at other approaches that might work more effectively.

Total remuneration

When discussing the overall level of remuneration I am talking about the total remuneration received by the executive under all the different pay schemes in the course of a year. In other words the total value transferred from a company's shareholders to an executive over a year, irrespective of whether that value was transferred as cash, pension entitlement, shares, share options or in some other form.

Several difficulties arise when we try to determine total remuneration. For example, if there is a significant element of variable pay then the total remuneration is likely to vary considerably from one year to the next, depending on performance. Also, because of the complexity of the schemes and the different time periods involved it is in fact very difficult to determine clear and meaningful numbers for the total remuneration in any one year.

We saw in the last chapter that these difficulties and uncertainties have the effect of reducing transparency on executive pay, and indeed some of the complexity in executive pay may actually have arisen because of a desire to reduce transparency. For this reason it is very important that remuneration committees do not allow such problems to prevent them from understanding and discussing the overall level of remuneration. Appendix 2 suggests a way of presenting executive pay that would make it far easier for a remuneration committee to understand how much it is actually paying in total, and how those payments arise.

Current practice on determination of the level of executive pay

Remuneration reports set out policies on remuneration and these usually include reassuring statements about alignment of executives' incentives with shareholder interests and a high proportion of executive pay being linked to performance. On the specific issue of the level of total remuneration for executives they usually say something like this:

"The Remuneration Committee aims to set executive pay at a level that allows the company to recruit, motivate and retain executives of the high calibre required to run the company and deliver good returns to shareholders. The Committee is mindful of the intensely competitive and increasingly international market from which executive directors are recruited. To ensure that our remuneration packages remain competitive the Committee benchmarks against a group of comparable companies. Executive benefits are adjusted to ensure that they remain at around median level in the comparison group."

In many cases the report does not refer to median level, but instead says, "the company aims to provide remuneration packages that are highly competitive in the market," or, "the level is set to retain a recruitment advantage." There are some companies where the reports explicitly state that they use a higher than median level of remuneration and such companies usually give some justification for this.

It is clear from remuneration reports that the market comparison approach is the approach typically used by remuneration committees to determine the level of executive pay. The central justification for the current level of executive pay is therefore the need to recruit and retain executives in a competitive market for executive talent. This justification requires some examination from a shareholders perspective.

Shareholder problems with executive remuneration set at market levels

From a shareholder perspective, there are fundamental problems with the strategy of offering executive salaries that appear competitive in the market place. In the public sector, the UK public certainly require top politicians and civil servants to earn significantly less than their talents could command in the open market. This policy ensures that a person seeking public office is motivated by some sense of public service because self-interested people would be more attracted by higher paid jobs elsewhere. Why do shareholders not apply the same argument to executive directors who hold fiduciary responsibility for the shareholders' company? An executive who genuinely puts the shareholder interest first would certainly settle for salary below market level. In fact, if the executive requires a salary at market levels or above then this strongly suggests that he or she is working to optimise his or her own financial interests rather than those of the shareholders. Using market rates as a basis for executive pay therefore creates a conflict of interests for the company board as both buyer and provider of executive services. Such a conflict compromises all other efforts to create alignment of interests between executives and shareholders through executive pay. Shareholders should not accept such a basic conflict and should seek to minimise the influence that market rates have on executive pay.

There is here a fundamental issue about trust. It should always be possible to find high performing executives who can be trusted to work effectively for the interests of shareholders. Such people are far more suitable for board level positions than less trusted people, even if the less trusted people might appear to perform better. Trust is difficult to quantify and this can make it hard to assign it appropriate value. However in the long term trust is fundamental to the whole business environment. Avinash Persaud and John Plender explain it like this. "Economies contract when trust breaks down. The more transactions have to be governed by contract the more cumbersome and costly business becomes as everything has to be negotiated, agreed, litigated and enforced. Put crudely, ethical standards are a low cost-substitute for internal control within the company and for outside external regulation."[34] This is particularly true in the case of executive pay, because it is extremely difficult to formally define good executive behaviours.

Executive benefits are set at high enough levels that companies now have the opportunity to offer very attractive packages that are clearly below the current market level. Would it not be better to use such a package to recruit a chief executive who shareholders are 100% confident is working for their interests, rather than to recruit one who is more marketable, but is motivated more by self-interest? The latter option only looks attractive if shareholders are confident that they can harness the chief executive's self-interest to deliver shareholder returns. However the first ten chapters of this book have shown that the alignment between executive incentives and shareholder interests is not nearly as close as it needs to be for this strategy to work effectively.

Even for the chief executive there are significant potential upsides in being paid demonstrably less than market value! The pay could still be very good and it is unlikely that any reduction in the chief executive's standard of living would be required. There could however be significant benefits to the chief executive's quality of life at work, where a great deal of his or her time is spent. It would be far easier to build relationships of trust with shareholders and with the company board, because it would be clearer that the chief executive was giving top priority to the needs of the company. Better working relationships reduce stress and make the working environment more enjoyable. The chief executive would become free from the rat race of using salary to prove self-worth. His or her motivation could start to focus on the self-actualising needs identified by Maslow, rather than slavishly addressing basic financial needs one hundred times over. The chief executive's leadership position within the company could also be significantly enhanced. It would be far easier and more credible for him or her to focus on non-financial motivational factors for other employees such as the taking of responsibility, the chance to make a difference and achieve results, public recognition, better working relationships and the belief that something worthwhile is being done for the benefit of many different people. As we saw in the previous chapter, financial compensation is an important consideration, but it is other factors that determine whether or not a top executive will take a job. Non-financial motivation helps a chief executive to develop higher human values both personally and in the business culture, enhancing integrity and trust and marginalising unethical behaviour.

From a shareholder perspective another big risk with using high pay to recruit an executive is that the executive might accept the job because of the high pay, even though he or she is aware of serious problems with the job that should really be addressed before an appointment is made. High pay takes the focus off reporting lines, working relationships, board level attitudes and other factors that should be essential in determining whether or not a job should be accepted. I once accepted a job because of good pay, despite serious reservations about the reporting lines. The result was that I was completely ineffective in the new post. The mistake was expensive for the company.

Another reason why shareholders should not want to use market forces to determine executive pay is that the market for executive talent does not behave like a normal market in respect of supply and demand. In a normal market if the price of a commodity goes up then the economics of supply are improved and supply is increased. However the market for executive talent does not train up more potential chief executives because they are getting paid more. In fact the higher reward packages have the effect of reducing the number of potential candidates who could fill the post. The higher the reward package the more important it is that the person appointed is well known to the company board, the wider industry and the financial press. This restricts the pool of candidates. Also higher executive remuneration makes it far harder for executives to perform effectively in executive posts. Levels of trust are much lower, expectations of performance are much higher and more immediate, and there are more hounds baying for blood at the first hint of a slip.

The fact that high executive pay makes it harder rather than easier to recruit suitable executives is most clearly seen in the US, where executive pay is much higher than in the UK. Coke, Boeing, McDonalds and Delta all filled the CEO position with retired former executives during 2003 or 2004. The expectations on the CEO position have become so extreme and immediate that it is increasingly impossible to find candidates with the required credibility. Lower executive pay would help to build more realistic expectations with a longer term focus and this would make it much easier to find suitable candidates.

The argument that a company should pay more to recruit a better chief executive might appear reasonable to people who own shares in that one company alone. However most shareholders own shares in many different UK companies, typically through pension schemes or investment products. To these shareholders the argument clearly does not work. The higher pay simply causes a good chief executive to move from one company to another. The damage to the losing company, where the chief executive has a proven track record, is likely to be greater than the benefit to the recruiting company where the new appointment carries significant risk. (See chapter 7.)

In real life the supply of new executive talent is the responsibility of executives who are currently in post and of chief executives in particular. Remuneration committee members should make sure that their companies have good plans and procedures for developing future leaders and giving them the opportunities and exposure required to become great leaders of the future. This process requires high levels of trust because it is not comfortable for executives to have highly capable successors waiting in the wings. It is important to notice that it is not market forces that develop new executive talent; in fact market forces work against its development. Executives would clearly have greater market value if they had no obvious successors.

As we saw in chapter 7, healthy companies normally appoint new chief executives from within. They have a succession plan with two or three potential future chief executives always under development. Hopefully the existing chief executive also has some FILLIP style incentives to ensure the success of the company after his or her departure. If a tradable market in executive talent does exist, then it is really a market in executive potential and it takes place in the two or three levels immediately below chief executive level. The risks involved in changing company at these levels are much lower, both for executives and companies. It is at these levels that reward packages can really make a big difference to the quality of candidates available. However, even at these levels, higher reward packages do not increase the overall supply of potential executive talent. Executive talent has to be specifically nurtured and developed by more senior managers.

The difficulty of determining market levels

Even if shareholders did want to set executive salaries at competitive market levels then it is far from clear that this could actually be done. Certainly it could not possibly be achieved through the current benchmarking procedure. By definition, half of all reward packages would have to be set below median level.

Meaningful price discovery is almost impossible in a market for executive talent. The poaching of a senior executive by another company is a relatively rare event, and when it does occur the financial aspect is only one of a very large number of considerations. The quality of opportunity, timing, business relationships and personal considerations are all likely to be more important than the detail of the reward package. Headhunting organisations would be best placed to comment on price discovery, but their fees are defined as a proportion of the executive salary so they have very strong incentives to force salaries upwards.

The unexpected departure of a senior executive is a very significant event that can easily be very damaging to a company. It is therefore very understandable that remuneration committees want to pay enough to make sure that unexpected departures do not happen on account of pay. This pressure makes remuneration committees want instinctively to pay above average remuneration. The extra money paid is easily justified when you consider how badly criticised a remuneration committee would be if an important executive was lost for want of pay. However it is also abundantly clear that not all remuneration committees can pay above average, much as they might all like to. This is one of the factors that are continually forcing executive remuneration upwards in an unsustainable way.

There is another important factor that prevents normal market levels of pay from becoming clear in the case of executive remuneration. Normally, when a senior manager is hired the remuneration package is determined as part of a negotiation. This negotiation will also cover many other topics such as responsibilities, reporting lines, travel arrangements and office locations. These factors are at least as important as pay in any final deal. One outcome of the negotiation is a good understanding of what the important issues are in the recruitment, motivation and retention of that particular senior manager. In particular it will be known if the proposed level of remuneration is satisfactory, or whether it needs to be increased to secure the appointment. This information is obviously essential if a market driven salary is to be set.

However, in the case of executive directors, it is very unclear how this essential market information can properly be brought together. The Combined Code requires that, "No director should be involved in deciding his or her own remuneration."[35] Similarly it requires that, "Where executive directors or senior management are involved in advising or supporting the remuneration committee, care should be taken to avoid conflicts of interest."[36] The Combined Code also envisages a separation of responsibilities between the Nomination Committee, who recommend board level appointments and the Remuneration Committee who set remuneration. All this separation is intended to avoid conflicts of interest, but it has the unintended consequence of preventing the information necessary for setting remuneration at an efficient market level from all coming together in one place at one time. In the absence of full information the remuneration committees have to pay more than would be required by the market, in order to be on the safe side. If all the necessary information does come together in one place then this is likely to be with an external head hunting agency and such agencies have incentives to inflate salaries, so are unlikely to recommend efficient market levels of remuneration.

Different approaches to setting the level of executive pay

As we have seen, there are several big problems associated with attempting to use market levels to determine executive salaries. These problems are further compounded by the use of comparative pay positioning that was discussed in chapter 11. These methods that are currently in use can only force the overall average executive remuneration upwards. It is not the case that executive pay will stabilise when it reaches an appropriate level. The dynamic which is driving it upwards has nothing to do with the current level of pay and looks certain to continue for the foreseeable future.

The current approach continually compares executive pay in one company with executive pay in another. These comparisons have little meaning because all other companies are also using the same approach. There are however other comparisons that might be more relevant.

For example comparisons can be made on a historical basis. Current levels of executive pay appear extremely high from a historical perspective. This is because executive pay has risen very dramatically since the mid 1980s and is still rising.

Another possible comparison is with executive pay in other countries. Usually executive pay in the US is much higher than it is in the UK, although the US companies are often bigger and the US has a very strong record on productivity. Directors of US companies also have extraordinarily little accountability to shareholders. Pay in other countries is often less transparent than the UK and US, making international comparisons difficult.

Another comparative measure is the ratio of total remuneration for the chief executive to total remuneration for an average employee. This ratio is difficult to determine but in the US it has reportedly grown from about 40 in 1980 to over 400 by the year 2000.[37] The ratio to the total remuneration of an average working citizen also seems relevant.

However all comparative measures have their limitations. Executive pay is much higher than it was in 1985, but this might simply mean that it was far too low in 1985. Executive pay is much lower in the UK than it is in American, but this might simply mean that it is far too high in America. Religious values have always cautioned against comparison as a means of determining entitlements.[38] These problems with comparisons raise the question of whether there are means of determining the level of executive pay that are not based on comparisons. What more absolute indicators are there for the right level of executive pay?

This is a tough question, but it is certainly one that remuneration committees should spend time considering. I do not pretend to have a simple answer, but I do think there is one important way of assessing the level of executive pay that gets far too little attention. This arises from the role of executives and chief executives in particular as company leaders. Executive pay is one of the most telling statements made by a company's leadership. The level of executive pay should enhance and reinforce other aspects of the leadership message. If it does this, then this is evidence to suggest that the level of pay is appropriate. However if the level of executive pay undermines and discredits the leadership message then this is evidence to suggests that the level of pay is inappropriate.

Executive pay and the leadership message to employees

The level of executive pay gives out very important messages to employees. Surveys can be used to identify the messages received and to check their consistency with other parts of the leadership message.

A low level of executive pay can be used to convey the message that the company needs to be very cost conscious and prudent with money. It can be used to emphasise the importance of non-financial values and the sense that both executives and employees are all in the same boat with interests that are well aligned. However, depending on other leadership actions, a low level of executive pay could also convey a message of stinginess, false economy and reluctance to invest. It might suggest that the company does not value people's talents, skills and experience. It might say that salary aspirations in the company are limited, and this could be demotivating and encourage employees, especially employees with high potential, to move on.

A high level of executive pay can convey very positive messages to employees. It can say that the company believes in its top people and is prepared to set them up as examples. The company wants to reward people who perform well. It suggests that the company is serious about performance and it is prepared to invest money in people to help them to develop and perform better. It values the talents, skills and experience of employees and is committed to recruiting, training, developing and retaining the best people.

However, if executive pay is too high relative to the company's real belief in and actions towards its employees then the employees will pick up a different message. They will perceive that the company values its executives far more than its employees. They might also perceive that the executives are mainly motivated by self-interest. Both these perceptions can cause great cynicism and are very damaging to the company. If these perceptions are strong then it suggests that the level of executive pay is too high.

Whether middle and lower management respond well or badly to high executive pay depends on how they themselves are treated. An important part of this is the question of who gets promoted. High executive pay creates a strong incentive to rise to higher levels in the organisation. If this is well managed it can be a very good thing. If the people who rise up the organisation are those people who have genuinely made an outstanding contribution and who have helped other people to contribute then this suggests that the high executive pay is working. However if the people who rise up the organisation are self-interested people who have prioritised their own agendas at the expense of their colleagues then the high executive pay is very damaging. The message to other managers is that they should work to their own self-interest. Trust and collaboration are diminished. The organisations culture is weakened and becomes more individualistic.

The Anglo Dutch oil and gas group Shell is a good example of a company that became great based on some very strong collaborative values such as trust and integrity. These values then became seriously eroded and problems started to emerge in 2004. As John Plender observed, "For most of the last century Shell worked well [...] demonstrating a strong, cohesive culture and a capacity for self-renewal. The problems set in after it shifted to US-style quantitative performance targets for managers and to stock options, while shedding the old system of controls needed to check and balance ambitious managers."[39]

The other big question for managers, and indeed all employees, about high executive pay is the extent to which it cascades down the organisation. If everybody is perceived to benefit then the response to the leadership is likely to be positive. However if the chief executive earns 400 times more than the average employee then areas where their common interests are aligned are few and far between. To the average employee the message from the top appears to be "You need to do this better, so that I can get paid more."

The potential for this problem is most acute at times when a company needs to make expenditure cut backs. How can an executive team lead and promote cost cutting initiatives when their own salaries are very high? Such situations have the potential to generate internal conflict and resentment. Sometimes executives waive an annual bonus to show willing, but this is usually a one year only initiative, and its impact is likely to be as confined as its generosity. If a year later the executives earn even bigger bonuses for having successfully pushed through the cut-backs then cynicism, resentment and mistrust are certain to fester amongst the people who were adversely affected. The suspicion is always that executives are rewarded for difficulties and sufferings that have been borne by other people.

The high performance, high reward culture

The misalignment of interests that arises when executives are paid far more than other staff is most typically addressed by allowing high financial rewards to cascade down to as many people as possible within the organisation. The cost implications of this are sometimes controlled by outsourcing posts where pay is necessarily low. The idea is to create a high performance, high reward culture so that each person within the organisation can experience rewards that are high, relative to their position in the organisation.

The credibility of the high performance, high reward culture rests on the credibility of the high performance. The performance needs to be very good for the company's competitive position to withstand the higher costs. It is difficult to attain high performance but to sustain it is even harder. When a dip in performance does occur the company's problems are amplified because variable pay is reduced, and this has a demotivating effect. Of course to the extent that pay is not reduced, the company's competitive position is further weakened. The high performance, high reward company culture is therefore inherently unstable.

The high performance, high reward culture is particularly hard to sustain in organisations that employ a lot of people. The focus on high financial rewards to motivate employees can easily reduce focus on the other motivating factors such as clear common objectives, effective teams and appreciation from customers.

Outsourcing and the development of high performance organisations have become central to many company strategies over the recent years. However from a shareholder perspective it is not clear to what extent these strategies have been motivated by the need for higher shareholder value and to what extent they have been motivated by the need to create environments that can withstand higher executive pay.

Executive pay and the leadership message to customers

Sometimes executive pay can provide a leadership message to customers. An unfortunate example of this occurred at MG Rover in 2003. When four Birmingham businessmen bought Rover from BMW for £10 in 2000, there was significant enthusiasm for their innovative, entrepreneurial initiative which preserved the last large scale British car manufacturer and many thousands of jobs in the Midlands. However public credibility was rocked when the company set aside £12.95 million as a trust fund for directors' pensions. The public concern appeared to reflect straight through into sales. In December 2003 the Financial Times reported that, "MG Rover's share of the car market dropped by almost a third last month as sales at the last British owned mass producer were hit by accusations of corporate greed by its directors...The sharp decline in Rover's sales confirms the worst fears of trade unions, which warned the privately owned company two weeks ago that controversy over a £12.95m trust fund for directors could deter buyers."[40]

By the time that MG Rover finally collapsed in April 2005 it was clear that the directors' strategy had been to extract value from the company through directors' fees, reported to total £47m[41], rather than through profits and dividends. This strategy was disastrous for all other stakeholders, and it is regrettable that high levels of executive pay elsewhere in the UK made it appear relatively acceptable.

Executive pay as a leadership message to other stakeholders

Professional firms of accountants, lawyers and consultants are sensitive to executive pay when they set their fees. Executive pay is now relatively transparent and it provides a ready benchmark against which to compare profits per partner. Rising executive pay suggests that professional fees have scope to rise; falling executive pay is a call for restraint in professional fees.

Popular culture is very sensitive to the message of executive pay. Films and TV shows frequently depict senior executives as self serving company drones with no capability to evaluate a proposal beyond the financial perspective. For example in the children's TV show "Biker Mice from Mars" the principal villain is an absurd company boss who panders to his own greed and is devoid of all other values. Such caricatures may be completely unfair but they remain extremely damaging. How will our children learn to create wealth if they grow up with such negative impressions of big business? The leadership message of big business to popular culture is currently in disastrous shape, and the high level of executive pay is a big part of the problem.

Executive pay and the leadership message to shareholders

Executive pay is a matter of great concern to shareholders not least because they bear its direct cost. Higher costs mean lower profit and lower earnings to return to shareholders.

However shareholders' concerns about getting the level of executive pay right go far beyond the direct cost.

The more significant problem for shareholders occurs when inappropriate executive pay starts to damage the leadership message and consequently reduce the effectiveness of the business. We have seen how executive pay that is too high can damage relationships both inside and outside of the company. It weakens the internal values and culture of the company. It creates pressure for higher salaries within the business. It leads to environments in which losses through fraud or lack of Corporate

Social Responsibility (CSR) are more likely. All this leads to weaker financial performance and lower returns to shareholders.

The other more profound problem for shareholders is the loss of clarity on the principle that the business is being run by the executives for the benefit of the shareholders. High executive pay suggests that, at least in part, the business is being run for the personal benefit of the executives. This then raises the question of what other parts of the business are being optimised for the personal benefit of executives rather than for the benefit of shareholders? Are personal expenses being authorised for executive benefit? Are company resources being used, or much worse specified for executive benefit? Is the company strategy really designed to generate value for shareholders or is it compromised in ways that make it convenient and profitable for executives?

This clearly raises major challenges for shareholders. In the next chapter we look at the various ways that shareholders have responded to this challenge. In particular we will look at the increasingly active approach that shareholders are adopting in their capacity as company owners.

Effect of high executive pay on company leadership

Shareholder activism and other responses to high executive pay have made the jobs of company chairman and chief executive much more difficult in recent years. Levels of trust are much lower and expectations of performance are much higher and more immediate. Highly paid individuals have a very high profile and are subjected to a great deal of scrutiny. Executives complain about operating in a goldfish bowl and being smothered by red tape, but many of these problems arise directly or indirectly from the very high levels of executive pay. Ironically the greater difficulties have caused some executives and company chairmen to argue that they now deserve to be paid more! In reality however higher pay would just make all the problems worse. The problems can only really be addressed by reducing executive pay. On the whole executives keep their heads down, quietly suffering the company problems caused by high executive pay, and quietly enjoying the personal benefits!

Summary

In FTSE 350 companies today the overall level of executive pay is typically set to appear appropriate when compared to the executive pay in other comparable organisations. This is justified by saying that there is a competitive market in executive talent and a company that pays less than market rates will quickly fall behind in the recruitment and retention of high quality executive talent.

From a shareholder perspective this market based approach to recruiting executive talent is extremely unsatisfactory. It creates an unnecessary and very problematic conflict of interest for the company board as buyer and provider of executive services. This has the effect of undermining the relationship of trust, which executives need to build with their shareholders. Executives can build shareholder trust by accepting remuneration that is demonstrably less than what they otherwise could command in the market.

Even if shareholders accept the market approach, the market for executive talent is extremely complex and depends on many other things besides money. The supply and demand rules are quite different from normal markets. It is doubtful whether the market in executive talent could ever be made truly competitive or efficient from a buyer's point of view. Certainly the current comparative pay positioning approach is extremely unsatisfactory as a way of determine market levels, because by definition half of all executives should be paid lower than median salaries.

Remuneration committees need to look for ways of determining the level of executive pay that do not resort to comparative methods. This is not easy, but one powerful and very important consideration is the consistency of executive pay with the leadership message from the company board. If the level of executive pay supports the leadership message of the board and increases its credibility then this is evidence to suggest that the level of executive pay is appropriate. If the level of executive pay is inconsistent with the leadership message and undermines the credibility of the leadership then this suggests that the level of pay is not right.

Notes

34. Financial Times 23/08/05: An extract from Plender 2005
35. Combined Code 2003: Main Principle B.2
36. Combined Code 2003: Supporting Principles B.2
37. William McDonough, Chairman of Public Company Accounting Oversight Board, in testimony before US congress in June 2004, reported in Financial Times 24/08/04, page 15
38. For example Exodus 20:17 or Matthew 20:1-16
39. Financial Times 21/06/04: Page 22
40. Financial Times 04/12/03: Front page
41. Financial Times 22/04/05: Front page

13

The shareholder response

As we saw in the last chapter, high executive pay raises many issues for shareholders. Financial returns to shareholders are damaged when executive pay is excessive. High executive pay also makes shareholders question whether their ownership rights are being properly respected. This chapter is about the shareholder response to these issues. What have shareholders done in response to high executive pay?

Selling the shares

Traditionally shareholders respond to executive practices that they do not like by selling the company shares. This response has certainly happened in a very big way. The bear market in the first years of the new century has made investors very cautious about endorsing equity investments. Many actuaries have advised pension funds to diversify their investment risk away from equities, and in particular to buy more index linked bonds because they fit more accurately to the liabilities arising from providing pensions. This has caused large flows of capital out of equities and into other investments such as bonds. Standard Life reported that it had reduced the proportion of equity assets in its £31bn with-profits fund from 77% at the start of 2002 to 35% by February 2004. In May 2004 the Financial Times reported that the UK's biggest fund managers planned to move £150bn out of equities over three years.[42] This scenario is extremely disheartening for the equity investor. In particular it could significantly reduce equity valuations causing greater pension deficits and serious problems for all of us who expect to live off a pension at some time in the future.

Requests for more information

The problem with the "sell the shares" response is that equities form such an important part of the UK investment market that shareholders cannot simply sell up and walk away. Shareholders themselves would be easily the biggest losers if equity prices were to collapse. Shareholders have been forced to develop other responses to the problems.

One of these responses has been to request more information. Shareholders need to satisfy themselves that the large sums of money being paid to executives are justified. They want details of executive remuneration and how it is linked to performance. They want to know that the performance criteria are justified. They want to understand strategy, to see that the company really is being run to create value. They want to understand the risks and see that these are being managed. They want to see more detailed external audits and stronger internal control procedures. They want more information about CSR risks and what is being done to manage them.

The requests for more information generate significant amounts of work for companies, which for the most part is not value adding. Executive time is absorbed by such activities and to some extent executive reputations are judged on compliance. All this diverts focus and resources from the creation of shareholder value. Shareholders' informational requirements have grown in an overwhelming way such that annual reports are typically two or three times as thick as they were in 1990. In general the government has been very supportive of shareholders' desires for more information. In particular it has introduced the Directors Remuneration Report Regulations 2002 and encouraged development of Operating and Financial Reviews.

Corporate governance

A third shareholder response has been to request company boards to comply with codes of conduct and best practice guidance. This has been a massive growth area! A whole new profession of corporate governance advisors has been born. Consultancies specialising in corporate governance are now big businesses[43], with their own commercial agendas. The number of regulations, codes and best practice guides has mushroomed. The most important such documents are discussed in the "Regulation and compliance" section of chapter 4, but it should also be remembered that many financial institutions have developed their own guidelines. It is very difficult for a company board to know whether to comply with all, or some or none of these guides. Whilst the guides contain many consistent themes they are far from completely consistent on the detail. The focus on whether or not a company complies, and how well it explains any non-compliance all takes focus off the real challenge of creating shareholder value.

Closely linked to the growth in corporate governance is a big new trend of shareholder activism. Institution shareholders increasingly want to be consulted about executive pay and key appointments. They want to discuss and challenge the strategy and are prepared to vote against the company board at annual meetings. Shareholder activism has been strongly supported by the government[44] who perhaps see it as a market based mechanism for ensuring best practice in listed companies, particularly on issues such as executive pay. Shareholder activism is discussed in more detail later in this chapter.

The cycle of vested interests surrounding the level of executive pay

Given that there is so much shareholder concern to constrain executive pay it might at first sight appear rather surprising that executive pay continues to rise. The most obvious conflicts of interest have been eliminated by the Combined Code which insists that no director should be involved in deciding his or her own remuneration.[45] The Combined Code has also substantially eliminated mutual back scratching arrangements such as the one that contributed to Richard Grasso's infamous $187.5 million proposed remuneration at the New York Stock Exchange (NYSE). Mr Grasso was on the board of Home Depot where the founder was Kenneth Langone, chairman of the NYSE compensation committee.

The most obvious conflicts of interest and mutual back scratching may have been removed, but they have been replaced by more sophisticated interrelationships with common, self-reinforcing vested interests. Shareholders and remuneration committees need to be aware of these vested interests and take proper account of them. Let us therefore examine the incentives on the various parties involved in setting executive pay in the UK.

The incentives on executives

Executives themselves clearly have very strong incentives to see executive pay continue to spiral upwards. They are the most direct beneficiaries. Everyone likes to get a pay rise! Most executives are very happy to see executive pay moving upwards.

Paradoxically however I suspect it is the executives themselves who are most conscious of the damage that current practise on executive pay is doing to UK companies. It is the executives whose jobs become more difficult as conflict increases, trust diminishes, and red tape increases.

Before the 1992 Cadbury Report many companies had a single person acting as chairman and chief executive. Such people had very strong and direct control over executive pay including their own pay. This obvious conflict of interests was not always well handled, but in most cases it was handled very responsibly with great attention to the good of the company and to fiduciary duty. Certainly the growth in executive pay before the mid 1980s was very small compared to what has happened since. When company leadership meant, amongst other things, controlling executive pay, many leaders felt the need to do this effectively, even though they could have justified paying themselves more. It is much more difficult for executives today to show leadership through restraint on executive pay. To do so they would have to work very hard to influence the other executives, the chairman, the remuneration committee and the remuneration consultants involved. Each of these groups has good reasons for dismissing calls for restraint as misplaced, idealistic or impractical. To try and influence the remuneration committee could even constitute a breach of the Combined Code.[46] It is one thing to accept lower personal benefits; it is quite another to fight for lower personal benefits! Very few executives are going to attempt this.

The incentives on company chairmen

There is some correlation between rises in executive pay and rises in the pay of company chairmen. Company chairmen therefore have a personal financial incentive to see executive pay move upwards. In fact they sometimes express the view that executive pay in public companies in the UK is inadequate.[47] However, if institutional shareholders take exception to executive pay proposals then they can cause embarrassment and a great deal of hard work for company chairmen. Sir Christopher Hogg spent much of 2003 sorting out the problems arising from the shareholder vote against the GlaxoSmithKline plc remuneration report for 2002. Chairmen may benefit from executive pay rising, but they are sensitive to the views of institutional investors.

The incentives on remuneration committees

Remuneration committees hold direct responsibility for executive pay. They are made up of independent non-executive directors but this does not mean that they are exempt from pressures and incentives. If they are to be effective, remuneration committees need to take account of these pressures and incentives as they exercise their duties. The first pressure is the pressure of time. Non-executive directors typically have substantive other jobs and so have very limited time to spend on their remuneration duties. The Higgs review identified lack of time as the biggest barrier to the effectiveness of non-executive directors.[48] This is particularly true for members of the remuneration committee because there is huge complexity and detail involved in executive pay. The committee has to consider the incentive regime, the performance conditions, the overall level of executive pay and considerations surrounding external presentation. Ideally they would also discuss proposals with shareholder representatives. All these issues require time for thought and dialogue between the committee members. It obviously cannot all happen in the day or two of time available each month. The committee is necessarily very dependent on the remuneration consultancy or management group that manages the detail and comes up with the proposals. This makes the remuneration committee far less independent than it appears to be at first sight.

It is also important to remember that most remuneration committee members have been executive directors of other companies in the past. Many still have executive style responsibilities, most commonly as company chairmen, but often as executive directors either in the UK or abroad. People with this background are almost certain to benefit if the general level of executive pay rises. They are naturally sympathetic to the message that executive talent is a scarce resource that needs to be better remunerated. The remuneration consultancies know this, and consequently make it a central component of their sales pitch.

As independent non-executive directors the remuneration committee members do not have executive responsibility for the company. They consequently have little responsibility for the company ethos, culture and values which are primarily set by the chairman and executive directors. This means that policy on executive pay, even though it makes statements that are central to the company's leadership, culture and values has become separated from the actual leadership. The remuneration committee have some accountability to shareholders for problems caused by excessive executive pay, but most of the difficulties with relationships and trust that arise from excessive executive remuneration fall on the executives. Of course the executives have very strong incentives to manage these problems quietly and play down their significance.

Even if a remuneration committee did feel the need to fight hard to exercise restraint on executive pay it is very difficult for it to do this. All the data and proposals that are prepared and presented for discussion come from the remuneration consultancy and the executives, all of whom have financial incentives to see executive pay move upwards. The company chairman also has incentives to see pay move upwards and the chairman is normally very influential on the question of the future reappointment of the non-executive directors. For the remuneration committee to take a strong stand it would need to devote both time and resources and neither of these two things are available to it.

Sadly, the primary incentive on the remuneration committee is therefore to take the path of least resistance through the problem. The remuneration committee inevitably therefore focuses on "What will appear acceptable?" rather than "What is best for the company?" Often the only really compelling reason for a remuneration committee to oppose a remuneration proposal arises when failure to take on a fight now would result in even bigger problems later with external stakeholders.

Incentives on remuneration consultancies

The incentives on remuneration consultancies were discussed in detail in chapter 11. It is clear that they have incentives to propose rises in executive pay, because it is a very effective way of securing engagement with management. They also have incentives to increase the scope of their role by making executive pay an ever bigger, more complicated and more important issue.

Shareholder activism on executive pay

In the previous section we saw that most of the people who have direct involvement in executive remuneration have a clear incentive to see the overall levels of executive pay move upwards. It is therefore no surprise that the levels of executive pay do continue to move upwards, sometimes quite rapidly.

Of course the people who lose out when executive pay increases are the people who own shares in the in the companies concerned. They lose out because of the direct cost of executive pay, but they lose out much more in other ways as we saw in chapter 12. We have already looked at some of the ways that shareholders have responded to these problems. Now let us look in more detail at the ways that shareholders can exercise their voting rights in order to influence company boards on issues such as executive pay.

Some listed companies have large shareholdings owned by a single person or family; very often the founder of the business. In these companies the major shareholders have real voting power and they are often represented on company boards. In situations like this the major shareholders have strong incentives to act as effective owners. They have tremendous financial incentives to make sure that the company is well run and delivers shareholder value. In most cases this works to the benefit of all shareholders. Problems can arise if actions are taken that favour the major shareholder over the others, or if the executive team has family links to the major shareholder, but the really important point is that the natural incentives arising from ownership are fully present and they create an environment in which effective ownership is likely to be exercised.

However the overwhelming bulk of equity in UK listed companies is owned by a very large number of very small shareholdings. Even a big financial institution is only likely to own a very small proportion of any one FTSE 350 company. How do these shareholders exercise effective ownership? How do they actively make sure that companies are being run for the benefit of the shareholders rather than for the benefit of the management?

Shareholder activism and the individual investor

The individual investor is in a weak position as an activist shareholder. The proportion of a company's shares owned by any one private individual is usually extremely small, certainly far too small to have any effective voting power. This is rather discouraging for private investors, and they often do not use the small amount of voting power that they have.

Private investors can attend annual general meetings and ask company directors awkward questions. This is probably their most powerful weapon and it can cause some discomfort to a company board for a couple of hours each year. There is however very little incentive on company boards to take notice of the points raised once the meeting is over.

The private investor's influence, even for a very wealthy private investor, is seriously weakened by the investor's need to diversify risk. Investing in just one company exposes the investor to excessive risk. The investor therefore tends to invest a smaller amount in several different companies. This means he or she has less voting influence for each company covered, and has less time to spend examining the annual report and getting to grips with the issues affecting each company. This therefore makes the private investor a very ineffective owner. It is usually very easy for company boards to ignore the interests of private investors.

One way of making the ownership of private investors more effective is for the investors to act collectively. Organisations like the UK Shareholders Association (UKSA) strive to make this happen. Whilst much is said about shareholder value and huge tomes are produced on the way that businesses should be run it is often relatively small organisations such as UKSA who most accurately and consistently express what it means to run a company in the interests of its shareholders.

The other huge problem which makes the private investor very ineffectual as a company owner is that his or her shares are much more commonly held through some form of pension or investment fund than held directly. There are thousands of pension and investment funds covering all different forms of investment. The Financial Times publishes prices for about 13,000 funds every day. Legally it is these funds who own the shares of UK listed companies rather than the underlying investors. That means that it is the funds, the fund managers and the institutional investors who must exercise the rights associated with share ownership rather than the underlying investors themselves.

Shareholder activism and the institutional investor

UK financial institutions have been large scale investors in UK equities for many years. In 1999 they collectively owned just over half of the entire UK equity market.[49] This means that, where they act collectively, their voting power is easily sufficient to have an impact at shareholder meetings and at company annual general meetings in particular.

Historically however the institutions have not usually exercised the considerable powers that they retain as large scale share owners. Often they did not even vote at annual general meetings. This passive approach to investing gave rise to a huge gap in the role of ownership. For company boards the role of owner only really became important in the event of a takeover bid; the rest of the time management had a very free hand.

A gradual move towards greater shareholder activism became more purposeful with the arrival of the new Labour government in 1997. Many of the incoming government's MPs and trade union supporters regarded high executive pay as an abuse of board room power. However when they started to address this problem it quickly became clear that the abused parties were in fact the company owners, and unless the company owners started to act in their own best interests any solution imposed by government would be at best partial. The government therefore started to take measures to encourage shareholders, and institutional shareholders in particular, to exercise their ownership powers in the ownership interest.

The government made various changes to ensure that shareholder voting was both easier and more necessary. The National Association of Pension Funds (NAPF) and the Association of British Insurers (ABI) developed a joint statement on responsible shareholder voting.[50] Despite this shareholder activism developed more slowly than expected. The reasons for this were specifically examined by the 2001 Myners review of institutional investment.[51] The review identified four factors which discouraged activism amongst institutional investors.

Firstly the selection and assessment of fund managers is largely based on the quarterly performance of the funds which they manage. This gives the fund manager a very short term focus. Activities such as shareholder activism, which might deliver long term benefits are not sufficiently taken into account or rewarded. The short term focus of the incentives on fund managers is a very serious problem that is proving very damaging to capitalism as we know it today.

Secondly the culture in the financial community wants to avoid public confrontation with management. The review does not seek to explain this, but it is clear that City institutions are very dependent on their contacts in listed companies to provide them with information, to improve their understanding of the businesses and to help them outperform their competitors. Clearly getting help from the company is very difficult in a confrontational environment, but much easier when interests are aligned and trust is high.

Thirdly conflicts of interest arise because the institutions often need to sell services, especially pension fund management services, to listed companies. Clearly this selling of services, and the retaining customers, will go much better if the fund managers are not actively challenging the company management!

Fourthly effective shareholder intervention requires persistence and a thick skin over a long period of time. The cost and effort to a particular fund manager might be significant, but the benefits would be equally shared by all investors in that company. To the extent that fund managers are seeking to outperform their peers this free-ride effect is a big disincentive to intervention.

The Myners review concludes that, "effective intervention, when appropriate, is in the best financial interests of the beneficiaries. As such it is arguably already a legal duty of both pension fund trustees and their fund managers to pursue such strategies." The report highlights the US situation where a Department of Labor bulletin from 1994 makes it very clear that the fiduciary duties of plan managers include the voting of proxies on issues that may affect the value of the plan's investment. The Myners report recommends that investment mandates and UK law should be modified to make it very clear that this same principle also applies in the UK.

Since the Myners report shareholder activism has continued to develop in the UK. The ABI and NAPF have been at the forefront, coordinating and articulating investor opinion and making recommendations on the ways that shareholder votes should be cast. There were some significant successes. In May 2003 shareholders rejected the GlaxoSmithKline remuneration report. In October 2003 shareholders blocked the appointment of Michael Green as chairman of ITV and in February 2004 they similarly blocked Sir Ian Prosser at Sainsbury. Concerned about the problems that shareholder activism was causing in UK boardrooms, the Confederation of British Industry (CBI), asked to meet some leading institutional investors at the RAC club for "peace talks" in March 2004. The Financial Times reported that at this private meeting, "Digby Jones, the director-general of the CBI, banged on about one of his favourite topics: that fund managers should disclose their salaries."[52] The fact is that the UK fund management industry takes far more value from UK investors than executive pay does. Digby Jones's important comment made the institutional investors realise that they live in glass houses and should not throw stones. Shareholder activism has been far less confrontational and has had a far lower profile ever since.

Limitations of shareholder activism

Shareholder activism is probably better developed in the UK than anywhere else in the world. However even in the UK shareholder activism falls a very long way short of providing listed companies with effective ownership. However effective the work of the ABI and NAPF, the institutional investors are not in a position to provide the proactive ownership attention that is required.

In today's model of shareholder activism it is the responsibility of the companies to produce proposals and for the shareholders to say "Yes" or "No". This negotiating structure (perhaps quite rightly!) limits the input that shareholders can have. However, in a confrontational situation it is very difficult for shareholders to continually say "No" because it becomes possible to blame the shareholders for the company's failure to move forward. If such a confrontation damages the company, then shareholders are likely to be at least as worried as the company board is. If shareholders start to produce proposals of their own then many further questions are raised. Do shareholders have time to do this properly? Do they understand the company well enough to do it effectively? What if the message from the different shareholders is not consistent? Is this micromanagement? Is it consistent with equal information for all shareholders?

The present structure requires large numbers of institutional shareholders to agree about their interventions. This is intrinsically difficult, although the ABI and NAPF appear to be surprisingly effective at making it happen. However company boards can undermine shareholder interventions by making complicated proposals that are difficult for shareholders to agree upon. They can also exploit the short term focus of institutional investors. For example, in August 2004 Berkeley Group put forward a complicated scheme that linked very high executive remuneration in six years time, with a huge payback of cash to investors in the short term. Presented in this way, it was always going to be difficult for the shareholders to agree that the proposed remuneration was inappropriate. The ABI came out firmly against the proposal and a significant protest vote was lodged. Even so the proposal was comfortably approved by the shareholder vote. Probably shareholders felt that, given the directors enthusiasm for the scheme, it represented the most realistic route forward for shareholders. This is quite different from believing that the scheme was developed with the shareholder interest at heart.

There are also very deep problems with the incentive regime for fund managers. Even if they had a very clear fiduciary duty to be activist shareholders, the incentive regime discourages them from being effective owners. The four points from the Myners report are all very relevant here, but there are also some deeper problems.

First of all the financial services industry itself enjoys very high levels of pay. It is difficult for fund managers to argue externally that executives should be paid less, whilst at the same time arguing internally that fund managers should be paid more. In particular comparisons with executive pay, which is now relatively transparent, can easily be used to support notions of what it is reasonable for a fund manager to earn. Fund managers particularly like the "exceptional pay for exceptional performance" argument because it is an argument that they themselves frequently use in support of their own pay. As we saw in chapter 7 this argument only works for the underlying shareholder if the performance measures are based on long term growth in Total Shareholder Return (TSR), and this is very seldom the case. Short term measures are all too common.

The high pay mentality in fund management was illustrated at the Hermes Focus Asset Management (HFAM) funds, which had a particular reputation for shareholder activism and for being at the forefront of initiatives on corporate governance. The funds had a ground breaking strategy of investing in companies where the share price appeared to be depressed because of poor arrangements for corporate governance. By buying the shares and actively engaging with the company board, HFAM frequently managed to improve the company's governance and financial performance. Significant rises in the share price would follow and the HFAM investment strategy proved to be very successful. Then in August 2004 two directors of HFAM resigned after Hermes refused their request for personal slices of equity in HFAM. The very good performance of the HFAM funds meant that the two directors were each paid a total of £2.3million in 2003, but it would seem that they thought this was not enough.[53] From the point of view of the underlying owners of a unit trust or a pension fund the level of fees charged by fund managers is in fact a much bigger problem than executive pay. Such fees can easily amount to 3% or more of the total investment every year! The very high costs and other difficulties that institutional investors thrust upon underlying investors are increasingly well understood[54] and it is very clear that many people in the financial services industry have a great deal to lose if all the conflicts of interest are properly resolved. With so much vested interest at stake the financial services industry is in no position to criticise executives for creaming off too much shareholder value. Supporters of high executive pay can undermine the financial services industry's credibility on this point, as the RAC club meeting of March 2004 demonstrates.

A further problem for institutional investors seeking to control executive pay is that most institutional funds are controlled directly or indirectly by large listed companies, many of them in the FTSE 100. This means that the fund managers who are being encouraged to take a firm stand against excessive executive pay, ultimate report to executives who directly benefit from high levels of executive pay. This is bound to cause problems, even where the individuals concerned act with the highest possible integrity. Clearly it is not a good career move to publicly criticise or create embarrassment for your own bosses! Also increases or decreases in executive pay tend to get cascaded down the organisation and to a greater or lesser extent they start to affect the pay of other senior people. Restricting your bosses pay therefore has the effect of restricted your own pay. Of course if the bosses start to seek revenge then that restriction could be very severe!

This loop of ownership control is a very general problem, but it was well illustrated in April 2004 when Keith Jones, chief executive of Morley Fund Management accepted new responsibilities at the ABI. In keeping with the new role, Morley issued tough statements about companies with poor corporate governance. However it subsequently became clear that Morley's parent company, Aviva plc, offered retesting of its long term incentive schemes and paid guaranteed bonuses to executives; two of the very practices that Morley was objecting to.[55] Even with the best will in the world, this cannot have helped Keith Jones or his stand on corporate governance.

It is clear that even if fund managers have the best of intentions and the highest integrity, all the incentives that they face discourage them from devoting time and effort to the long term interests of the underlying owners of the funds. In such a situation those fund managers who do try to act as effective company owners are likely to be less competitive and effective in their own industry than those who do not.

Corporate governance and effective ownership

The UK system of corporate governance, as articulated in the Combined Code, depends critically on the role of the non-executive director. The Higgs Guidance sets out what is expected of a non-executive director.[56] This is summarised in one particular sentence; "Non-executive directors should constantly seek to establish and maintain confidence in the conduct of the company."

It is possibly the intention of the Combined Code that the ownership interest of shareholders should be represented on the company board by the non-executive directors. Unfortunately non-executive directors have no effective power to do this. The main problem they face is that they have very limited time to devote to their duties. Often proposals that come before the board have been developed without their input. This, together with the fact that they have no staff reporting to them, restricts their ability to pursue their own agenda. Another big power limiting factor is that most non-executive directors are independent. By definition an independent non-executive director has a very limited relationship with the company. He or she is most unlikely to have a sufficiently detailed knowledge of the company or its historical background to be able to represent the ownership interest effectively. A further power restriction arises from the appointment and re-election of non-executive directors which is mainly in the gift of the board itself, particularly of the chairman. This means that a successful non-executive director is very unlikely to pursue an agenda that creates conflict with the company chairman. The only real power that a non-executive can exercise comes when he or she threatens to resign. Unfortunately resignation is likely to hurt the non-executive at least as much as it is likely to hurt the board. Post-resignation the non-executive, particularly if he or she is independent, usually has very little incentive to pursue the issue that lead to the resignation.

In fact a closer study of the Combined Code 2003 shows that it does not envisage that the non-executives have any specific responsibility to represent the ownership interest. On the contrary the code envisages that contact with shareholders is much more the business of the chairman than of the non-executives (A.3.3, D.1). Further, non-executives who have a significant shareholding in the company, or who have any longstanding relationship with the company are unlikely to be considered as independent in accordance with the codes criteria (A.3.1). A non-executive who is not independent cannot serve on the remuneration committee (B.2.1) or on the audit committee (C.3.1) and can only be in a minority on the nomination committee (A.4.1) and on the board as a whole (A.2). Non-executive directors who are not independent therefore have very limited scope in their role, and consequently can have only limited influence.

Unfortunately therefore the Combined Code has the, perhaps unintended, consequence of decreasing rather than increasing owner representation on company boards. This is a very serious problem. The voice of the underlying ownership interest has become extremely marginalised. This means that the most important market related control on executive pay has become ineffective.

The consequences of no effective ownership

In FTSE 350 companies the lack of effective ownership is a problem that is very closely related to the problem of excessive executive pay. It is noticeable that in the US, where the ownership interest is even more marginalised than it is in the UK, executive pay is even higher than in the UK[57]. Unfortunately the lack of effective ownership has consequences that stretch well beyond executive pay. With no effective ownership, the shareholders' requirement for sustained long term growth and a reasonable return on investment can only become more and more marginalised as a business goal. Instead we can expect to see companies run more and more for the benefit of directors, executives, consultants, professional advisors and wider management. This is a very depressing prospect. If business is run in a self-serving way then the high values, trust and strong sense of purpose that are essential to business success all become undermined. An environment is created in which more regulation and red tape is required. This in turn makes financial performance harder to achieve. Listed companies are likely to look less attractive to investors. Private equity investments, where ownership is more effective, will start to look more attractive.

Summary

Investors in UK equities have spent the first years of the twenty-first century attempting to reduce their exposure to the stock market by selling shares. They have also requested far more information from companies and have become very interested in issues of corporate governance.

Despite these signs of disquiet and mistrust, the overall level of executive pay has continued to rise, sometimes quite rapidly. This surprising occurrence can be explained by looking at the incentives affecting those people who are directly involved in the setting of executive remuneration. Executives, company chairmen, remuneration committee members, remuneration consultancies and senior company managers all benefit directly or indirectly when the overall level of executive pay in the UK rises.

The people who lose out because of this upward growth cycle in executive pay are company shareholders. This has lead to disquiet and mistrust on the part of shareholders. Shareholders have become far more prepared to challenge company management and much more active in voting of their shareholdings. This new shareholder activism has won some significant victories, but still falls a long way short of the effective ownership necessary to guarantee that companies are run for the benefit of their shareholders.

The lack of effective ownership has become a very significant problem. The biggest shareholdings are controlled by fund managers who usually have no incentives to act as effective company owners. In fact there are many practical problems that make it very difficult for them to take company ownership seriously. Effective ownership is also made difficult by the Combined Code. The code requires many important functions to be handled by independent non-executive directors, who by definition have only limited interests in the company. Non-executive directors with significant shareholdings are marginalised.

Notes

42. Financial Times 27/05/04: Page 3

43. On 14/07/05 FT.com reported that Institutional Shareholder Services forecasted that its cashflow would top $100m per year from 2006.
44. For example Government 2003: Pages 5-6
45. Combined Code 2003: Main Principle B.2
46. Combined Code 2003: Main Principle and Supporting Principles B.2
47. For example the remarks of Allan Leighton reported in the Financial Times 13/05/04, page 23
48. Higgs 2003: Paragraph 12.12
49. Myners 2001: Page 27
50. ABI and NAPF 1999
51. Myners 2001: Pages 89-93
52. Financial Times 31/03/04: Page 7
53. Based on reports in the Financial Times 10/08/04 to 12/08/04
54. For example John Sunderland speech to Investor Relations Society 21/04/05, Myners 2001 and Sykes 2004
55. Financial Times 05/04/04: Page 16
56. Combined Code 2003: Page 63-4
57. Bubchuk 2004

14

The future of executive pay

This book has looked at many of the difficulties associated with current arrangements for executive pay in the UK. In this chapter we look briefly at some of the things that can be done to help resolve these problems.

Reforming the structure of executive pay

The first ten chapters of this book were primarily concerned with the way that executive pay is structured, and the incentives that arise from those structures. A great many difficulties were identified and some solutions suggested. This was illustrated by the restructuring of Joe Figment's remuneration package from that shown at the start of chapter 4 to that shown at the end of chapter 8. This restructuring can be achieved without changing the expected annual average value of remuneration, and as such remuneration committees should find such changes relatively achievable. Let us remind ourselves of the key changes in six simple steps.

Step 1 - Move from defined benefit pensions to defined contribution pensions
This can be done without changing the pension entitlement earned to date. The company's annual contribution to an executive's pension might still remain large. The change is needed to break the link between basic salary and pension so as to weaken the incentives associated with basic salary. The incentives arising from basic salary tend to work against the interests of shareholders. In particular it is not realistic to attempt to reduce basic salary until this link has been broken.

Step 2 - Break the link between salary and awards under variable pay schemes

Awards under variable pay schemes need to be defined independently of basic salary. This change is also needed to break the link between basic salary and variable pay so as to weaken the incentives associated with basic salary.

Step 3 - Replace a proportion of basic salary, and ALL variable pay schemes with a single variable pay scheme that properly aligns executive and shareholder interests. I would suggest a PRER FILLIP.

This ensures that incentives are properly aligned with shareholder interests, that the incentive arrangements are relatively simple, transparent, consistent over time and consistent over all possible performance outcomes.

Step 4 – Minimise the number and size of benefits provided irrespective of performance

The main fixed benefits should be basic salary and pension. Other benefits (cars, insurance etc) should be few and small. There should be a good reason why the benefit is provided by the company rather than being the responsibility of the executive.

Step 5 – Double check that all variable pay schemes beyond the FILLIP have gone.

Step 6 – Check that the changes have not changed overall expected remuneration

The above changes massively increase confidence that the incentives faced by executives are in alignment with the interests of shareholders. Transparency, objectivity and the robustness of the performance link will all be much improved leading to far greater trust between shareholders and executives. Trust inside the company, and with its other stakeholders is also likely to benefit, particularly as all executive variable pay will be based on the common corporate goals of long term growth in shareholder value.

It is realistic to hope that changes similar to those suggested above can be implemented by many companies to the great benefit of many, many people. The proposed changes are realistic because they would result in lots of net winners and few net losers. Shareholders would be immediate net winners, executives who are genuinely effective at adding shareholder value over the longer term would also be net winners. While the changes were taking place remuneration consultancies would be very big winners, although they will want to keep best practice moving onwards even when all the necessary changes have been made. Remuneration committees would need to resist this. The main losers would be executives who are not really effective in building long term shareholder value. These are the people who can be expected to object most vociferously to the proposals.

Re-establishing effective ownership

As we saw in the last chapter the problem of very high executive pay is closely linked to the lack of effective ownership that we see in many listed companies in the UK today.

Re-establishing effective ownership in listed companies might be an important agenda item for a very brave government, but it is a goal substantially beyond the reach of even the noblest and best people in corporate life today. However, given the importance of effective ownership, I would like to mention some realistic developments that would help to move things in the right direction.

Appoint large shareholders as non-executive directors
Michael Skapinker has argued convincingly[58] that non-executives who have significant amounts of their own capital wrapped up in the companies shares are the most effective at improving company performance. He quotes research by Donald Hambrick and Eric Jackson published as "Outside Directors with a Stake: The Linchpin in Improving Governance" in the California Management Review 2000. He also refers to the famously successful investment company Berkshire Hathaway run by Warren Buffet. When appointing non-executive directors Mr Buffet sees a large personal shareholding as more important than any other criteria. Mr Buffet says, "Charlie and I love such honest-

to-God ownership. After all, who ever washes a rental car?"[59] A significant personal shareholding makes a non-executive more, rather than less, eligible to serve on important board committees. The Combined Code rules about independence for non-executive directors need to take this into account.

Outsourcing of corporate governance by investment and pension funds

In August 2004 both the Wellcome Trust and British Coal Staff Superannuation Scheme outsourced their corporate governance activities to more activist shareholder bodies. This practise makes it much easier for activist shareholder bodies to act as effective owners. First of all their voting power is increased because they vote the outsourced shares as well as their own. Secondly the exercising of shareholder rights becomes a core activity in their business so is more likely to get proper focus. Thirdly, as money is paid for the service, there are more resources available to do it properly. However this is still only a partial solution. Most of the incentive problems associated with shareholder activism by financial institutions (see chapter 13) are still relevant and still damaging to the effectiveness of ownership. It might be possible to partially address this by linking the outsourcing fee to long term growth (with dividends reinvested) in the FTSE 350 index with a FILLIP style structure, although this might then raise further issues.

Consolidation in the financial services industry

Many problems about effective ownership arise from problems in the financial services industry. Such problems are beyond the scope of this book, but it is not clear to me why we need 13,000 possible investment funds. The requirements of competition and choice could be very well covered by 130 different funds. This suggests that the costs of the fund management industry are at least 100 times higher then they need to be. Consolidation of the funds would leave each remaining fund with a greater percentage share of the ownership of each listed company. This would make effective ownership both easier and more important for the fund.

Better training and support for pension fund trustees

Pension fund trustees are the buyers of fund management services.

Unfortunately most of the advice and training that they get comes form the financial services industry. This means that the actions of pension fund trustees as buyers sometimes appear to be more influenced by the needs of the service providers than by the needs of the underlying owners of shares. As buyers, pension trustees should always seek to invest in the very largest funds, and they should insist that the benefits of lower unit costs arising from large scale fund management are passed back to the underlying owners. Buyers should always seek much lower and more transparent pay for fund managers. They should insist that any performance related pay for fund managers is based only on long term performance measured over at least five years. Similarly a performance related fund management fee should only be accepted if the performance is measured over at least five years.

Others measures to help remuneration committees control the level of executive pay

Reduce influence of market levels in the determination of executive directors pay

Being a director is fundamentally about trust. Executive directors must provide evidence that they are working for the benefit of the company and are not solely interested in their own personal rewards. The best demonstration of this occurs when a director accepts a total reward package that is demonstrably below what the individual could command elsewhere in the market. A complete culture change is required here, but the culture change is essential if trust in company boards is to be re-established. The benefits of moving away from market based pay are examined in chapter 12.

Stop the practise of comparative pay positioning

As we saw in chapter 11, comparative pay positioning, as currently practiced, is very damaging to the interests of shareholders, and especially to shareholders who own shares across many UK companies. When remuneration committees "judge where to position their company relative to other companies" as they are required to do by supporting principle B.1 of the Combined Code, they should be making no more than a sense check to ensure that obvious problems are avoided. Remuneration committees should be far more concerned about doing the right thing for their own company than about what other companies are doing. Executive pay should be set to enhance the leadership message of the board. On the question of recruiting and retaining executive directors the discussions should mainly concern matters other than pay. If individuals insist on pay that is too high to be consistent with the leadership message of the board then this suggests that they are not the right people for the job.

Make comparative pay positioning independent and consistent

If comparative pay positioning cannot be stopped then it should at least be improved by making it genuinely independent of the company and consistent between companies. The present arrangements are far from consistent and objective because each company wants to select and present data in a way that makes it look good. This is well illustrated by the performance graphs that companies are required to present in their remuneration reports. The vast majority of performance graphs show that performance has been above the benchmark. However if the benchmarks really were objective presentations of median performance then half of all performance graphs would be below benchmark.

Remuneration committees should seek to co-operate with other groups to improve the objectivity, consistency and independence of comparative pay data. Ultimately there could be a single pay-data body to provide complete, consistent, transparent and independent data for use by all companies in the setting of executive pay. The body could publish TSR index data for FTSE 350 companies and relevant overseas companies. It could publish estimates of total remuneration for chief executives based on remuneration reports, and ranking positions within its own independently defined comparator groups. Institutional shareholders would encourage companies to use the standard data, which because of its transparency, consistency and independence would have far higher credibility than anything the company could produce for itself. Of course it would be legitimate for the company to attempt to influence the pay-data body on issues such as comparator groups, and in such cases the body could publish the representations made, the view received from shareholders, its own thinking and the decisions it made.

There is a difficult question of who should pay for such a body, because its costs would be significant. However the cost would make sense for shareholders collectively because there would be a very large cost saving to all FTSE 350 companies each of which currently generates this same data independently. The government might consider paying for the body because corporation tax revenues would benefit from cost savings within the companies and from better company performance arising from more accurate links between performance and executive pay. This is very much a public interest issue because of the widespread ownership of shares, especially through investment products and pension schemes.

Seek to reduce dependence on remuneration consultants

As discussed in chapter 11, remuneration committees need to be aware that most of the incentives faced by remuneration consultancies work against the shareholder interest. It therefore makes sense to minimise dependence on remuneration consultancies. One very good way of doing this is to move to simpler and more transparent structures for executive pay, and to review this less frequently. Remuneration committees may wish to explore ways in which they could directly control their own people and resources to do the necessary work on executive pay.

Summary of key messages

Here is summary of the key messages contained in this book.

Long term growth in shareholder value

For shareholders, performance is all about long term growth in shareholder value. The financial measure that really matters is the percentage growth in the TSR index over a long period of time. Almost all other financial or operational measures within the business are important because of their direct or indirect contribution to long term shareholder value. Companies should certainly strive to improve their performance on safety, the environment and social impact, and additional measures may be relevant for these business objectives, but in the long term even these objectives are almost certain to contribute to shareholder value.

Incentives

The principal reason for linking performance to pay is to provide the correct incentives. Incentives should be a central consideration in all discussions about executive pay. Incentives do not arise solely from performance related pay. They also rise from fixed pay and career progression. Remuneration committees also need to be aware of the incentives on commercial bodies outside the company, such as consultancies and institutional shareholders.

The single, common, financial incentive for executives

The very top managers in a company should have a single, common, financial incentive to grow shareholder value in the long term. Any other financial incentive starts to affect goals, targets, priorities, team work, performance measures and communications in ways that are not optimal for long term shareholder value.

Short term targets

Short term targets, especially targets based on annual profit or earnings, are already far too important to executives even before the targets are linked to financial reward. This is because shareholders have to look at short term performance when trying to access likely long term performance. The problem is accentuated by the short term focus of measures used by financial institutions.

LTIPs

The incentives arising from LTIPs could and should be far better aligned with shareholders interests than they are at present. The incentives to manipulate share prices, to create medium term share price volatility and to destroy and recreate value are all particularly damaging. This is a matter for the detailed design of the plan. A PREP FILLIP would provide incentives that are much better aligned with shareholder interests.

Share Options

Share options are popular for all the wrong reasons. They should be replaced by forms of remuneration that are better aligned with shareholders interests such as PREP FILLIPs.

Fixed Pay

Very strong and usually undesirable incentives arise from fixed pay. Significant improvements in the incentive regime can be made by defining pension benefits and variable pay benefits independently of basic salary. In particular, executive pension schemes should work on a defined contribution basis, not on a defined benefit basis.

Total Remuneration

Remuneration committees should make sure that they know how much, in total, they have paid their executives in each recent year. The report format in appendix 2 can help them do this. Without this information it is difficult to see how a remuneration committee can make informed decisions about future pay.

Trust

In recent years company boards have faced a huge growth in red tape and regulation. This arises from a perceived lack of trust, much of which is directly or indirectly attributable to high levels of executive pay. As Warren Buffet put it, "In judging whether Corporate America is serious about reforming itself, CEO pay remains the acid test."[60] Executives have an important opportunity to build trust with shareholders by accepting a level of remuneration that is demonstrably below market levels.

Comparative pay positioning

Comparative pay positioning causes the general level of executive pay to ratchet upwards without providing any benefits to shareholders. The ratchet mechanism cannot lead to stabilisation at an appropriate level; it can only force pay upwards. Remuneration committees need to make less use of comparisons with other companies and focus rather on finding the right level of pay for their own company. The level of executive pay should enhance the leadership message from the company board. If the leadership message is discredited by executive pay then this suggests that the level of pay is not appropriate.

Effective ownership

The natural incentives of ownership would be essential to any market based mechanism for establishing appropriate levels of executive pay. Unfortunately many FTSE 350 companies suffer from a lack of effective ownership. This is a serious problem which directly or indirectly causes much disillusionment for investors in listed companies. The problem is hard to fix, but it would help if the directors' financial wellbeing depended more on the long term performance of the company shares and less on the directors' fees and salaries.

Conclusion

Executive pay remains a controversial subject which it is difficult for remuneration committees to get right. However the key messages set out above will significantly aid remuneration committees who want to move executive pay in a direction that will work better for shareholders. The proposals would also help executives by making their jobs easier and more enjoyable. Executives who are effective at creating long term value for shareholders have nothing to fear from the any of the proposals. The biggest beneficiaries would however be shareholders, especially small shareholders and shareholders who own shares indirectly as part of a pension scheme or investment product. Such shareholders form a substantial part of the population of the United Kingdom, so there is huge scope for a large scale collective benefit.

Remuneration committees should make the most of this opportunity!

Notes

58. FT.com 08/06/04
59. Berkshire Hathaway Chairman's letter to shareholders 2003
60. Berkshire Hathaway Chairman's letter to shareholders 2003

Appendix 1
TSR definition and example

Rules for determining a TSR index

For a quoted company the TSR index value on any one day is a measure the value of an investment in that company relative to the value on the base day when the original investment was made. The percentage increase in TSR for the company between any two dates can therefore be determined by dividing the index on the second date by the index on the first date, subtracting 1 and then multiplying by 100. It will be negative if value has been lost.

The index is calculated assuming that any dividends are immediately reinvested in shares of the company. In the event of a capital restructuring the index should continue to track the value of any securities coming out of the restructure, after any cash has been reinvested. If the share is bought out and there is no successor security in which to invest the cash (because of a private equity buyer for example), then the cash can be assumed to gather interest at the Bank of England base rate.

Example

On 31st December 1999 Company X has a share price of £4.28. It pays a dividend of 11p on 30th June each year. Consider the value of £100 invested in the shares of the company on 31st December 1999.

Date	Share Price (£s)	No. of Shares	Investment Value (£s)	
31/12/1999	4.28	23.36449	100.00	
31/03/2000	4.38	23.36449	102.34	
30/06/2000	4.10	23.36449	95.79	Plus dividend: £2.570093

30/06/2000	4.10	23.99134	98.36	Buying shares with dividend
30/09/2000	4.41	23.99134	105.80	
31/12/2000	4.32	23.99134	103.64	
31/03/2001	4.51	23.99134	108.20	
30/06/2001	4.40	23.99134	105.56	Plus dividend £2.639047
30/06/2001	4.40	24.59112	108.20	Buying shares with dividend
30/09/2001	4.56	24.59112	112.14	
19/10/2001	4.70	24.59112	115.58	

On 19th October 2001 Company X was taken over by Company Y. Each of Company X's shares was converted into 0.45 of a Company Y share plus 48 pence. On 19th October Company Y's shares closed at £9.38. The Company X TSR index therefore tracks Company Y shares after 19th October.

19/10/2001	9.38	11.0660	103.80	Plus cash £11.80374
19/10/2001	9.38	12.3244	115.60	Buying shares with cash
31/12/2001	9.30	12.3244	114.62	
31/03/2002	9.42	12.3244	116.10	

The percentage increase in TSR from 31/12/2000 to 31/12/2001 is 10.6 %. This is calculated from the index values on the two days in question: $(114.62/103.64 - 1)*100$.

This way of calculating a TSR index ensures that the performance of an investment can be tracked even after the share itself has ceased to exist. This might have limited meaning in terms of performance, but it ensures that the incentives provided to executives remain consistent. It ensures that executives have the incentive necessary to accept a reasonable offer in the event of a takeover. It removes the need to have special change of control provisions in the share incentive plan. Such provisions frequently result in LTIP plans paying out prematurely, or being bought out at a premium.

The TSR index is clearly very sensitive to share price. This might cause problems if the closing share price on the last day of a performance period turns out to be higher or lower than expected. This problem can be partially mitigated by using the 5-day share price to calculate the TSR index. This ensures that the TSR index on any one day depends on the mean closing share price over the last five business days. Clearly this is less volatile than the share price on a single day. The problem can also be mitigated by ensuring that the same TSR index is used to end one performance period and to start the next performance period. This ensures that any distortion in the share price cannot change the total TSR growth recorded overall. It can only change the period during which the TSR growth is recorded.

Appendix 2
Layout for executive pay report

The following table is based on that included in the Greenbury Report of 1995. It seeks to increase transparency by making greater use of Fair Market Value (FMV), Expected Present Value (EPV), annual charges in these values, totals and comparisons with earlier years.

Summary Remuneration Table for Financial Year ending 31/12/2005

This table seeks to bring together in one place the value of all the various elements of remuneration received by each director during the year. Where remuneration schemes cover different years the change in FMV over the year is included.

	Basic Salary & fees (£s)	Annual Bonus (£s)	Value from Deferred Bonus (£s)	Value from Pension Scheme (£s)	Value from SOS (£s)	Value from LTIP (£s)	Other (£s)	Total (£s)
Executive A	752,500	231,005	376,663	612,862	12,858	-224,492	72,547	1,833,944
Executive B	344,000	82,135	117,671	142,743	46,069	-123,471	154,779	763,927
Executive C	317,125	86,535	147,126	157,868	130,227	24,256	35,053	898,190
Chairman	430,000						56,342	486,342
Non-exec A	64,000							64,000
Non-exec B	67,000							67,000
Non-exec C	54,000							54,000
Non-exec D	57,000							57,000

Basic Salary

	Annual Salary to 31/03/05 (£s)	Annual Salary from 31/03/05 (£s)	Salary Paid to 31/03/05 (£s)	Salary Paid from 31/03/05 (£s)	Total, Carried to Summary (£s)
Executive A	700,000	770,000	175,000	577,500	752,500
Executive B	320,000	352,000	80,000	264,000	344,000
Executive C	295,000	324,500	73,750	243,375	317,125
Chairman	400,000	440,000	100,000	330,000	430,000

Fees for Non-executives

	Basic (£s)	Committee Fees (£s)	Committee Chair Fee (£s)	Total, Carried to Summary (£s)
Non-exec A	40,000	14,000	10,000	64,000
Non-exec B	40,000	7,000	20,000	67,000
Non-exec C	40,000	14,000		54,000
Non-exec D	40,000	7,000	10,000	57,000

Annual Bonus

	Maximum Annual Bonus (£s)	Actual Annual Bonus (£s)	Transfer to Deferred Bonus (£s)	Bonus Paid (Carried to Summary) (£s)
Executive A	770,000	693,000	461,995	231,005
Executive B	352,000	246,400	164,265	82,135
Executive C	324,500	259,600	173,065	86,535

Value from Deferred Bonus

Executive A

	Value of Bonus Deferred (£s)	Share Price on Bonus Day (Pence)	Number of Shares Bought	EPS Growth over Inflation to 31/12/05	Matching Shares Award	Value at 31/12/05 (£s)	Value at 31/12/04 (£s)	Total Value Increase during 2005 (£s)
2003	362,349	192	188,723	24.00%	188,723	797,166	805,138	-7,972
2004	402,787	210	191,803	10.00%	159,836	742,661	818,278	-75,616
2005	461,995	212	217,922	1.00%	0	460,251	0	460,251
					Total (Carried to Summary):			376,663

Executive B

	Value of Bonus Deferred (£s)	Share Price on Bonus Day (Pence)	Number of Shares Bought	EPS Growth over Inflation to 31/12/05	Matching Shares Award	Value at 31/12/05 (£s)	Value at 31/12/04 (£s)	Total Value Increase during 2005 (£s)
2003	199,291	192	103,797	24.00%	103,797	438,439	442,823	-4,384
2004	221,532	210	105,491	10.00%	87,909	408,461	450,050	-41,589
2005	164,265	212	77,483	1.00%	0	163,644	0	163,644
					Total (Carried to Summary):			117,671

Executive C

	Value of Bonus Deferred (£s)	Share Price on Bonus Day (Pence)	Number of Shares Bought	EPS Growth over Inflation to 31/12/05	Matching Shares Award	Value at 31/12/05 (£s)	Value at 31/12/04 (£s)	Total Value Increase during 2005 (£s)
2003	109,610	192	57,088	24.00%	57,088	241,140	243,551	-2,411
2004	121,842	210	58,020	10.00%	48,350	224,653	247,527	-22,874
2005	173,065	212	81,634	1.00%	0	172,411	0	172,411
					Total (Carried to Summary):			147,126

Notes on Deferred Bonus:
The Chairman and Non-executives do not participate in the bonus or deferred bonus scheme.
Bonuses are awarded on 1st April each year based on performance in the previous financial year.
Bonus that is deferred is immediately used to buy shares, which are released back to the executive after three years.
At release matching shares are added to the extent that EPS growth targets have been met.
The matching shares award for bonus deferred in 2003 is final. The matching shares award for bonus deferred in 2004 and 2005 is not yet determined. The number displayed is implied from the EPS growth rate in the years to 31/12/2005.
The values at 31/12/2004 are as reported last year.

Value from Pension Scheme

	Age in Years at 31/12/05	Pensionable Service in Years at 31/12/05	Accrued Pension (£s/annum) at 31/12/05	Transfer Value of Pension (£s) at 31/12/05	Transfer Value of Pension (£s) at 31/12/04	Personal Contributions in 2005 (£s)	Net Increase in Transfer Value (£s)
Executive A	55	30.2	378,758	5,340,493	4,713,117	14,513	612,862
Executive B	44	21.45	122,980	1,229,800	1,072,544	14,513	142,743
Executive C	45	24.76	130,867	1,400,276	1,227,895	14,513	157,868

Notes on Pensions:
The Chairman and Non-executives do not participate in the pension scheme.
Accrued pension is that payable annually from retirement at age 65, based on service until 31/12/05.
The effect of additional voluntary contributions made by directors (at no net cost to shareholders) is excluded.
Etc.

Value from Share Options Scheme

Issues of options under the SOS

Issue Date	Exercise Price (Pence)	Total Number Issued	Total Number Lapsed at 31/12/05	Total Number Exercised at 31/12/05	Total Number Outstanding at 31/12/05	Expiry Date	Fair Market Value per Option as at 31/12/04 (£s)	Fair Market Value per Option as at 31/12/05 (£s)
1/10/00	146.6	8,995,783	1,076,876	7,097,567	821,340	1/10/10	1.38	1.30
1/10/01	155.4	8,185,320	3,458,523	2,684,653	2,042,144	1/10/11	1.41	1.35
1/10/02	167.2	9,056,201	2,876,203	1,408,327	4,771,671	1/10/12	1.29	1.55
1/10/03	195.6	9,103,204	50925	67,302	8,984,977	1/10/13	1.04	0.81
1/10/04	211.2	8,563,293	104304	0	9,052,279	1/10/14	1.04	0.67
1/10/05	209.0	8,864,937	23086	0	8,458,989	1/10/15		0.98

Options for Executive A

Issue Date	Number Held at 31/12/04	Fair Market Value of Outstanding Options at 31/12/04	Number Issued/(Lapsed) during 2005	Number Exercised during 2005	Net Value Realised from Exercise in 2005 (£s)	Number Held at 31/12/05	Fair Market Value of Outstanding Options at 31/12/05	Total Value Increase during 2005 (£s)
1/10/00	124,281	171,508	0	124,281	149,137	0	0	-22,371
1/10/01	715,429	1,008,755	0	137,149	150,864	578,280	780,678	-77,213
1/10/02	705,974	909,295	-224,213	0	0	481,761	746,730	-162,565
1/10/03	667,953	696,341	0	0	0	667,953	541,042	-155,299
1/10/04	654,098	676,991	0	0	0	654,098	434,975	-242,016
1/10/05	0	0	684,297	0	0	684,297	672,322	672,322

Total (Carried to Summary): 12,858

Options for Executive B

Issue Date	Number Held at 31/12/04	Fair Market Value of Outstanding Options at 31/12/04	Number Issued/(Lapsed) during 2005	Number Exercised during 2005	Net Value Realised from Exercise in 2005 (£s)	Number Held at 31/12/05	Fair Market Value of Outstanding Options at 31/12/05	Total Value Increase during 2005 (£s)
1/10/00	324,268	447,490	0	0	0	324,268	421,548	-25,941
1/10/01	315,375	444,679	0	0	0	315,375	425,756	-18,923
1/10/02	305,857	393,944	-97,138	0	0	208,719	323,514	-70,429
1/10/03	297,352	309,989	0	0	0	297,352	240,855	-69,134
1/10/04	304,080	314,723	0	0	0	304,080	202,213	-112,510
1/10/05	0	0	349,116	0	0	349,116	343,006	343,006

Total (Carried to Summary): 46,069

Options for Executive C

Issue Date	Number Held at 31/12/04	Fair Market Value of Outstanding Options at 31/12/04	Number Issued/(Lapsed) during 2005	Number Exercised during 2005	Net Value Realised from Exercise in 2005 (£s)	Number Held at 31/12/05	Fair Market Value of Outstanding Options at 31/12/05	Total Value Increase during 2005 (£s)
1/10/03	245,128	255,546	0	0	0	245,128	198,554	-56,992
1/10/04	286,932	296,975	0	0	0	286,932	190,810	-106,165
1/10/05	0	0	298,610	0	0	298,610	293,384	293,384

Total (Carried to Summary): 130,227

Notes on the SOS:
The Chairman and Non-executives do not participate in the SOS.
Several senior executives below board level also participate in the SOS.
Fair Market Value has been calculated using the Black-Scholes model using the following assumptions...
The Fair Market Values as at 31/12/05 of options issued in 2003, 2004 and 2005, take account of a proportion of options expected to be lost when performance conditions are tested. The proportions estimated as lost are 40%, 50% and 25% respectively. Fair market values as at 31/12/04 are as stated in last years report.

Value from LTIP

Issues of shares under the LTIP

Conditional Issue Date	Share Price at Conditional Issue Date (Pence)	Total Number of Shares Conditionally Issued	Comparator Group Position	Percentage of Shares Transferred	Number of Shares Transferred	Number of Shares Released	Share Price at Release Date (Pence)	EPV of each Share at 31/12/2005 (Pence)
1/10/00	145.2	8,995,783	4/18	100.00%	8,945,125	8,945,125	209.4	
1/10/01	156.7	8,185,320	6/17	82.50%	6,695,321			211.20
1/10/02	170.2	9,056,201	10/19	30.00%	2,656,202			211.20
1/10/03	194.0	9,103,204	13/18	0.00%				0.00
1/10/04	211.8	8,563,293	8/16	39.33%				83.07
1/10/05	209.4	8,864,937	6/15	70.00%				147.84

LTIP Shares for Executive A

Conditional Issue Date	Number of Shares Conditionally Issued	Number of Shares Transferred	Number of Shares Released	Value of Shares at Release Date (£s)	EPV of Un-released Shares at 31/12/2005 (£s)	EPV of Un-released Shares at 31/12/2004 (£s)	Total Value Increase during 2005 (£s)
1/10/00	320,397	320,397	320,397	670,911		683,445	-12,534
1/10/01	315,869	260,591			550,368	555,872	-5,504
1/10/02	310,724	93,217			196,874	463,968	-267,094
1/10/03	298,098				0	190,764	-190,764
1/10/04	301,001				250,048	449,450	-199,402
1/10/05	304,928				450,806	0	450,806

Total (Carried to Summary): -224,492

LTIP Shares for Executive B

Conditional Issue Date	Number of Shares Conditionally Issued	Number of Shares Transferred	Number of Shares Released	Value of Shares at Release Date (£s)	EPV of Un-released Shares at 31/12/2005 (£s)	EPV of Un-released Shares at 31/12/2004 (£s)	Total Value Increase during 2005 (£s)
1/10/00	176,218	176,218	176,218	369,000		375,894	-6,894
1/10/01	173,727	143,324			302,700	305,727	-3,027
1/10/02	170,898	51,269			108,280	255,182	-146,902
1/10/03	163,953				0	104,919	-104,919
1/10/04	165,550				137,526	247,197	-109,671
1/10/05	167,710				247,942	0	247,942

Total (Carried to Summary): -123,471

LTIP Shares for Executive C

Conditional Issue Date	Number of Shares Conditionally Issued	Number of Shares Transferred	Number of Shares Released	Value of Shares at Release Date (£s)	EPV of Un-released Shares at 31/12/2005 (£s)	EPV of Un-released Shares at 31/12/2004 (£s)	Total Value Increase during 2005 (£s)
1/9/03	119,239				0	76,305	-76,305
1/9/04	120,400				100,019	179,779	-79,761
1/9/05	121,971				180,322	0	180,322

Total (Carried to Summary): 24,256

Notes on the LTIP
The Chairman and Non-executives do not participate in the LTIP
Several executives below board level also participate in the LTIP
Share price at issue is the average closing share price for the five business days immediately before the issue date.
Comparator group positions are final for conditional issues in 2000, 2001 and 2002, measured three years after issue.
Comparator group positions for conditional issues in 2003, 2004 and 2005 are current positions as at 31/12/2005.
Percentage of Shares Transferred is final for the conditional issues of 2000, 2001 and 2002. For subsequent years the percentage is not yet determined. The percentage displayed is the one implied by the comparator group position as at 31/12/2005.
Share price at release is the average closing share price for the five business days immediately before the release date.
EPV of each share at 31/12/2005 is based on the 5-day share price for 31/12/2005 (211.2 pence) and the transfer percentage implied by the 31/12/2005 comparator group position. It is assumed that the value of the share will increase between 31/12/2005 and the release date by an amount exactly sufficient to offset the time value of money over this period.
EPV of unreleased shares from each conditional share issue for an executive as at 31/12/2004 is as reported last year.

Other Remuneration

The values shown under "Other" represent company cars, health and life assurance schemes. In 2005 Executive B was paid an additional allowance of £120,000, in consideration for four months spent based in China. This is included under "Other".

Historical Comparison of Total Remuneration (£s)

	Three Year Average Total Remuneration	Total Remuneration by Year					
		2005	2004	2003	2002	2001	2000
Executive A	2,939,856	1,833,944	2,487,784	4,497,839	2,283,766	2,097,300	2,709,808
Executive B	1,224,593	763,927	1,036,283	1,873,569	951,300	873,628	1,128,767
Executive C	1,439,821	898,190	1,218,415	2,202,857	1,118,495	1,027,172	1,327,153
Chairman	470,849	486,342	486,342	439,863	436,852	420,032	420,186
Non-exec A	62,000	64,000	64,000	58,000	58,000	58,000	52,000
Non-exec B	65,000	67,000	67,000	61,000	61,000	61,000	49,000
Non-exec C	52,333	54,000	54,000	49,000	49,000	49,000	41,000
Non-exec D	55,333	57,000	57,000	52,000	52,000	38,000	38,000

The historical comparison shows the total remuneration of each director over the last six financial years, and the average total remuneration over the three most recent financial years.
All historical values shown have been determined using consistent valuation methodologies for long term schemes.
In 2003 the valuation methodology for share options was changed. This means that SOS valuations in remuneration reports for years 2002 and before differ from those shown here.

Appendix 3
Research on immediate versus deferred rewards

In late 2003 I invited colleagues to take part in a simple survey investigating preference for immediate and deferred remuneration. A copy of the survey form follows. 18 people responded with useable data.

The survey form asks respondents to choose between an immediate bonus worth £5,000 and a bonus deferred for three years, on a very secure basis, worth more than £5,000. The survey investigates what considerations are made by employees when faced with this choice and how much more than £5,000 needs to be paid to make the deferred bonus attractive.

13 responses (72%) would accept a deferral of the bonus if £7,000 was paid in three years time. This is represents and annual growth rate of 11.9 % in the value of the bonus over the three year deferral period. Eight of these 13 responses would have accepted £6,000 (annual growth rate of 6.3%), and 12 of the 13 would have accepted £6,655 (annual growth rate 10%). It was clear that most of these respondents were thinking about the rates of return that they could get if they were to invest the money themselves. The survey form may have encouraged them to think in this way.

Five responses (28%) would prefer immediate payment of the bonus. Three of the five appeared to always want money now, for example to spend on holidays, whereas two of the five appeared more worried about somehow losing the bonus during the deferral period, despite the assurances about security that appeared on the survey form. Four of the five suggested that they would have accepted a three year deferral for £10,000 (annual growth rate 26%).

Overall the research shows a very strong preference on the part of managers to receive bonus type pay on a deferred basis provided that the bonus is secure and growing at a good enough rate of return.

Whilst the data examined was overwhelmingly in support of the above conclusion it is necessary to be aware of limitations arising from the returned sample of 18 usable forms. The 18 forms cover four nationalities and two FTSE 100 companies, both of which have a history of providing employees with profitable share saving schemes. All 18 forms are from senior managers rather than from executives as defined in this book. The style and manner of the survey will have appealed more to some managers than to others, and this may have had a selective effect on the responses received.

Survey on Preferences between Short Term Pay and Long Term Pay

This survey investigates whether people prefer to be paid now, or paid more later.
There are no right or wrong answers; it is about personal preferences.
Please fill in or amend the boxes below.

Name:

Company:

Country:

Suppose you are to be paid a bonus!
You can choose between accepting the bonus now (in your next monthly pay), or a bigger bonus in three years time
If you accept the bonus now it will be £5,000
If you opt to take the bonus in three years time it will be £7,500

If you opt to take £7,500 in three years time then this is guaranteed to you by the company, even if you retire, resign are dismissed or made redundant. If you die it will be paid to your estate. If the company is taken over or involved in a merger the payment will still be made in three years time. You can assume that the company is very credit worthy.

You can be confident that inflation will be negligible over the next three years.

Whichever option you choose you will have to pay tax on the payment when the payment is made.

| | I would take the £5,000 now |
| or | I would take the £7,500 in three years time |

What are the main reasons for your choice?
E.g. "I need the money now because I am buying a new kitchen."; or
"It is worth waiting 3 years for an extra £2,500."

If the choice was between £5,000 now and £5,100 in three years time most people would take the money now.
If the choice was between £5,000 now and £15,000 in three years time most people would wait three years.
Somewhere between £5,100 and £15,000 there is a cross over point where it is hard to chose between taking the money now, or taking more money in three years time.

Where is the cross over point for you personally, based on your circumstances right now?
How much money would need to be offered in three years time for you to find it difficult to chose between £5,000 now and that much later?

What are the main reasons for this?
E.g. "I always need money straight away."; or
"If I were to put the £5,000 in a building society it would not grow much in three years."

Thank you for completing this survey. Please return it by e-mail to *********@*****, or return a hard copy to: Patrick Gerard, ***************

Answers will be kept confidential, but aggregate information and typical attitudes will be published.

Appendix 4
Modelling the value of Typico's LTIP

Appendix 4: Modelling the value of Typico's LTIP

Scenario 1: Steady median performance

Parameters:

Annual conditional award value (£s):	937,500
Annual median TSR growth rate (%):	8.0%
Standard deviation on 3 yr TSR growth rate (%):	30.0%
Initial share price (£s):	5.00
Discount rate for executive savings (%):	8.0%
Number of companies in comparitor group (inc Typico):	16

Share price year 1:	£5.00
Share price year 2:	£5.40
Share price year 3:	£5.83
Share price year 4:	£6.30
Share price year 5:	£6.80
Share price year 6:	£7.35
Share price year 7:	£7.93
Share price year 8:	£8.57
Share price year 9:	£9.25
Share price year 10:	£10.00
Share price year 11:	£10.79
Share price year 12:	£11.66

	Year 1	Year 2	Year 3	Year 4	Year 5	Year 6	Year 7
Share price at conditional award (£s):	5.00	5.40	5.83	6.30	6.80	7.35	7.93
Number of shares conditionally awarded:	187,500	173,611	160,751	148,844	137,818	127,609	118,157
Share price after three years (£s):	6.30	6.80	7.35	7.93	8.57	9.25	10.00
Percentage TSR growth over three years:	26.0%	26.0%	26.0%	26.0%	26.0%	26.0%	26.0%
Position in comparitor group (1 is top):	8	9	8	9	8	9	8
Percentile position in comparitor group:	46.7	53.3	46.7	53.3	46.7	53.3	46.7
Percentage of conditional award that transfers:	39.3%	0.0%	39.3%	0.0%	39.3%	0.0%	39.3%
Number of shares that transfer:	73,750	0	63,229	0	54,208	0	46,475
Share price after five years (£s):	7.35	7.93	8.57	9.25	10.00	10.79	11.66
Values of released shares after five years (£s):	541,815	0	541,815	0	541,814	0	541,816
PV of released shares in award year (£s):	368,750	0	368,750	0	368,750	0	368,751
Average PV of shares released (£s):				Years 4 to 7: 184,375		Years 1 to 7:	210,714

Assumes no dividends paid, so share price is effectively a TSR index.

Assumes the percentage growth in TSR for comparitor group companies over the performace period is normally distributed.

Appendix 4: Modelling the value of Typico's LTIP

Scenario 2: Volatile median performance

Parameters:

Annual conditional award value (£s):	937,500	
Annual median TSR growth rate (%):	8.0%	
Standard deviation on 3 yr TSR growth rate (%):	30.0%	
Initial share price (£s):	5.00	
Discount rate for executive savings (%):	8.0%	
Number of companies in comparitor group (inc Typico):	16	

Share price year 1:	£5.00	Share price year 7:	£7.93
Share price year 2:	£6.30	Share price year 8:	£10.00
Share price year 3:	£5.83	Share price year 9:	£9.25
Share price year 4:	£7.35	Share price year 10:	£10.00
Share price year 5:	£6.80	Share price year 11:	£10.79
Share price year 6:	£8.57	Share price year 12:	£11.66

	Year 1	Year 2	Year 3	Year 4	Year 5	Year 6	Year 7
Share price at conditional award (£s):	5.00	6.30	5.83	7.35	6.80	8.57	7.93
Number of shares conditionally awarded:	187,500	148,844	160,751	127,609	137,818	109,404	118,157
Share price after three years (£s):	7.35	6.80	8.57	7.93	10.00	8.57	7.93
Percentage TSR growth over three years:	46.9%	46.9%	46.9%	46.9%	46.9%	46.9%	46.9%
Position in comparitor group (1 is top):	4	12	4	12	4	12	8
Percentile position in comparitor group:	20.0	73.3	20.0	73.3	20.0	73.3	46.7
Percentage of conditional award that transfers:	100.0%	0.0%	100.0%	0.0%	100.0%	0.0%	39.3%
Number of shares that transfer:	187,500	0	160,751	0	137,818	0	46,475
Share price after five years (£s):	8.57	7.93	10.00	9.25	10.00	10.79	11.66
Values of released shares after five years (£s):	1,606,710	0	1,606,710	0	1,377,494	0	541,816
PV of released shares in award year (£s):	1,093,500	0	1,093,500	0	937,499	0	368,751
Average PV of shares released (£s):			Years 4 to 7:	326,562		Years 1 to 7:	499,036

Assumes no dividends paid, so share price is effectively a TSR index.
Assumes the percentage growth in TSR for comparitor group companies over the performace period is normally distributed.

Appendix 4: Modelling the value of Typico's LTIP

Scenario 3: Steady top quartile performance

Parameters:

Annual conditional award value (£s):	937,500
Annual median TSR growth rate (%):	8.0%
Standard deviation on 3 yr TSR growth rate (%):	30.0%
Initial share price (£s):	5.00
Discount rate for executive savings (%):	8.0%
Number of companies in comparitor group (inc Typico):	16

Share price year 1:	£5.00	Share price year 7:	£10.69
Share price year 2:	£5.68	Share price year 8:	£12.13
Share price year 3:	£6.44	Share price year 9:	£13.77
Share price year 4:	£7.31	Share price year 10:	£15.63
Share price year 5:	£8.30	Share price year 11:	£17.74
Share price year 6:	£9.42	Share price year 12:	£20.13

	Year 1	Year 2	Year 3	Year 4	Year 5	Year 6	Year 7
Share price at conditional award (£s):	5.00	5.68	6.44	7.31	8.30	9.42	10.69
Number of shares conditionally awarded:	187,500	165,198	145,549	128,237	112,984	99,546	87,705
Share price after three years (£s):	7.31	8.30	9.42	10.69	12.13	13.77	15.63
Percentage TSR growth over three years:	46.2%	46.2%	46.2%	46.2%	46.2%	46.2%	46.2%
Position in comparitor group (1 is top):	4	4	4	4	4	4	4
Percentile position in comparitor group:	20.0	20.0	20.0	20.0	20.0	20.0	20.0
Percentage of conditional award that transfers:	100.0%	100.0%	100.0%	100.0%	100.0%	100.0%	100.0%
Number of shares that transfer:	187,500	165,198	145,549	128,237	112,984	99,546	87,705
Share price after five years (£s):	9.42	10.69	12.13	13.77	15.63	17.74	20.13
Values of released shares after five years (£s):	1,765,837	1,765,834	1,765,836	1,765,836	1,765,833	1,765,844	1,765,830
PV of released shares in award year (£s):	1,201,799	1,201,797	1,201,798	1,201,798	1,201,796	1,201,804	1,201,794

Years 4 to 7: 1,201,798

Years 1 to 7: 1,201,798

Average PV of shares released (£s): 1,201,798

Assumes no dividends paid, so share price is effectively a TSR index.
Assumes the percentage growth in TSR for comparitor group companies over the performace period is normally distributed.

Appendix 4: Modelling the value of Typico's LTIP

Scenario 4: Steady bottom quartile performance

Parameters:

Annual conditional award value (£s):	937,500
Annual median TSR growth rate (%):	8.0%
Standard deviation on 3 yr TSR growth rate (%):	30.0%
Initial share price (£s):	5.00
Discount rate for executive savings (%):	8.0%
Number of companies in comparitor group (inc Typico):	16

Share price year 1:	£5.00
Share price year 2:	£5.09
Share price year 3:	£5.19
Share price year 4:	£5.29
Share price year 5:	£5.38
Share price year 6:	£5.49
Share price year 7:	£5.59
Share price year 8:	£5.69
Share price year 9:	£5.80
Share price year 10:	£5.91
Share price year 11:	£6.02
Share price year 12:	£6.13

	Year 1	Year 2	Year 3	Year 4	Year 5	Year 6	Year 7
Share price at conditional award (£s):	5.00	5.09	5.19	5.29	5.38	5.49	5.59
Number of shares conditionally awarded:	187,500	184,058	180,679	177,363	174,107	170,911	167,774
Share price after three years (£s):	5.29	5.38	5.49	5.59	5.69	5.80	5.91
Percentage TSR growth over three years:	5.7%	5.7%	5.7%	5.7%	5.7%	5.7%	5.7%
Position in comparitor group (1 is top):	13	13	13	13	13	13	13
Percentile position in comparitor group:	80.0	80.0	80.0	80.0	80.0	80.0	80.0
Percentage of conditional award that transfers:	0.0%	0.0%	0.0%	0.0%	0.0%	0.0%	0.0%
Number of shares that transfer:	0	0	0	0	0	0	0
Share price after five years (£s):	5.49	5.59	5.69	5.80	5.91	6.02	6.13
Values of released shares after five years (£s):	0	0	0	0	0	0	0
PV of released shares in award year (£s):	0	0	0	0	0	0	0
Average PV of shares released (£s):			Years 4 to 7:			Years 1 to 7:	0

Assumes no dividends paid, so share price is effectively a TSR index.

Assumes the percentage growth in TSR for comparitor group companies over the performace period is normally distributed.

Appendix 4: Modelling the value of Typico's LTIP

Scenario 5: Steady 9% growth

Parameters:

Annual conditional award value (£s):	937,500	Share price year 1:	£5.00
Annual median TSR growth rate (%):	8.0%	Share price year 2:	£5.45
Standard deviation on 3 yr TSR growth rate (%):	30.0%	Share price year 3:	£5.94
Initial share price (£s):	5.00	Share price year 4:	£6.48
Discount rate for executive savings (%):	8.0%	Share price year 5:	£7.06
Number of companies in comparitor group (inc Typico):	16	Share price year 6:	£7.69
		Share price year 7:	£8.39
		Share price year 8:	£9.14
		Share price year 9:	£9.96
		Share price year 10:	£10.86
		Share price year 11:	£11.84
		Share price year 12:	£12.90

	Year 1	Year 2	Year 3	Year 4	Year 5	Year 6	Year 7
Share price at conditional award (£s):	5.00	5.45	5.94	6.48	7.06	7.69	8.39
Number of shares conditionally awarded:	187,500	172,018	157,815	144,784	132,830	121,862	111,800
Share price after three years (£s):	6.48	7.06	7.69	8.39	9.14	9.96	10.86
Percentage TSR growth over three years:	29.5%	29.5%	29.5%	29.5%	29.5%	29.5%	29.5%
Position in comparitor group (1 is top):	8	8	8	8	8	8	8
Percentile position in comparitor group:	46.7	46.7	46.7	46.7	46.7	46.7	46.7
Percentage of conditional award that transfers:	39.3%	39.3%	39.3%	39.3%	39.3%	39.3%	39.3%
Number of shares that transfer:	73,750	67,660	62,074	56,948	52,246	47,932	43,975
Share price after five years (£s):	7.69	8.39	9.14	9.96	10.86	11.84	12.90
Values of released shares after five years (£s):	567,368	567,366	567,368	567,366	567,369	567,367	567,367
PV of released shares in award year (£s):	386,141	386,140	386,141	386,140	386,142	386,140	386,140
			Years 4 to 7:	386,141		Years 1 to 7:	386,141
Average PV of shares released (£s):	386,141						

Assumes no dividends paid, so share price is effectively a TSR index.
Assumes the percentage growth in TSR for comparitor group companies over the performace period is normally distributed.

Appendix 4: Modelling the value of Typico's LTIP

Scenario 6: Volatile 9% growth

Parameters:

Annual conditional award value (£s):	937,500
Annual median TSR growth rate (%):	8.0%
Standard deviation on 3 yr TSR growth rate (%):	30.0%
Initial share price (£s):	5.00
Discount rate for executive savings (%):	8.0%
Number of companies in comparitor group (inc Typico):	16

Share price year 1:	£5.00
Share price year 2:	£6.48
Share price year 3:	£5.94
Share price year 4:	£7.69
Share price year 5:	£7.06
Share price year 6:	£9.14
Share price year 7:	£8.39
Share price year 8:	£10.86
Share price year 9:	£9.96
Share price year 10:	£10.86
Share price year 11:	£11.84
Share price year 12:	£12.90

	Year 1	Year 2	Year 3	Year 4	Year 5	Year 6	Year 7
Share price at conditional award (£s):	5.00	6.48	5.94	7.69	7.06	9.14	8.39
Number of shares conditionally awarded:	187,500	144,784	157,815	121,862	132,830	102,569	111,800
Share price after three years (£s):	7.69	7.06	9.14	8.39	10.86	9.96	10.86
Percentage TSR growth over three years:	53.9%	9.0%	53.9%	9.0%	53.9%	9.0%	29.5%
Position in comparitor group (1 is top):	3	12	3	12	3	12	8
Percentile position in comparitor group:	13.3	73.3	13.3	73.3	13.3	73.3	46.7
Percentage of conditional award that transfers:	100.0%	0.0%	100.0%	0.0%	100.0%	0.0%	39.3%
Number of shares that transfer:	187,500	0	157,815	0	132,830	0	43,975
Share price after five years (£s):	9.14	8.39	10.86	9.96	10.86	11.84	12.90
Values of released shares after five years (£s):	1,713,787	0	1,713,787	0	1,442,463	0	567,367
PV of released shares in award year (£s):	1,166,374	0	1,166,374	0	981,716	0	386,140

	Years 4 to 7:	Years 1 to 7:
Average PV of shares released (£s):	341,964	528,658

Assumes no dividends paid, so share price is effectively a TSR index.
Assumes the percentage growth in TSR for comparitor group companies over the performace period is normally distributed.

223

Appendix 4: Modelling the value of Typico's LTIP
Scenario 7: Volatile 9% growth with retesting

Parameters:

Annual conditional award value (£s):	937,500
Annual median TSR growth rate (%):	8.0%
Standard deviation on 3 yr TSR growth rate (%):	30.0%
Initial share price (£s):	5.00
Discount rate for executive savings (%):	8.0%
Number of companies in comparitor group (inc Typico):	16

Share price year 1:	£5.00
Share price year 2:	£6.48
Share price year 3:	£5.94
Share price year 4:	£7.69
Share price year 5:	£7.06
Share price year 6:	£9.14
Share price year 7:	£8.39
Share price year 8:	£10.86
Share price year 9:	£9.96
Share price year 10:	£10.86
Share price year 11:	£11.84
Share price year 12:	£12.90

	Year 1	Year 2	Year 3	Year 4	Year 5	Year 6	Year 7
Share price at conditional award (£s):	5.00	6.48	5.94	7.69	7.06	9.14	8.39
Number of shares conditionally awarded:	187,500	144,784	157,815	121,862	132,830	102,569	111,800
Share price after three years (£s):	7.69	7.06	9.14	8.39	10.86	9.96	10.86
Percentage TSR growth over three years:	53.9%	9.0%	53.9%	9.0%	53.9%	9.0%	29.5%
Position in comparitor group after three years:	3	12	3	12	3	12	8
Share price after four years (£s):	7.06	9.14	8.39	10.86	9.96	10.86	11.84
Percentage TSR growth over four years:	41.2%	41.2%	41.2%	41.2%	41.2%	18.8%	41.2%
Position in comparitor group after four years:	8	8	8	8	8	11	8
Better comparitor group position:	3	8	3	8	3	11	8
Better percentile position:	13.3	46.7	13.3	46.7	13.3	66.7	46.7
Percentage of conditional award that transfers:	100.0%	39.3%	100.0%	39.3%	100.0%	0.0%	39.3%
Number of shares that transfer:	187,500	56,948	157,815	47,932	132,830	0	43,975
Share price after five years (£s):	9.14	8.39	10.86	9.96	10.86	11.84	12.90
Values of released shares after five years (£s):	1,713,787	477,541	1,713,787	477,541	1,442,463	0	567,367
PV of released shares in award year (£s):	1,166,374	325,006	1,166,374	325,007	981,716	0	386,140
			Years 4 to 7:			Years 1 to 7:	
Average PV of shares released (£s):				423,216			621,517

Assumes no dividends paid, so share price is effectively a TSR index.
Assumes the percentage growth in TSR for comparitor group companies over the performace period is normally distributed.

Appendix 4: Modelling the value of Typico's LTIP

Scenario 8: Steady 9% growth with year 4 price spike

Parameters:

Annual conditional award value (£s):	937,500
Annual median TSR growth rate (%):	8.0%
Standard deviation on 3 yr TSR growth rate (%):	30.0%
Initial share price (£s):	5.00
Discount rate for executive savings (%):	8.0%
Number of companies in comparitor group (inc Typico):	16

Share price year 1:	£5.00	
Share price year 2:	£5.45	
Share price year 3:	£5.94	
Share price year 4:	£7.50	
Share price year 5:	£7.06	
Share price year 6:	£7.69	
Share price year 7:	£8.39	
Share price year 8:	£9.14	
Share price year 9:	£9.96	
Share price year 10:	£10.86	
Share price year 11:	£11.84	
Share price year 12:	£12.90	

	Year 1	Year 2	Year 3	Year 4	Year 5	Year 6	Year 7
Share price at conditional award (£s):	5.00	5.45	5.94	7.50	7.06	7.69	8.39
Number of shares conditionally awarded:	187,500	172,018	157,815	125,000	132,830	121,862	111,800
Share price after three years (£s):	7.50	7.06	7.69	8.39	9.14	9.96	10.86
Percentage TSR growth over three years:	50.0%	29.5%	29.5%	11.8%	29.5%	29.5%	29.5%
Position in comparitor group (1 is top):	4	8	8	11	8	8	8
Percentile position in comparitor group:	20.0	46.7	46.7	66.7	46.7	46.7	46.7
Percentage of conditional award that transfers:	100.0%	39.3%	39.3%	0.0%	39.3%	39.3%	39.3%
Number of shares that transfer:	187,500	67,660	62,074	0	52,246	47,932	43,975
Share price after five years (£s):	7.69	8.39	9.14	9.96	10.86	11.84	12.90
Values of released shares after five years (£s):	1,442,460	567,366	567,368	0	567,369	567,367	567,367
PV of released shares in award year (£s):	981,714	386,140	386,141	0	386,142	386,140	386,140

Average PV of shares released (£s):   Years 4 to 7: 289,606   Years 1 to 7: 416,060

Assumes no dividends paid, so share price is effectively a TSR index.
Assumes the percentage growth in TSR for comparitor group companies over the performace period is normally distributed.

Appendix 4: Modelling the value of Typico's LTIP

Scenario 9: Value destroyed then partially recovered

Parameters:

Annual conditional award value (£s):	937,500	Share price year 1:	£5.00
Annual median TSR growth rate (%):	8.0%	Share price year 2:	£5.40
Standard deviation on 3 yr TSR growth rate (%):	30.0%	Share price year 3:	£5.83
Initial share price (£s):	5.00	Share price year 4:	£3.00
Discount rate for executive savings (%):	8.0%	Share price year 5:	£2.00
Number of companies in comparitor group (inc Typico):	16	Share price year 6:	£2.00
		Share price year 7:	£4.30
		Share price year 8:	£5.00
		Share price year 9:	£5.40
		Share price year 10:	£5.83
		Share price year 11:	£6.30
		Share price year 12:	£6.80

	Year 1	Year 2	Year 3	Year 4	Year 5	Year 6	Year 7
Share price at conditional award (£s):	5.00	5.40	5.83	3.00	2.00	2.00	4.30
Number of shares conditionally awarded:	187,500	173,611	160,751	312,500	468,750	468,750	218,023
Share price after three years (£s):	3.00	2.00	5.83	4.30	5.00	5.40	5.83
Percentage TSR growth over three years:	-40.0%	-63.0%	-65.7%	43.3%	150.0%	170.0%	35.6%
Position in comparitor group (1 is top):	16	16	16	5	1	1	6
Percentile position in comparitor group:	100.0	100.0	100.0	26.7	0.0	0.0	33.3
Percentage of conditional award that transfers:	0.0%	0.0%	0.0%	95.3%	100.0%	100.0%	76.7%
Number of shares that transfer:	0	0	0	297,917	468,750	468,750	167,151
Share price after five years (£s):	2.00	4.30	5.00	5.40	5.83	6.30	6.80
Values of released shares after five years (£s):	0	0	0	1,608,750	2,733,750	2,952,450	1,137,035
PV of released shares in award year (£s):	0	0	0	1,094,888	1,860,544	2,009,388	773,847

Average PV of shares released (£s):	Years 4 to 7:	1,434,667	Years 1 to 7:	819,810

Assumes no dividends paid, so share price is effectively a TSR index.
Assumes the percentage growth in TSR for comparitor group companies over the performace period is normally distributed.

Appendix 4: Modelling the value of Typico's LTIP

Scenario 10: Value increased then partially lost

Parameters:

Annual conditional award value (£s):	937,500
Annual median TSR growth rate (%):	8.0%
Standard deviation on 3 yr TSR growth rate (%):	30.0%
Initial share price (£s):	5.00
Discount rate for executive savings (%):	8.0%
Number of companies in comparitor group (inc Typico):	16

Share price year 1:	£5.00
Share price year 2:	£5.40
Share price year 3:	£5.83
Share price year 4:	£9.00
Share price year 5:	£11.50
Share price year 6:	£10.00
Share price year 7:	£10.80
Share price year 8:	£11.66
Share price year 9:	£12.60
Share price year 10:	£13.60
Share price year 11:	£14.69
Share price year 12:	£15.87

	Year 1	Year 2	Year 3	Year 4	Year 5	Year 6	Year 7
Share price at conditional award (£s):	5.00	5.40	5.83	9.00	11.50	10.00	10.80
Number of shares conditionally awarded:	187,500	173,611	160,751	104,167	81,522	93,750	86,806
Share price after three years (£s):	9.00	11.50	10.00	10.80	11.66	12.60	13.60
Percentage TSR growth over three years:	80.0%	113.0%	71.5%	20.0%	1.4%	26.0%	26.0%
Position in comparitor group (1 is top):	1	1	2	10	13	8	9
Percentile position in comparitor group:	0.0	0.0	6.7	60.0	80.0	46.7	53.3
Percentage of conditional award that transfers:	100.0%	100.0%	100.0%	0.0%	0.0%	39.3%	0.0%
Number of shares that transfer:	187,500	173,611	160,751	0	0	36,875	0
Share price after five years (£s):	10.00	10.80	11.66	12.60	13.60	14.69	15.87
Values of released shares after five years (£s):	1,875,000	1,874,999	1,875,000	0	0	541,815	0
PV of released shares in award year (£s):	1,276,093	1,276,093	1,276,093	0	0	368,750	0

	Years 4 to 7:	92,188
	Years 1 to 7:	599,576
Average PV of shares released (£s):		

Assumes no dividends paid, so share price is effectively a TSR index.
Assumes the percentage growth in TSR for comparitor group companies over the performace period is normally distributed.

Appendix 5

Rules of a FILLIP including a pro rata rule

The following are the rules of a FILLIP for a director. The plan costs £1,000,000 per annum at median performance. The conditional award is therefore £2,000,000 per annum or £500,000 per quarter.

On the first day of each calendar quarter the company shall conditionally award the director a number of shares in the company, as part of the remuneration for the director's work over the quarter just ended.

The number of shares awarded will be a whole number such that the value of the conditional award is as close as possible to £500,000 when each share is valued at the 5-day share price for the last business day of the quarter just ended.

For any business day, the 5-day share price of the company on that day is the mean of the closing price for the company's shares, as reported by the Financial Times, for the five business days leading up to and including that business day.

Before a conditional award is made, the level of the 5-day TSR index for the company at the start of the new performance period (the "current index") shall be compared with level of the index at the end of all performance periods that have been completed within the last three years, including the one completed exactly three years ago. The highest index level at the end of a performance period within the last three years shall be called the maximum index. If the current index is greater than or equal to the maximum index then the conditional award shall be made in full. However if the maximum index exceeds the current index then the number of shares in the conditional award shall be reduced to the proportion (current index/maximum index) of what would otherwise have been conditionally awarded. This is the pro rata rule.

If the director did not work for the company for the whole period of the quarter for which he or she is being remunerated, then the number of shares conditionally awarded shall be reduced proportionate to the period of time not worked. The period of time not worked shall include any periods where the director is on gardening leave, suspended or not required to work but serving a contractual notice period.

Each time that the company makes a conditional award of shares under this plan, the company shall publish a list of companies who will form a comparator group for the purposes of assessing the relative performance of the company in respect of that conditional award. The comparator group will include companies with whom the financial performance of the company can be reasonably compared. The comparator groups shall be kept as large as practically possible, and should never contain less than 25 other companies.

For each company mentioned in a comparator group, including this company, the company shall maintain a TSR index showing the relative growth or fall in the shareholder value of that company over time. The TSR index used shall be calculated from the 5-day share price for the companies concerned, so as to reduce volatility.

For each conditional award, there shall be a three year performance period. The performance period shall cover precisely the 12 calendar quarters starting on the day that the award is made. A determination of relative performance shall be made immediately after the end of the performance period.

To determine relative performance the company shall calculate the percentage increase in TSR over the performance period for each company in the comparator group, including this company. The companies shall then be ranked in order, with the first ranked company showing the greatest percentage increase in TSR, and the last ranked showing the smallest. A TSR index and a ranking position shall be determined for all companies in the comparator group, even where the companies no longer exist, and even where the percentage increase in TSR is negative.

The proportion of conditionally allocated shares that the company shall transfer to the director shall be determined in accordance with the company's position in the ranking. If there are N companies in the comparator group (including this company) then the proportion of conditionally allocated shares that shall be transferred shall be $(N - n)/(N-1)$ where n is the position of the company in the ranking from 1 to

N. The number of shares to be transferred shall be rounded to the nearest whole number. Shares not transferred shall be returned to the company and lost to the director.

The company shall continue to hold the shares transferred to the director for a further period of two years. The company shall release these shares to the director with share certificates as soon as possible after the fifth anniversary of the conditional award. During the two year period the company shall pass onto the director any dividends it received in respect of the shares that it holds on his or her behalf.

The remuneration committee may increase or decrease the proportion of share to be transferred at the end of a performance period if they are satisfied that the comparator group ranking seriously misrepresents the companies underlying financial performance. This discretion should only be exercised in exceptional circumstances. When it is exercised, it should normally be done by declaration of an artificial share price for the purpose of determining the TSR index at the end of the performance period. This same artificial share price should then be used as the TSR index at the start of the next performance period. In this way the remuneration committee's intervention has the effect of transferring TSR index growth between periods rather than creating or destroying TSR growth.

The director shall be responsible for all personal taxation in respect of any shares or dividends received. The company may sell shares to cover a personal tax liability before releasing them into the director's name. Similarly dividend payments may be withheld if required to cover a personal tax liability.

In no circumstances shall the performance period or comparator group associated with a conditional award be modified after it has been defined. There will be no provision for the retesting of performance conditions.

If the director stops working for the company then the company shall stop making conditional allocations of shares to the director. The last conditional allocation of shares shall be made on the first day of the quarter following the quarter in which the director stopped working for the company. Once a conditional allocation of shares has been made then shares will normally be transferred to the director and released to the director in accordance with the rules of this plan, irrespective of whether or not the director continues to work for the company.

If the director stops working for the company in order to work for a competitor then a proportion of all shares (including any cash or other securities) held in the FILLIP shall be forfeit by the director. That proportion lost shall be 100% if the director has worked for the company for less than a year. It shall be 30% if the director has worked for the company for at least three years. It shall be determined on a straight line based between 100% and 30% if the director has worked for the company for between one and three years. Normally therefore a director retains an entitlement to 70% of the FILLIP benefits. This is the golden handcuffs rule.

At any time the remuneration committee may veto the transfer of conditionally allocated shares or the subsequent release of those shares to the director if it is satisfied that the director acted negligently in respect of his or her duties to the company, or knowingly mislead shareholders with information material to their valuation of the company.

In the event of a merger, demerger, acquisition, disposal or capital restructure of any of the companies in a comparator group, or this company, then the TSR index for the company concerned shall continue to be calculated, even if the company no longer exists. This ensures that a comparator group ranking can still be determined at the end of the performance period. Shares held within the FILLIP shall be restructured in the same way as other shares in the company. A proportion of the securities and cash so arising shall be transferred to the director after three years, and released to the director after five years in accordance with the normal rules. For cash balances within the FILLIP, simple interest shall be calculated at the Bank of England base rate and added to the cash amount immediately before the cash is released to the director on the fifth anniversary of the conditional award.

The enhanced return rule

The following enhanced return rule can be added to the rules of a FILLIP to increase the incentive to generate absolute returns to shareholders.

Each time that the company makes a conditional award of shares under this plan, the company shall publish a percentage rate of annual growth that the remuneration committee considers to be a reasonable target for TSR index growth in the two years between the third and fifth anniversary of the conditional award.

The number of shares in the conditional award shall be reduced by the equivalent of four years growth at the TSR index target growth rate. For example, if the target TSR index growth rate was 8%, and if 300,000 shares would have been conditionally awarded without this rule in place, then with this rule in place the number of shares to be conditional awarded would be 220,509 because this is $300,000/1.08^4$.

After the fifth anniversary of the conditional award the number of shares to be released to the director shall be increased (or decreased) twice over by the factor (TSR index on 5th anniversary/TSR index on 3rd anniversary). For example, if the number of shares transferred at the third anniversary was 110,255 and if the TSR index had risen from 207 to 246 between the 3rd and 5th anniversaries, then the number of shares to be released to the director would be 155,714 because this is $110,255*(246/207)^2$.

Setting the TSR index growth target rate

Where an enhanced return rule is used, remuneration committees have an interesting challenge in setting the TSR index growth rate target. Investors will certainly look to the target as a guide to the company's expectations about future growth. They will therefore hope to see a high target. Executive teams will be rewarded for out performing the target and punished for under performing against it, so they would prefer to see a low target. A realistic target is therefore necessary.

It is impossible to predict business conditions in three to five years time, so it is quite impossible to be confident that an appropriate target has been set. This disadvantage is inherent in an absolute performance measure and it means that such measures have to be used sparingly. Adjustments can never be made after the target has been set because this would undermine the incentives created by setting the target.

The length of the performance period

A remuneration committee may want to configure the length of the FILLIP performance period to fit the circumstances of its company, or even the individual under remuneration.

As a performance period, three years is probably sufficient in sectors such as retail where the effect of good or bad management shows through relatively quickly. In other sectors, such as pharmaceuticals or oil and gas, performance depends to a large extent on investment. It takes time for the value of investments to become apparent so a longer performance period might ensure better incentives. Longer performance periods are also important where bad ethical practices take time to mature into value destroying lawsuits and public relations disasters. Executives should not be allowed to depart from a company, taking with them large rewards whilst at the same time leaving a financial time bomb under a company's valuation.

Golden handcuffs

Instinctively a remuneration committee may wish to remove 100% of all shares in a FILLIP if a director leaves to work for a competitor. However such an arrangement is not practical because executives would perceive the value in their FILLIPs as being value at risk, rather than value already earned. It would become very hard to recruit executives externally without offering huge golden hellos. It would also create big pressure for higher base salaries and annual bonuses to mitigate the risks associated with FILLIP based remuneration. Ideally a FILLIP should replace a proportion of base salary as well as variable pay. This is not feasible if the value of the FILLIP is unreasonably put at risk.

The value in a FILLIP has in fact already been earned by the director. The only reason it is locked in the FILLIP is to provide a long term incentive and to determine its final value. Removing an executive's entitlement to the FILLIP is therefore more draconian than removing entitlement to a normal share based incentive scheme. Because of this it is not reasonable, in the case of a FILLIP, to remove entitlement if an executive chooses to leave for personal reasons or to change career. The golden handcuffs should only be used to defend the company from aggressive recruiting by competitors.

The remuneration committee should also remember that the executives who are most marketable outside the company are the ones who are most likely to persuade a competitor to pay a golden hello equivalent to the value lost by breaking the golden handcuffs. It is poor performing executives who find the golden handcuffs most restrictive. The golden handcuffs can therefore cause retention of the wrong people.

Share retention schemes

Some companies have share retention schemes whereby executives are prevented from selling shares until they have significant shareholdings in the company. If a company has a well developed share retention scheme then it may be possible to use this instead of the two year further retention period envisaged in the FILLIP. However this will only have the desired effect if the share retention scheme ensures that shares are retained for several years after the executive leaves the company. If executives' interests are to be properly aligned with shareholders then it is important that executives retain financial exposure to opportunities and problems that emerge in the company after they have left.

If an enhanced return rule is used in the FILLIP then the two year share retention period becomes an enhanced return period which cannot be replaced by a share retention scheme.

Appendix 6
Modelling value of three types of FILLIP

Appendix 6: Modelling value of three types of FILLIP

Scenario 1: Steady median performance

Annual conditional award value for FILLIP (£s):	937,500
Annual conditional award value for TP FILLIP (£s):	689,090
Annual median TSR growth rate (%):	8.0%
Standard deviation on 3 yr TSR growth rate (%):	30.0%
Initial share price (£s):	5.00
Discount rate for executive savings (%):	8.0%
Growth rate of conditional cash award (%):	8.0%

Share price year 1:	£5.00
Share price year 2:	£5.40
Share price year 3:	£5.83
Share price year 4:	£6.30
Share price year 5:	£6.80
Share price year 6:	£7.35
Share price year 7:	£7.93
Share price year 8:	£8.57
Share price year 9:	£9.25
Share price year 10:	£10.00
Share price year 11:	£10.79
Share price year 12:	£11.66

	Year 1	Year 2	Year 3	Year 4	Year 5	Year 6	Year 7
Share price at conditional award (£s):	5.00	5.40	5.83	6.30	6.80	7.35	7.93
FILLIP - number of shares in conditional award:	187,500	173,611	160,751	148,844	137,818	127,609	118,157
Pro rata FILLIP - number of shares in conditional award:	187,500	173,611	160,751	148,844	137,818	127,609	118,157
PRER FILLIP - number of shares in conditional award:	137,818	127,609	118,157	109,404	101,300	93,797	86,849
Share price after three years (£s):	6.30	6.80	7.35	7.93	8.57	9.25	10.00
Percentage TSR growth over three years:	26.0%	26.0%	26.0%	26.0%	26.0%	26.0%	26.0%
Percentage of conditional award that transfers:	50.0%	50.0%	50.0%	50.0%	50.0%	50.0%	50.0%
FILLIP - number of shares transferred:	93,750	86,805	80,375	74,422	68,909	63,804	59,078
Pro rata FILLIP - number of shares transferred:	93,750	86,805	80,375	74,422	68,909	63,804	59,078
PRER FILLIP - number of shares transferred:	68,909	63,804	59,078	54,702	50,650	46,898	43,424
Share price after five years (£s):	7.35	7.93	8.57	9.25	10.00	10.79	11.66
TSR growth in years 4 and 5 (%):	16.6%	16.6%	16.6%	16.6%	16.6%	16.6%	16.6%
FILLIP - value of shares released (£s):	688,748	688,743	688,743	688,750	688,747	688,740	688,743
Pro rata FILLIP - value of shares released (£s):	688,748	688,743	688,743	688,750	688,747	688,740	688,743
PRER FILLIP - value of shares released (£s):	688,747	688,740	688,743	688,745	688,745	688,743	688,741
FILLIP - PV of shares in award year (£s):	468,750	468,747	468,747	468,751	468,750	468,745	468,747
Pro rata FILLIP - PV of shares in award year (£s):	468,750	468,747	468,747	468,751	468,750	468,745	468,747
PRER FILLIP - PV of shares in award year (£s):	468,750	468,745	468,747	468,748	468,748	468,747	468,746

FILLIP - Average PV of shares released (£s):	Years 1 to 7:	468,748
Pro rata FILLIP - Average PV of shares released (£s):	Years 1 to 7:	468,748
PRER FILLIP - Average PV of shares released (£s):	Years 1 to 7:	468,747

Appendix 6: Modelling value of three types of FILLIP

Scenario 2: Volatile median performance

Parameters:

Annual conditional award value for FILLIP (£s):	937,500
Annual conditional award value for TP FILLIP (£s):	689,090
Annual median TSR growth rate (%):	8.0%
Standard deviation on 3 yr TSR growth rate (%):	30.0%
Initial share price (£s):	5.00
Discount rate for executive savings (%):	8.0%
Growth rate of conditional cash award (%):	8.0%

Share price year 1:	£5.00	Share price year 7:	£7.93
Share price year 2:	£6.30	Share price year 8:	£10.00
Share price year 3:	£5.83	Share price year 9:	£9.25
Share price year 4:	£7.35	Share price year 10:	£10.00
Share price year 5:	£6.80	Share price year 11:	£10.79
Share price year 6:	£8.57	Share price year 12:	£11.66

	Year 1	Year 2	Year 3	Year 4	Year 5	Year 6	Year 7
Share price at conditional award (£s):	5.00	6.30	5.83	7.35	6.80	8.57	7.93
FILLIP - number of shares in conditional award:	187,500	148,844	160,751	127,609	137,818	109,404	118,157
Pro rata FILLIP - number of shares in conditional award:	187,500	148,844	148,844	127,609	127,609	109,404	109,405
PRER FILLIP - number of shares in conditional award:	137,818	109,404	109,404	93,797	93,797	80,415	80,415
Share price after three years (£s):	7.35	6.80	8.57	7.93	10.00	9.25	10.00
Percentage TSR growth over three years:	46.9%	8.0%	46.9%	8.0%	46.9%	8.0%	26.0%
Percentage of conditional award that transfers:	75.8%	27.5%	75.8%	27.5%	75.8%	27.5%	50.0%
FILLIP - number of shares transferred:	142,057	40,869	121,791	35,038	104,416	30,039	59,078
Pro rata FILLIP - number of shares transferred:	142,057	40,869	112,770	35,038	96,681	30,039	54,702
PRER FILLIP - number of shares transferred:	104,416	30,039	82,888	25,754	71,064	22,080	40,207
Share price after five years (£s):	8.57	7.93	10.00	9.25	10.00	10.79	11.66
TSR growth in years 4 and 5 (%):	16.6%	16.6%	16.6%	16.6%	0.0%	16.6%	16.6%
FILLIP - value of shares released (£s):	1,217,304	324,270	1,217,304	324,264	1,043,640	324,260	688,743
Pro rata FILLIP - value of shares released (£s):	1,217,304	324,270	1,217,139	324,264	966,329	324,260	637,727
PRER FILLIP - value of shares released (£s):	1,217,302	324,260	1,127,121	324,265	710,286	324,266	637,717
FILLIP - PV of shares in award year (£s):	828,476	220,693	828,477	220,689	710,284	220,686	468,747
Pro rata FILLIP - PV of shares in award year (£s):	828,476	220,693	767,112	220,689	657,667	220,686	434,026
PRER FILLIP - PV of shares in award year (£s):	828,475	220,686	767,100	220,689	483,409	220,690	434,019
FILLIP - Average PV of shares released (£s):			Years 4 to 7:	405,101		Years 1 to 7:	499,722
Pro rata FILLIP - Average PV of shares released (£s):			Years 4 to 7:	383,267		Years 1 to 7:	478,478
PRER FILLIP - Average PV of shares released (£s):			Years 4 to 7:	339,702		Years 1 to 7:	453,581

237

Appendix 6: Modelling value of three types of FILLIP

Scenario 3: Steady top quartile performance

Parameters:

Annual conditional award value for FILLIP (£s):	937,500
Annual conditional award value for TP FILLIP (£s):	689,090
Annual median TSR growth rate (%):	8.0%
Standard deviation on 3 yr TSR growth rate (%):	30.0%
Initial share price (£s):	5.00
Discount rate for executive savings (%):	8.0%
Growth rate of conditional cash award (%):	8.0%

Share price year 1:	£5.00
Share price year 2:	£5.68
Share price year 3:	£6.44
Share price year 4:	£7.31
Share price year 5:	£8.30
Share price year 6:	£9.42
Share price year 7:	£10.69
Share price year 8:	£12.13
Share price year 9:	£13.77
Share price year 10:	£15.63
Share price year 11:	£17.74
Share price year 12:	£20.13

	Year 1	Year 2	Year 3	Year 4	Year 5	Year 6	Year 7
Share price at conditional award (£s):	5.00	5.68	6.44	7.31	8.30	9.42	10.69
FILLIP - number of shares in conditional award:	187,500	165,198	145,549	128,237	112,984	99,546	87,705
Pro rata FILLIP - number of shares in conditional award:	187,500	165,198	145,549	128,237	112,984	99,546	87,705
PRER FILLIP - number of shares in conditional award:	137,818	121,426	106,983	94,258	83,047	73,169	64,466
Share price after three years (£s):	7.31	8.30	9.42	10.69	12.13	13.77	15.63
Percentage TSR growth over three years:	46.2%	46.2%	46.2%	46.2%	46.2%	46.2%	46.2%
Percentage of conditional award that transfers:	75.0%	75.0%	75.0%	75.0%	75.0%	75.0%	75.0%
FILLIP - number of shares transferred:	140,640	123,912	109,174	96,188	84,747	74,668	65,786
Pro rata FILLIP - number of shares transferred:	140,640	123,912	109,174	96,188	84,747	74,668	65,786
PRER FILLIP - number of shares transferred:	103,375	91,079	80,246	70,701	62,292	54,883	48,355
Share price after five years (£s):	9.42	10.69	12.13	13.77	15.63	17.74	20.13
TSR growth in years 4 and 5 (%):	28.8%	28.8%	28.8%	28.8%	28.8%	28.8%	28.8%
FILLIP - value of shares released (£s):	1,324,519	1,324,520	1,324,525	1,324,518	1,324,516	1,324,534	1,324,518
Pro rata FILLIP - value of shares released (£s):	1,324,519	1,324,520	1,324,525	1,324,518	1,324,516	1,324,534	1,324,518
PRER FILLIP - value of shares released (£s):	1,615,654	1,615,648	1,615,652	1,615,645	1,615,654	1,615,660	1,615,658
FILLIP - PV of shares released (£s):	901,445	901,446	901,450	901,445	901,443	901,456	901,445
Pro rata FILLIP - PV of shares in award year (£s):	901,445	901,446	901,450	901,445	901,443	901,456	901,445
PRER FILLIP - PV of shares in award year (£s):	1,099,587	1,099,583	1,099,586	1,099,581	1,099,587	1,099,591	1,099,589

FILLIP - Average PV of shares released (£s):	Years 4 to 7: 901,447		Years 1 to 7: 901,447
Pro rata FILLIP - Average PV of shares released (£s):	Years 4 to 7: 901,447		Years 1 to 7: 901,447
PRER FILLIP - Average PV of shares released (£s):	Years 4 to 7: 1,099,587		Years 1 to 7: 1,099,586

Appendix 6: Modelling value of three types of FILLIP

Scenario 4: Steady bottom quartile performance

Parameters:

Annual conditional award value for FILLIP (£s):	937,500
Annual conditional award value for TP FILLIP (£s):	689,090
Annual median TSR growth rate (%):	8.0%
Standard deviation on 3 yr TSR growth rate (%):	30.0%
Initial share price (£s):	5.00
Discount rate for executive savings (%):	8.0%
Growth rate of conditional cash award (%):	8.0%

Share price year 1:	£5.00	Share price year 7:	£5.59
Share price year 2:	£5.09	Share price year 8:	£5.69
Share price year 3:	£5.19	Share price year 9:	£5.80
Share price year 4:	£5.29	Share price year 10:	£5.91
Share price year 5:	£5.38	Share price year 11:	£6.02
Share price year 6:	£5.49	Share price year 12:	£6.13

	Year 1	Year 2	Year 3	Year 4	Year 5	Year 6	Year 7
Share price at conditional award (£s):	5.00	5.09	5.19	5.29	5.38	5.49	5.59
FILLIP - number of shares in conditional award:	187,500	184,058	180,679	177,363	174,107	170,911	167,774
Pro rata FILLIP - number of shares in conditional award:	187,500	184,058	180,679	177,363	174,107	170,911	167,774
PRER FILLIP - number of shares in conditional award:	137,818	135,288	132,805	130,367	127,974	125,625	123,318
Share price after three years (£s):	5.29	5.38	5.49	5.59	5.69	5.80	5.91
Percentage TSR growth over three years:	5.7%	5.7%	5.7%	5.7%	5.7%	5.7%	5.7%
Percentage of conditional award that transfers:	25.0%	25.0%	25.0%	25.0%	25.0%	25.0%	25.0%
FILLIP - number of shares transferred:	46,833	45,974	45,130	44,301	43,488	42,690	41,906
Pro rata FILLIP - number of shares transferred:	46,833	45,974	45,130	44,301	43,488	42,690	41,906
PRER FILLIP - number of shares transferred:	34,424	33,792	33,172	32,563	31,965	31,378	30,802
Share price after five years (£s):	5.49	5.59	5.69	5.80	5.91	6.02	6.13
TSR growth in years 4 and 5 (%):	3.8%	3.8%	3.8%	3.8%	3.8%	3.8%	3.8%
FILLIP - value of shares released (£s):	256,894	256,898	256,897	256,894	256,895	256,897	256,895
Pro rata FILLIP - value of shares released (£s):	256,894	256,898	256,897	256,894	256,895	256,897	256,895
PRER FILLIP - value of shares released (£s):	203,352	203,351	203,353	203,353	203,351	203,350	203,350
FILLIP - PV of shares in award year (£s):	174,838	174,840	174,840	174,838	174,839	174,840	174,838
Pro rata FILLIP - PV of shares in award year (£s):	174,838	174,840	174,840	174,838	174,839	174,840	174,838
PRER FILLIP - PV of shares in award year (£s):	138,398	138,397	138,399	138,398	138,397	138,396	138,396

FILLIP - Average PV of shares released (£s):	Years 1 to 7:	174,839
Pro rata FILLIP - Average PV of shares released (£s):	Years 1 to 7:	174,839
PRER FILLIP - Average PV of shares released (£s):	Years 1 to 7:	138,398

Appendix 6: Modelling value of three types of FILLIP

Scenario 5: Steady 9% growth

Parameters:

Annual conditional award value for FILLIP (£s):	937,500
Annual conditional award value for TP FILLIP (£s):	689,090
Annual median TSR growth rate (%):	8.0%
Standard deviation on 3 yr TSR growth rate (%):	30.0%
Initial share price (£s):	5.00
Discount rate for executive savings (%):	8.0%
Growth rate of conditional cash award (%):	8.0%

Share price year 1:	£5.00
Share price year 2:	£5.45
Share price year 3:	£5.94
Share price year 4:	£6.48
Share price year 5:	£7.06
Share price year 6:	£7.69
Share price year 7:	£8.39
Share price year 8:	£9.14
Share price year 9:	£9.96
Share price year 10:	£10.86
Share price year 11:	£11.84
Share price year 12:	£12.90

	Year 1	Year 2	Year 3	Year 4	Year 5	Year 6	Year 7
Share price at conditional award (£s):	5.00	5.45	5.94	6.48	7.06	7.69	8.39
FILLIP - number of shares in conditional award:	187,500	172,018	157,815	144,784	132,830	121,862	111,800
Pro rata FILLIP - number of shares in conditional award:	187,500	172,018	157,815	144,784	132,830	121,862	111,800
PRER FILLIP - number of shares in conditional award:	137,818	126,439	115,999	106,421	97,634	89,572	82,176
Share price after three years (£s):	6.48	7.06	7.69	8.39	9.14	9.96	10.86
Percentage TSR growth over three years:	29.5%	29.5%	29.5%	29.5%	29.5%	29.5%	29.5%
Percentage of conditional award that transfers:	54.7%	54.7%	54.7%	54.7%	54.7%	54.7%	54.7%
FILLIP - number of shares transferred:	102,536	94,069	86,302	79,176	72,639	66,641	61,139
Pro rata FILLIP - number of shares transferred:	102,536	94,069	86,302	79,176	72,639	66,641	61,139
PRER FILLIP - number of shares transferred:	75,367	69,144	63,435	58,197	53,392	48,983	44,938
Share price after five years (£s):	7.69	8.39	9.14	9.96	10.86	11.84	12.90
TSR growth in years 4 and 5 (%):	18.8%	18.8%	18.8%	18.8%	18.8%	18.8%	18.8%
FILLIP - value of shares released (£s):	788,822	788,816	788,817	788,816	788,821	788,817	788,823
Pro rata FILLIP - value of shares released (£s):	788,822	788,816	788,817	788,816	788,821	788,817	788,823
PRER FILLIP - value of shares released (£s):	818,445	818,445	818,447	818,443	818,447	818,439	818,429
FILLIP - PV of shares in award year (£s):	536,859	536,855	536,856	536,855	536,858	536,856	536,860
Pro rata FILLIP - PV of shares in award year (£s):	536,859	536,855	536,856	536,855	536,858	536,856	536,860
PRER FILLIP - PV of shares in award year (£s):	557,020	557,020	557,021	557,019	557,021	557,016	557,009
FILLIP - Average PV of shares released (£s):			Years 4 to 7:	536,857		Years 1 to 7:	536,857
Pro rata FILLIP - Average PV of shares released (£s):			Years 4 to 7:	536,857		Years 1 to 7:	536,857
PRER FILLIP - Average PV of shares released (£s):			Years 4 to 7:	557,016		Years 1 to 7:	557,018

Appendix 6: Modelling value of three types of FILLIP

Scenario 6: Volatile 9% growth

Parameters:

Annual conditional award value for FILLIP (£s):	937,500
Annual conditional award value for TP FILLIP (£s):	689,090
Annual median TSR growth rate (%):	8.0%
Standard deviation on 3 yr TSR growth rate (%):	30.0%
Initial share price (£s):	5.00
Discount rate for executive savings (%):	8.0%
Growth rate of conditional cash award (%):	8.0%

Share price year 1:	£5.00
Share price year 2:	£6.48
Share price year 3:	£5.94
Share price year 4:	£7.69
Share price year 5:	£7.06
Share price year 6:	£9.14
Share price year 7:	£8.39
Share price year 8:	£10.86
Share price year 9:	£9.96
Share price year 10:	£10.86
Share price year 11:	£11.84
Share price year 12:	£12.90

	Year 1	Year 2	Year 3	Year 4	Year 5	Year 6	Year 7
Share price at conditional award (£s):	5.00	6.48	5.94	7.69	7.06	9.14	8.39
FILLIP - number of shares in conditional award:	187,500	144,784	157,815	121,862	132,830	102,569	111,800
Pro rata FILLIP - number of shares in conditional award:	187,500	144,784	144,784	121,862	121,862	102,569	102,569
PRER FILLIP - number of shares in conditional award:	137,818	106,421	106,421	89,572	89,572	75,391	75,391
Share price after three years (£s):	7.69	7.06	9.14	8.39	10.86	9.96	10.86
Percentage TSR growth over three years:	53.9%	9.0%	53.9%	9.0%	53.9%	9.0%	29.5%
Percentage of conditional award that transfers:	82.4%	28.6%	82.4%	28.6%	82.4%	28.6%	54.7%
FILLIP - number of shares transferred:	154,451	41,379	129,998	34,828	109,417	29,314	61,139
Pro rata FILLIP - number of shares transferred:	154,451	41,379	119,264	34,828	100,382	29,314	56,091
PRER FILLIP - number of shares transferred:	113,526	30,415	87,663	25,599	73,784	21,546	41,228
Share price after five years (£s):	9.14	8.39	10.86	9.96	10.86	11.84	12.90
TSR growth in years 4 and 5 (%):	18.8%	18.8%	18.8%	18.8%	0.0%	18.8%	18.8%
FILLIP - value of shares released (£s):	1,411,712	346,984	1,411,709	346,985	1,188,210	346,984	788,823
Pro rata FILLIP - value of shares released (£s):	1,411,712	346,984	1,295,143	346,985	1,090,095	346,984	723,693
PRER FILLIP - value of shares released (£s):	1,464,727	360,017	1,343,788	360,007	801,255	360,004	750,861
FILLIP - PV of shares in award year (£s):	960,788	236,151	960,785	236,152	808,676	236,152	536,860
Pro rata FILLIP - PV of shares in award year (£s):	960,788	236,151	881,453	236,152	741,900	236,152	492,534
PRER FILLIP - PV of shares in award year (£s):	996,869	245,021	914,560	245,015	545,321	245,013	511,024

FILLIP - Average PV of shares released (£s):	Years 4 to 7: 454,460	Years 1 to 7: 567,938
Pro rata FILLIP - Average PV of shares released (£s):	Years 4 to 7: 426,684	Years 1 to 7: 540,733
PRER FILLIP - Average PV of shares released (£s):	Years 4 to 7: 386,593	Years 1 to 7: 528,975

Appendix 6: Modelling value of three types of FILLIP
Scenario 7: Very volatile 9% growth

Parameters:

Annual conditional award value for FILLIP (£s):	937,500
Annual conditional award value for TP FILLIP (£s):	689,090
Annual median TSR growth rate (%):	8.0%
Standard deviation on 3 yr TSR growth rate (%):	30.0%
Initial share price (£s):	5.00
Discount rate for executive savings (%):	8.0%
Growth rate of conditional cash award (%):	8.0%

Share price year 1:	£5.00
Share price year 2:	£8.39
Share price year 3:	£5.94
Share price year 4:	£9.96
Share price year 5:	£7.06
Share price year 6:	£11.84
Share price year 7:	£8.39
Share price year 8:	£14.06
Share price year 9:	£9.96
Share price year 10:	£10.86
Share price year 11:	£11.84
Share price year 12:	£12.90

	Year 1	Year 2	Year 3	Year 4	Year 5	Year 6	Year 7
Share price at conditional award (£s):	5.00	8.39	5.94	9.96	7.06	11.84	8.39
FILLIP - number of shares in conditional award:	187,500	111,800	157,815	94,100	132,830	79,202	111,800
Pro rata FILLIP - number of shares in conditional award:	187,500	111,800	111,800	94,100	94,100	79,202	79,202
PRER FILLIP - number of shares in conditional award:	137,818	82,176	82,176	69,166	69,166	58,216	58,216
Share price after three years (£s):	9.96	7.06	11.84	8.39	14.06	9.96	10.86
Percentage TSR growth over three years:	99.3%	-15.8%	99.3%	-15.8%	99.3%	-15.8%	29.5%
Percentage of conditional award that transfers:	99.3%	8.2%	99.3%	8.2%	99.3%	8.2%	54.7%
FILLIP - number of shares transferred:	186,134	9,139	156,665	7,692	131,862	6,474	61,139
Pro rata FILLIP - number of shares transferred:	186,134	9,139	110,985	7,692	93,414	6,474	43,312
PRER FILLIP - number of shares transferred:	136,814	6,717	81,577	5,654	68,662	4,759	31,836
Share price after five years (£s):	11.84	8.39	14.06	9.96	10.86	11.84	12.90
TSR growth in years 4 and 5 (%):	18.8%	18.8%	18.8%	18.8%	-22.8%	18.8%	18.8%
FILLIP - value of shares released (£s):	2,203,234	76,635	2,203,231	76,634	1,431,951	76,632	788,823
Pro rata FILLIP - value of shares released (£s):	2,203,234	76,635	1,560,818	76,634	1,014,426	76,632	558,817
PRER FILLIP - value of shares released (£s):	2,285,975	79,508	1,619,428	79,514	444,596	79,516	579,810
FILLIP - PV of shares released in award year (£s):	1,499,484	52,157	1,499,482	52,156	974,562	52,154	536,860
Pro rata FILLIP - PV of shares in award year (£s):	1,499,484	52,157	1,062,267	52,156	690,401	52,154	380,322
PRER FILLIP - PV of shares in award year (£s):	1,555,796	54,112	1,102,156	54,116	302,585	54,118	394,609

	Years 4 to 7:	Years 1 to 7:
FILLIP - Average PV of shares released (£s):	403,933	666,693
Pro rata FILLIP - Average PV of shares released (£s):	293,758	541,277
PRER FILLIP - Average PV of shares released (£s):	201,357	502,499

Appendix 6: Modelling value of three types of FILLIP

Scenario 8: Steady 9% growth with year 4 price spike

Parameters:

Annual conditional award value for FILLIP (£s):	937,500
Annual conditional award value for TP FILLIP (£s):	689,090
Annual median TSR growth rate (%):	8.0%
Standard deviation on 3 yr TSR growth rate (%):	30.0%
Initial share price (£s):	5.00
Discount rate for executive savings (%):	8.0%
Growth rate of conditional cash award (%):	8.0%

Share price year 1:	£5.00
Share price year 2:	£5.45
Share price year 3:	£5.94
Share price year 4:	£7.50
Share price year 5:	£7.06
Share price year 6:	£7.69
Share price year 7:	£8.39
Share price year 8:	£9.14
Share price year 9:	£9.96
Share price year 10:	£10.86
Share price year 11:	£11.84
Share price year 12:	£12.90

	Year 1	Year 2	Year 3	Year 4	Year 5	Year 6	Year 7
Share price at conditional award (£s):	5.00	5.45	5.94	7.50	7.06	7.69	8.39
FILLIP - number of shares in conditional award:	187,500	172,018	157,815	125,000	132,830	121,862	111,800
Pro rata FILLIP - number of shares in conditional award:	187,500	172,018	157,815	125,000	125,000	121,862	111,800
PRER FILLIP - number of shares in conditional award:	137,818	126,439	115,999	91,879	91,879	89,572	82,176
Share price after three years (£s):	7.50	7.06	7.69	8.39	9.14	9.96	10.86
Percentage TSR growth over three years:	50.0%	29.5%	29.5%	11.8%	29.5%	29.5%	29.5%
Percentage of conditional award that transfers:	78.8%	54.7%	54.7%	31.8%	54.7%	54.7%	54.7%
FILLIP - number of shares transferred:	147,829	94,069	86,302	39,801	72,639	66,641	61,139
Pro rata FILLIP - number of shares transferred:	147,829	94,069	86,302	39,801	68,357	66,641	61,139
PRER FILLIP - number of shares transferred:	108,659	69,144	63,435	29,255	50,245	48,983	44,938
Share price after five years (£s):	7.69	8.39	9.14	9.96	10.86	11.84	12.90
TSR growth in years 4 and 5 (%):	2.6%	18.8%	18.8%	18.8%	18.8%	18.8%	18.8%
FILLIP - value of shares released (£s):	1,137,266	788,816	788,817	396,530	788,821	788,817	788,823
Pro rata FILLIP - value of shares released (£s):	1,137,266	788,816	788,817	396,530	742,321	788,817	788,823
PRER FILLIP - value of shares released (£s):	879,530	818,445	818,447	411,423	770,207	818,439	818,429
FILLIP - PV of shares in award year (£s):	774,004	536,855	536,856	269,872	536,858	536,856	536,860
Pro rata FILLIP - PV of shares in award year (£s):	774,004	536,855	536,856	269,872	505,211	536,856	536,860
PRER FILLIP - PV of shares in award year (£s):	598,593	557,020	557,021	280,007	524,190	557,016	557,009

	Years 4 to 7:	Years 1 to 7:
FILLIP - Average PV of shares released (£s):	470,111	532,594
Pro rata FILLIP - Average PV of shares released (£s):	462,200	528,073
PRER FILLIP - Average PV of shares released (£s):	479,556	518,694

Appendix 6: Modelling value of three types of FILLIP

Scenario 9: Value destroyed then partially recovered

Parameters:	
Annual conditional award value for FILLIP (£s):	937,500
Annual conditional award value for TP FILLIP (£s):	689,090
Annual median TSR growth rate (%):	8.0%
Standard deviation on 3 yr TSR growth rate (%):	30.0%
Initial share price (£s):	5.00
Discount rate for executive savings (%):	8.0%
Growth rate of conditional cash award (%):	8.0%

Share price year 1:	£5.00
Share price year 2:	£5.40
Share price year 3:	£5.83
Share price year 4:	£3.00
Share price year 5:	£2.00
Share price year 6:	£2.00
Share price year 7:	£4.30
Share price year 8:	£5.00
Share price year 9:	£5.40
Share price year 10:	£5.83
Share price year 11:	£6.30
Share price year 12:	£6.80

	Year 1	Year 2	Year 3	Year 4	Year 5	Year 6	Year 7
Share price at conditional award (£s):	5.00	5.40	5.83	3.00	2.00	2.00	4.30
FILLIP - number of shares in conditional award:	187,500	173,611	160,751	312,500	468,750	468,750	218,023
Pro rata FILLIP - number of shares in conditional award:	187,500	173,611	160,751	160,751	160,751	160,751	218,023
PRER FILLIP - number of shares in conditional award:	137,818	127,609	118,157	118,157	118,157	118,157	160,253
Share price after three years (£s):	3.00	2.00	2.00	4.30	5.00	5.40	5.83
Percentage TSR growth over three years:	-40.0%	-63.0%	-65.7%	43.3%	150.0%	170.0%	35.6%
Percentage of conditional award that transfers:	1.4%	0.2%	0.1%	71.9%	100.0%	100.0%	62.6%
FILLIP - number of shares transferred:	2,613	263	180	224,568	468,742	468,750	136,533
Pro rata FILLIP - number of shares transferred:	2,613	263	180	115,518	160,748	160,751	136,533
PRER FILLIP - number of shares transferred:	1,921	193	133	84,910	118,155	118,157	100,356
Share price after five years (£s):	2.00	4.30	5.00	5.40	5.83	6.30	6.80
TSR growth in years 4 and 5 (%):	-33.3%	115.0%	150.0%	25.6%	16.6%	16.6%	16.6%
FILLIP - value of shares released (£s):	5,226	1,131	900	1,212,667	2,733,703	2,952,450	928,758
Pro rata FILLIP - value of shares released (£s):	5,226	1,131	900	623,797	937,482	1,012,500	928,758
PRER FILLIP - value of shares released (£s):	1,708	3,836	4,156	723,108	937,486	1,012,502	928,760
FILLIP - PV of shares in award year (£s):	3,557	770	613	825,321	1,860,513	2,009,388	632,097
Pro rata FILLIP - PV of shares in award year (£s):	3,557	770	613	424,546	638,035	689,090	632,097
PRER FILLIP - PV of shares in award year (£s):	1,162	2,611	2,829	492,135	638,037	689,092	632,098

FILLIP - Average PV of shares released (£s):	Years 4 to 7:	1,331,830	Years 1 to 7: 761,751
Pro rata FILLIP - Average PV of shares released (£s):	Years 4 to 7:	595,942	Years 1 to 7: 341,244
PRER FILLIP - Average PV of shares released (£s):	Years 4 to 7:	612,841	Years 1 to 7: 351,138

Appendix 6: Modelling value of three types of FILLIP

Scenario 10: Value increased then partially lost

Parameters:

Annual conditional award value for FILLIP (£s):	937,500	
Annual conditional award value for TP FILLIP (£s):	689,090	
Annual median TSR growth rate (%):	8.0%	
Standard deviation on 3 yr TSR growth rate (%):	30.0%	
Initial share price (£s):	5.00	
Discount rate for executive savings (%):	8.0%	
Growth rate of conditional cash award (%):	8.0%	

Share price year 1:	£5.00
Share price year 2:	£5.40
Share price year 3:	£5.83
Share price year 4:	£9.00
Share price year 5:	£11.50
Share price year 6:	£10.00
Share price year 7:	£10.80
Share price year 8:	£11.66
Share price year 9:	£12.60
Share price year 10:	£13.60
Share price year 11:	£14.69
Share price year 12:	£15.87

	Year 1	Year 2	Year 3	Year 4	Year 5	Year 6	Year 7
Share price at conditional award (£s):	5.00	5.40	5.83	9.00	11.50	10.00	10.80
FILLIP - number of shares in conditional award:	187,500	173,611	160,751	104,167	81,522	93,750	86,806
Pro rata FILLIP - number of shares in conditional award:	187,500	173,611	160,751	104,167	81,522	81,522	81,522
PRER FILLIP - number of shares in conditional award:	137,818	127,609	118,157	76,566	59,921	59,921	59,921
Share price after three years (£s):	9.00	11.50	10.00	10.80	11.66	12.60	13.60
Percentage TSR growth over three years:	80.0%	113.0%	71.5%	20.0%	1.4%	26.0%	26.0%
Percentage of conditional award that transfers:	96.4%	99.8%	93.5%	42.1%	20.7%	50.0%	50.0%
FILLIP - number of shares transferred:	180,777	173,287	150,352	43,866	16,845	46,875	43,403
Pro rata FILLIP - number of shares transferred:	180,777	173,287	150,352	43,866	16,845	40,761	40,761
PRER FILLIP - number of shares transferred:	132,877	127,371	110,513	32,243	12,381	29,960	29,960
Share price after five years (£s):	10.00	10.80	11.66	12.60	13.60	14.69	15.87
TSR growth in years 4 and 5 (%):	11.1%	-6.1%	16.6%	16.6%	16.6%	16.6%	16.6%
FILLIP - value of shares released (£s):	1,807,770	1,871,500	1,753,706	552,585	229,174	688,748	688,751
Pro rata FILLIP - value of shares released (£s):	1,807,770	1,871,500	1,753,706	552,585	229,174	598,913	646,826
PRER FILLIP - value of shares released (£s):	1,640,457	1,213,238	1,753,702	552,588	229,164	598,902	646,814
FILLIP - PV of shares in award year (£s):	1,230,338	1,273,711	1,193,543	376,080	155,972	468,750	468,752
Pro rata FILLIP - PV of shares in award year (£s):	1,230,338	1,273,711	1,193,543	376,080	155,972	407,610	440,219
PRER FILLIP - PV of shares in award year (£s):	1,116,467	825,710	1,193,540	376,082	155,965	407,602	440,211

	Years 4 to 7:	Years 1 to 7:
FILLIP - Average PV of shares released (£s):	367,389	738,164
Pro rata FILLIP - Average PV of shares released (£s):	344,970	725,353
PRER FILLIP - Average PV of shares released (£s):	344,965	645,083

Appendix 7
Cost of option based remuneration v cost of share based remuneration

Appendix 7: Cost of option based remuneration v cost of share based remuneration

Scenario 1: Company with 8% per annum target for share price growth

Assumes no dividends paid.	
Intended present value of remuneration for target perfromance (£s):	100,000
Target annual growth rate for share price:	8.0%
Executive savings discount rate:	8.0%
Initial value of share (£s):	5.00

Required value of award at year 10:	215,892
Target value of a share at year 10:	10.79
Number of shares in award:	20,000
Target value of an option at year 10:	5.79
Number of options in award:	37,257

Actual Share Price Growth Rate	Actual Share Price at Year 10	Value of shares at year 10	Value of options at year 10
-5.0%	2.99	59,874	0
-2.5%	3.88	77,633	0
0.0%	5.00	100,000	0
2.5%	6.40	128,008	52,176
5.0%	8.14	162,889	117,154
7.5%	10.31	206,103	197,654
10.0%	12.97	259,374	296,890
12.5%	16.24	324,732	418,642
15.0%	20.23	404,556	567,342
17.5%	25.08	501,624	748,166
20.0%	30.96	619,174	967,143
22.5%	38.05	760,958	1,231,266
25.0%	46.57	931,323	1,548,629
27.5%	56.76	1,135,277	1,928,566
30.0%	68.93	1,378,585	2,381,812

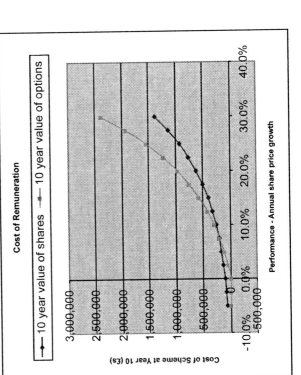

Cost of Remuneration

Legend: 10 year value of shares — 10 year value of options

Appendix 7: Cost of option based remuneration v cost of share based remuneration

Scenario 2: Company with 25% per annum target for share price growth

Assumes no dividends paid.

Intended present value of remuneration for target perfromance (£s):	100,000
Target annual growth rate for share price:	25.0%
Executive savings discount rate:	8.0%
Initial value of share (£s):	5.00

Required value of award at year 10:	215,892
Target value of a share at year 10:	46.57
Number of shares in award:	4,636
Target value of an option at year 10:	41.57
Number of options in award:	5,194

Actual Share Price Growth Rate	Actual Share Price at Year 10	Value of shares at year 10	Value of options at year 10
-5.0%	2.99	13,879	0
-2.5%	3.88	17,995	0
0.0%	5.00	23,180	0
2.5%	6.40	29,672	7,274
5.0%	8.14	37,758	16,332
7.5%	10.31	47,775	27,555
10.0%	12.97	60,123	41,389
12.5%	16.24	75,273	58,363
15.0%	20.23	93,776	79,093
17.5%	25.08	116,277	104,302
20.0%	30.96	143,524	134,829
22.5%	38.05	176,390	171,651
25.0%	46.57	215,881	215,894
27.5%	56.76	263,157	268,861
30.0%	68.93	319,556	332,049
32.5%	83.39	386,609	407,172
35.0%	100.53	466,070	496,197
37.5%	120.78	559,939	601,364
40.0%	144.63	670,492	725,224
42.5%	172.63	800,317	870,675
45.0%	205.42	952,343	1,040,999

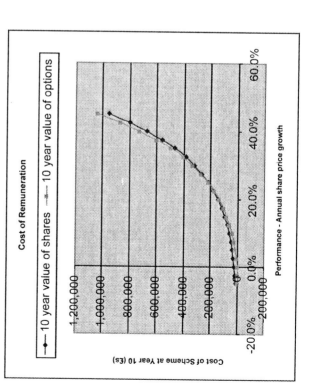

Cost of Remuneration

10 year value of shares — 10 year value of options

Performance - Annual share price growth

Cost of Scheme at Year 10 (£s)

Reference material and further reading

ABI 2005

    Association of British Insurers – Principles and Guidelines on Remuneration – 28 November 2005 (available from: http://www.ivis.co.uk/pages/gdsc2_1.pdf)

ABI and NAPF 1999

    Responsible Voting – A Joint ABI – NAPF Statement, July 1999, available from: http://www.ivis.co.uk/pages/framegu.html

Bebchuk 2004 (Lucian Bebchuk, Jesse Fried)

    Pay without Performance: The Unfulfilled Promise of Executive Compensation (USA: Harvard University Press)

Cadbury 1992a

    The Report of the Committee on The Financial Aspects of Corporate Governance – 1st December 1992 (London: Gee and Co. Ltd) available from: http://www.ecgi.de/codes/code.php?code_id=132

Cadbury 1992b

    The Financial Aspects of Corporate Governance – The Code of Best Practice (London: Gee and Co. Ltd) (see also p. 58 of Cadbury 1992a)

Cohn 2003 (Jeffrey M. Cohn, Rakesh Khurana)

    Strategy Maps for CEO Succession Planning (Harvard Business Online, Product Number B0307C)

Combined Code 1998 (superseded in 2003)

    The Combined Code: Principles of Good Governance and Code of Best Practice Derived by the Committee on Corporate Governance from the Committee's Final Report and from the Cadbury and Greenbury Reports. Available from: http://www.fsa.gov.uk/pubs/ukla/lr_comcode.pdf

Combined Code 2003

    The Combined Code on Corporate Governance – July 2003 (London: Accounting Standards Board, Financial Reporting Council) Available from: http://www.frc.org.uk

Ellig 2001 (Bruce R. Ellig)

    The Complete Guide to Executive Remuneration (New York: McGraw-Hill).

Government 1999

Company Law – Directors' Remuneration – A Consultative Document (London: DTI, July 1999, URN 99/923) Available from: http://www.dti.gov.uk/cld/payfinal.pdf

Government 2001

Company Law – Directors' Remuneration – A Consultative Document (London: DTI, December 2001, URN 01/1400) Available from: http://www.dti.gov.uk/cld/dir_rem.pdf

Government 2003

Company Law – "Rewards for Failure" Directors' Remuneration – Contracts, Performance and Severance – A Consultative Document – June 2003 (London: DTI) Available from: http://www.dti.gov.uk/cld/4864rewards.pdf

Greenbury 1995

Directors' Remuneration: Report of a Study Group chaired by Sir Richard Greenbury – 17th July 1995 (London: Gee Publishing Ltd). Available from: http://www.ecgi.org/codes/code.php?code_id=131

Hampel 1998

Committee on Corporate Governance: Final Report – January 1998 (London: Gee Publishing Ltd) Available from: http://www.ecgi.org/codes/documents/hampel_index.htm

Hemscott 2003

The current population of non-executive directors – Full dataset – 20th January 2003 Available from: http://www.dti.gov.uk/cld/non_exec_review/pdfs/finalcensus.pdf

Higgs 2003

Review of the role and effectiveness of non-executive directors – January 2003 (London: DTI) Available from: http://www.dti.gov.uk/cld/non_exec_review/pdfs/higgsreport.pdf?pubpdfdload=03%2F636

McNulty 2003 (Dr Terry McNulty, Dr John Roberts & Dr Philip Stiles)

Creating accountability within the board: The work of the effective non-executive director available from: http://www.dti.gov.uk/cld/non_exec_review/pdfs/stilesreport.pdf

Myners 2001

Institutional Investment in the United Kingdom: A Review (London: HM Treasury) available from http://www.hm-treasury.gov.uk./media/2F9/02/31.pdf

Paddock 2003 (Jane Paddock, Alicia Ash)

Tolley's Directors' Remuneration: A Practical Guide (Oxford: Butterworths)

Plender 2005 (John Plender, Avinash Persaud)
  The Missing Moral Compass: A reality Check on Business and Finance Ethics (for publication in 2005)
Regulations 2002
  Statutory Instrument 2002 No. 1986: The Directors' Remuneration Report Regulations 2002 (London: The Queen's printer of Acts of Parliament)
Sykes 2004
  Restoring Trust - Investment in the twenty-first century (London: Tomorrow's Company) Available for order from:
  http://www.tomorrowscompany.com/publications.htm

Glossary

5-day Share Price - For a particular share at a particular date, the 5-day share price is the average closing share price for that share taken on each of the last five working days up to and including that date.

ABI – See Association of British Insurers

Association of British Insurers – A trade association representing many of the UK's biggest investment institutions

Balanced Scorecard – A way of measuring the performance of a business, described in detail in chapter 1

Basic Salary – The annual salary paid to an executive in 12 monthly instalments over a year without any reference to performance considerations.

Bonus – an additional lump sum paid to an executive for good performance. An annual bonus is a bonus paid each year, the size of which depends on how well the executive has performed that year.

Business Plan – A plan showing how a business is expected to develop over the next five years, especially from a financial perspective. (See chapter 1.)

Chairman – The person who chairs the meeting of the board of directors for a company. The chairman is responsible for the management of the company board, as described in the Combined Code 2003.

Chief Executive – The member of the company board who has day to day responsibility for the management of the company.

Combined Code – A set of guidelines for good corporate governance maintained by the UK's Financial Reporting Council. (See chapter 4.)

Comparative Pay Positioning – The practice of setting the levels of executive pay in a company by reference to the levels of pay in comparable companies. (See chapter 11.)

Comparator Group - A defined group of comparable companies used for comparative pay positioning (see chapter 11) or for determination of relative performance in an LTIP (see chapter 6).

Corporate Governance – The system of rules, procedures and structures used to govern a company.

Corporate Social Responsibility (CSR) – A company's responsibilities to wider society in respect of social, ethical and environmental matters.

CSR – See Corporate Social Responsibility.

Defined Benefit Pension Scheme – A pension scheme in which the company manages the financial uncertainty of the pension fund so that executives have a high level of certainty about their future pension benefits. (See chapter 10.)

Defined Contribution Pension Scheme – A pension scheme to which executives and the company contribute at a defined rate. There is uncertainty about how big the future pension benefits will be. (See chapter 10.)

Demotivation Problem – The problem of demotivation that arises when an executive works hard to achieve a particular target, linked to a reward, but then narrowly fails to hit the target (perhaps through no fault of his or her own) and so is not paid the reward.

Director – A member of the board of directors, which is the top level decision making committee of the company. A director is usually designated as "Chairman", "Executive" or "Non-executive". The members of the board are collectively responsible for the success of the company.

Directors' Remuneration Report Regulations 2002 – Regulations that require a company to make a detailed disclosure of all directors remuneration in an annual remuneration report. A shareholders vote to approve the remuneration report has to take place at a general meeting of the company. (See chapter 4.)

Dividend – A payment, usually in cash, made by the company to its shareholders. Company earnings are typically distributed to shareholders through dividends.

Earnings – A company's profit in a financial year, after the deduction of interest and tax. It is the money that the company has actually earned for its shareholders.

Earnings Per Share (EPS) – The company earnings in a financial year, divided by the number of outstanding shares. EPS is a key measure used to estimate the value of a share.

Enhanced Return Rule – A rule that can be included in the rules of a FILLIP to make the payouts under the FILLIP more sensitive to the absolute growth in value of the TSR index. (See chapter 8 and appendix 5.)

EPS – See earnings per share.

Equity – An investment in company shares. Each investor has an equitable claim on the company in proportion to the number of shares owned. An equity investment provides a good financial return if the shares pay out good dividends or if they become significantly more valuable.

Executive – A member of the executive team; one of the very top managers in the company. Outside of this book the word "executive" is sometimes used to denote any senior manager. In this book the word is used much more specifically to mean one of a very small number of managers who are on the company board, or very close to that level.

Executive Team – The small group of managers at the top of the company's organisation, which has day to day responsibility for running the company. The executive team includes executive directors, excludes the non-executive directors and may include the chairman.

FILLIP – A Fully Invariable, Linear Long term Incentive Plan. (See chapter 7.)

Financial Services Authority – The government agency responsible for regulation of the UK's financial services industry.

FTSE 100 – An index measuring the share price growth (or contraction) of the 100 largest companies on the London Stock Exchange.

FTSE 350 – An index measuring the share price growth (or contraction) of the 350 largest companies on the London Stock Exchange.

Golden Handcuff – Remuneration that will be paid at a future date, providing that the executive is still working for the company at that time. Golden handcuffs provide incentives for executives to stick with the company that they currently work for, rather than going off to work for a competitor. (See chapter 7 and appendix 5.)

Golden Hello – A one time payment made to an executive as part of his or her recruitment process. Golden hellos are sometime paid to compensate new recruits who have lost out because of golden handcuffs in the company that they are leaving. (See chapter 7.)

Incentive – A personal benefit that an individual hopes to receive if he or she behaves in a particular way. Company remuneration systems always provide incentives whether or not they have been intentionally designed to do so.

Institutional Investor – An investor who is routinely investing large amounts of money on behalf of other people.

Listed Company – A company whose shares can be bought or sold through the London Stock Exchange, the Alternative Investment Market (AIM) or some other exchange.

Long term – five years or more

Long Term Incentive Plan (LTIP) – A form of remuneration designed to provide incentives over the long term. (See chapter 6.)

LTIP – See Long Term Incentive Plan.

Manager – Any person with significant responsibility within a company's organisation. Executive directors are managers. Non-executive directors are not managers.

Management – A company's managers, collectively.

Median Position – If a group of values are put in order with the highest first and the lowest last then the value in the middle is in median position. More precisely, Median Position is the 50th Percentile Position. (See definition of percentile position.) Note that if there is an even number of values in the group then (unless the two middle numbers have the same value) none of the values are strictly in median position; all are either above median position or below median position.

Motivational Dead Zone – A wide range of performance outcomes which all lead to the same remuneration outcome within a performance related pay scheme. There is no incentive to change the performance outcome if the change still falls inside the motivational dead zone.

Non-Executive Director – A company director, who is usually part time, and has no direct involvement with the management of the company.

Percentile Position – If a group of values are put in order with the highest first and the lowest last then the percentile position of a particular value is that percentage N (where $0 =< N =< 100$) such that N% of the values which are not equal to the particular value are greater than it and (100-N)% are less than it. For example, if the values are (18, 17, 15, 15, 14, 12, 10, 7, 3) then 12 is in 62.5th percentile position because 5 out of 8 of the other values are bigger than 12, and 3 out of 8 are smaller. By contrast 15 is in the 28.57th percentile position because 2 out of 7 of the other values are bigger than 15 and 5 out of 7 of the other values are smaller.

Performance – Performance is the level of success in doing what was intended. For executives, performance is how effectively they have done their jobs. For investments, performance is the level of financial return to the investor. There are many different ways of quantifying performance and these are examined in chapter 1.

Performance Related Pay – Pay that is linked to performance, such that the pay is high when performance (of the individual, team or company) has been good, and is low when performance has been bad.

Performance Period – A period of time over which performance is measured. For LTIPs and SOSs the performance period is often three years. Meaningful measurement of performance can only be achieved if the start and end date of the performance period is predefined and fixed.

Personal Performance Contract (PPC) – A set of between six and 12 performance targets for an individual manager that are documented at the start of the year and signed off by both the individual and his or her line manager. (See chapter 1.)

Phased Awards – Awards made under a LTIP or SOS that are made on a regular annual or quarterly basis, as opposed to a single large award made every three to five years.

PPC – See Personal Performance Contract.

PRER FILLIP – A FILLIP that incorporates both a pro rata rule and a enhanced return rule. (See chapter 8 and appendix 5.)

Profit – The money that a company makes in a year. This is its income during the year less all of its costs. Profit is usually calculated in accordance with accounting standards before interest and tax costs have been deducted. Profit after income and tax has been deducted is known as "earnings".

Pro Rata Rule - A rule that can be included in the rules of a FILLIP to prevent the FILLIP from paying large rewards to executive teams which destroy and then partially restore value.

Quartile – When examining a group of values, a value is in the top quartile if it is bigger than 75% of the other values. More precisely, a value is in the top quartile if its percentile position (see definition) is less than or equal to 25th. Similarly a value is in the bottom quartile if its percentile position is 75th or higher. Note that there may be no value that is strictly in the quartile positions. For example, if the values are (18, 17, 15, 15, 14, 12, 10, 7, 3) then 17 is in 12.5^{th} percentile position because 1 out of 8 of the other values are bigger than 17, and 7 out of 8 are smaller. However 15 is in the 28.57^{th} percentile position because 2 out of 7 of the other values are bigger than 15 and 5 out of 7 of the other values are smaller. Therefore only the values 18 and 17 are top quartile. In contrast, 10 is in the 75th percentile position because 6 out of 8 of the other values are bigger than it and 2 out of 8 are smaller. This means that the values 10, 7 and 3 are all bottom quartile.

Rate of Return – The percentage growth in the value of an investment over a year. For example if £1,000 is invested on a particular date and is worth £1,082 on that date the following year then the rate of return for that year of investment is 8.2 %.

Remuneration Committee – A sub-committee of the company board which is responsible for determining the remuneration of the executive directors and other top managers. The remuneration committee is made up of non-executive directors.

Remuneration Report – An annual report produced by the remuneration committee in accordance with the requirements of the Directors' Remuneration Report Regulations 2002.

Share – A share is a share in the ownership of a company. Most listed companies have millions or even billions of shares so one share is only a very tiny proportion of the full ownership. However an individual shareholder may own thousands or even millions of shares in which case that part ownership becomes significant.

Share Price – The price at which a share in a listed company can be bought or sold. Share prices change by the minute. Share prices at the end of each working day are published in the Financial Times and other newspapers.

Share Option – the right to buy a share in a particular company at a particular price before a particular date. Share options are explained more fully at the start of chapter 9.

Share Option Scheme (SOS) – A form of remuneration in which executives are awarded share options. This gives the executives incentives to grow the share price of the company. Usually the options are awarded on a conditional basis and only become fully available to the executive if predefined performance conditions have been met three years after the conditional award. SOSs are discussed in detail in chapter 9.

Shareholder – A person, institution or fund which owns shares in a company. It is important to notice that a large proportion of the population of the UK own shares indirectly through pension schemes or investment products. These people may not be legal owners of the shares but they are the people who ultimately benefit or lose out if a share performs well or badly as an investment.

Shareholder Activism – Shareholders actively seeking to influence the direction of a company by making use of the legal rights of shareholders. The most important of these rights is the right to vote on company resolutions. Shareholder activism is discussed in chapter 13.

Shareholder Value – The financial value that a shareholder derives from investing in shares. Shareholder value, and the way in which it can be measured, is discussed in chapter 1.

Short term – Within the next year or 18 months.

Single Hurdle – A performance condition which can be either "met" or "not met" without any possibility of it being partially met. For example, old fashioned SOSs used to pay out a full reward if performance was determined to be top quartile, and nothing at all otherwise. (See chapter 6.)

Sliding Scale – A performance condition that can be partially met. For example most SOSs pay out a full reward for performance that is top quartile and no reward for performance that is below median. For percentile positions between 25 and 50 they pay out on a sliding scale. Performance on the 26th percentile, receives rewards only slightly less than the rewards for top quartile performance. Performance on the 37.5th percentile receives reward half way between reward for top quartile and median performance. (See chapter 6.)

SOS – See Share Option Scheme.

Stakeholder – Someone with a legitimate interest in the activities of a company. Stakeholders include shareholders, directors, employees, customers, suppliers and regulators.

Total Shareholder Return (TSR) – The total shareholder value that accumulates to an investor in company shares, irrespective of whether that value arises from dividends, growth in the value of the shares or from other sources. (See chapter 1 and appendix 1.)

TSR – See Total Shareholder Return.

TSR Index – An index that tracks over time the growth (and fall) of the value of an investment in a particular company's shares. (See chapter 1 and appendix 1.)

Variable Pay – See Performance Related Pay.

Volatility – the tendency of share prices to rise and fall in an apparently random way over the short and medium term. Volatility can make it hard to see the underlying long term pattern of change in a share price.

Volatility Problem – The problem that occurs when an executive team can increase the benefits they receive from SOSs and LTIPs by increasing medium term volatility without increasing underlying long term performance. (See chapter 6.)

Index

ABI *see* Association of British Insurers

absolute performance 28, 35–42, 100, 101, 112, 231, 254

accountability 7, 10, 11, 19, 22–24, 29, 30, 67, 181, 251

accounting 4, 20, 54, 55, 59, 95, 106, 116, 117, 126, 127, 146, 175

Accounting Standards Board (ASB) 55

actuary 134, 136, 176

alignment 3, 14, 16, 22, 24, 27–30, 37, 38, 41, 42, 47, 48, 58, 68, 72, 83, 84, 86, 88, 89, 91–93, 98, 100, 101, 104, 109, 112, 119–121, 123, 125, 128, 138, 140, 142, 143, 160–162, 168, 170, 185, 195, 201, 234

Allfirst Financial 4

Andersen Consulting 36

appointment 89–91, 96, 163, 164, 166, 181

Ash, Alicia 251

assessment 7, 10, 11, 22–24, 32, 35–37, 47, 64, 65, 88, 139, 185, 201

Association of British Insurers (ABI) 45, 47, 56, 62, 69, 72, 80, 83, 85, 96, 97, 185–187, 189, 193, 250, 253

audit 4, 45, 59, 177

Aviva 189

Balance 28, 32, 48, 66, 132, 169

balanced scorecard 8, 9, 12, 57, 253

Barings Bank 4

basic salary 13, 43, 63, 70, 98, 105, 108, 111, 128–131, 133, 134, 136–138, 140, 141, 194, 195, 208, 233, 253

Bebchuk, Lucian 193, 250

behaviour 4, 16, 26, 29, 33, 59, 86, 102, 121, 142, 159, 162, 163, 176

benchmark 41, 45, 46, 71, 130, 133, 148, 149, 160, 165, 172, 199

Berkeley Group 187

Berkshire Hathaway 196, 203

best practice 44, 52, 145, 147, 149, 155, 177, 178, 196

Black Scholes 117, 210

BMW 171

board 14, 18, 44, 62, 90, 93, 156, 161, 162, 163, 174, 177, 178, 182–184, 186–188, 190, 197–199, 202

Boeing 164

Bonanza 71, 72, 78–80, 115, 131

bonus 13, 15, 21, 23, 29, 31, 43, 48, 51, 52, 54, 55–60, 63, 65–68, 98, 129, 133, 137, 142, 144, 156, 170, 189, 208, 209, 213, 215, 233, 253

Brent Spa 4

British Coal 197

Buffet, Warren 196, 202

business plan 5–7, 9, 12, 57, 235

Cadbury, Sir Adrian 44, 45, 56, 147, 157, 179, 250

California Management Review 196

capital gains tax 113

capital investment 6, 106, 233

capital restructure 122, 127, 131,

205, 231
capital structure 23
Carling lager 59
Carlton Communications 94, 99
CBI see Confederation of British
    Industry
Cellum, Pete 60, 61, 136–138
chairman 9, 44, 45, 48, 57, 63, 55, 90,
    94, 173, 179, 180, 181, 190–192,
    196, 208–211, 251, 253, 254, 256
Chancellor of the Exchequer 102
change of control 93, 94, 206
chief executive 9, 18–20, 22, 30, 35,
    38, 63, 70, 73, 89–93, 96, 121,
    122, 129–131, 162–164, 167, 168,
    173, 179, 199, 253
City 19, 58, 61, 103, 106
Cohn, Jeffrey M. 250
Coke 151, 164
Combined Code 44, 45, 56, 65, 69,
    72, 85, 92, 97, 128, 134, 141, 149,
    152, 154, 157,158, 166, 175, 177–
    179, 188–193, 197, 250, 251, 253
company car 44, 111, 128, 129, 139,
    195
comparative pay positioning 143,
    147–157, 167, 174, 198, 199, 202,
    253
comparison 167, 174, 202, 212
comparator group 36, 71, 75–79, 81,
    96, 148, 160, 199, 211, 218, 229,
    230, 253
competition 31, 33, 34, 37–40, 47, 94,
    100, 118, 150–152, 160, 161, 165,
    170, 174, 185, 189, 231, 234
complexity 47, 53, 55, 108, 144–147,
    151, 155–157, 160, 180, 182

Confederation of British Industry 186
Conflict 29, 31, 64, 68, 91, 170, 179,
    185–187, 190
conflict of interest 94, 152, 153, 161,
    166, 174, 178, 179
Coors 59
corporate governance (see also
    Combined Code) 44, 177, 178,
    188–192, 197, 251, 253
corporate performance 28, 29, 31, 32,
    34, 35
Corporate Social Responsibility 4, 66,
    172, 177, 200, 253
costs 14, 37, 55, 56, 65, 106, 123,
    124, 127, 155, 172, 173, 188, 189,
    200, 247
CSR see Corporate Social
    Responsibility
culture 4, 32–35, 68, 89, 90, 169, 170,
    181, 185, 188, 198
customer service 4, 8, 9, 30, 59, 64, 66

Davies, Sir Peter 63
deferred payment 47, 67, 90, 108,
    146, 208, 209, 213, 215
defined benefit 132–135, 137–139,
    141, 142, 194, 253
defined contribution 132, 134, 135,
    137, 139, 141, 143, 194, 254
Delta 164
demotivation 23, 24, 117, 170
demotivation problem 78–80, 82, 83,
    85, 116, 168, 254
design 16, 17, 24, 25, 50, 75, 80, 83,
    98, 101, 103–107, 112, 117, 126,
    201
dilution 95, 123

director 18, 25, 44, 46, 62, 116, 130, 150, 157, 166, 171, 191, 198, 212, 228, 254
    executive 5, 18, 30, 44, 46, 62, 128, 147, 152, 156, 160, 161, 166, 180, 181, 198, 199, 254
    independent 44, 48, 80, 152, 180, 181, 190–192, 197
    non-executive 9, 44, 45, 48, 57, 63, 65, 90, 180, 181, 190, 191, 192, 196, 197, 208–211, 251, 254, 256
    (*see also* chairman)
Directors' Remuneration Report Regulations 45, 53, 133, 145, 177, 252, 254, 258
discretion 53, 54, 59, 56, 66, 79, 80, 116, 117
disproportionate incentive problem 78, 82, 83, 85, 116, 117, 126
dividend 2, 72, 95, 120, 124, 127, 171, 197, 204, 218, 230, 248, 254
diversity 29, 34, 38, 41, 152, 176, 183

earnings 9, 19, 20, 49, 58, 59, 66, 105–107, 116, 120, 123, 127, 142, 172 201, 254
earnings per share (EPS) 36, 39, 86, 105, 106, 115, 116, 117, 126
economy 36–41
electricity 38
Ellig, Bruce 250
employees 4, 8, 15, 25, 36, 95, 134, 135, 152, 163, 167, 168, 169
enhanced return rule 100, 101, 109, 112, 231, 254
Enron 4, 33

Equity 1–3, 149, 150, 176, 177, 183, 184, 192, 254
Ethics 4, 162, 163, 233, 251, 253
exceptional items 59, 106, 116
exceptional reward 84, 85, 109, 110, 134, 188
executive 5, 10, 15, 16, 21–23, 26, 29–31, 41–43, 47, 64, 66–68, 72, 74, 78, 82, 83, 85, 87–90, 95, 96, 104, 108, 109, 111, 112, 117–120, 122–124, 127, 128, 130, 132, 137, 139, 140, 142, 149, 151, 152, 154, 157, 159, 162–165, 168, 172, 173, 174, 176, 177, 179, 181, 191, 192, 195, 196, 200–204, 208–210, 214, 254
executive team 5–9, 11, 14, 15, 18, 19, 22, 29–31, 34, 37, 38–40, 48, 58, 59, 61, 64, 88, 93, 95, 98, 99, 103, 104, 110, 114, 121, 170, 180, 255
expected value 47, 88, 94, 100, 101, 146, 147, 156, 194, 208, 211

fair market value 31, 45–47, 117, 118, 121–125, 127, 133, 142, 145, 146, 162, 208, 210
fast food 38
feedback 35, 52
fiduciary duty 179, 186, 187
Figment, Joe 43, 47–50, 52, 55, 57, 58, 60, 61, 70, 75, 110, 111, 112, 128,135, 116, 138, 194
FILLIP 84, 85, 87–89, 91–94, 96, 98–101, 103–105, 107, 109, 110, 112, 122, 133, 141, 146, 164, 179, 228, 235, 236, 254, 355, 257

Finance Act 2003 95
Financial Reporting Council (FRC)
  44, 250, 253
Financial Services Authority (FSA)
  45, 255
Financial Times 158, 171, 175, 184,
  186, 192, 193, 203, 228, 258
fixed pay 13, 15, 20, 43, 44, 96, 110,
  111, 128, 129, 134, 139, 144, 201,
  202
fraud 4, 20, 33, 172
free-ride 30, 185
Fried, Jesse 250
FRS20 55, 123
FSA see Financial Services Authority
FTSE companies 17, 24, 32, 34, 43,
  44, 50, 55, 58, 64, 70, 75, 83, 87,
  89, 93, 98, 104, 107, 110,112,
  114, 115, 133, 142, 143, 174, 183,
  189, 191, 197, 199, 200, 203, 214,
  255
fund manager 102, 110, 184,
  186–189, 192, 197, 198

GlaxoSmithKline 180, 186
golden handcuff 90, 91, 94, 231, 233,
  234, 255
golden hello 91, 92, 96, 233, 255
Google 19
government 59, 92, 153, 154, 177,
  178, 184, 193, 196, 200, 251
Granada 94
Grasso, Richard 146, 178
Green, Michael 94, 99, 186
Greenbury, Sir Richard 45, 56, 66,
  69, 144, 147, 148, 150, 153, 157,
  158, 208, 250, 251

Hambrick, Donald 196
Hampel, Sir Ronald 45, 56, 146, 148,
  157, 251
head hunter 151, 165, 166
heath insurance 44, 111, 128, 129,
  139, 195
hedge 125, 126, 247
hedge fund 3, 117
Hemscott 251
Hermes Focus Asset Management
  (HFAM) 188
Higgs, Derek 45, 180, 190, 193, 251
Hogg, Sir Christopher 180
Home Depot 178

IFRS2 55
in the money 113
incentive 7, 8, 13–17, 19–21, 24–30,
  33, 36, 38, 39, 40, 42, 48–50,
  53–55, 61–64, 66–68, 72–74, 76,
  79, 80, 82–84, 86–89, 91, 96, 98,
  100, 101, 104, 105, 107, 108, 111,
  112, 114, 115, 121, 122, 124,
  126–132, 134–143, 154, 156, 159,
  160, 162, 164, 169, 179, 180–183,
  185, 187, 190, 192, 194, 195, 197,
  201, 202, 204, 232, 233, 255
individual 9, 14, 16, 24, 30–34, 36,
  37, 48, 66, 68, 86, 129, 173, 199
individual performance 28, 29, 31–37
individualism 14, 34–36, 169
information 44, 54, 107, 148, 150,
  157, 166, 177, 185, 192
Institutional Shareholder Services 193
Invariable 75, 8–84, 103, 104, 255
investor 1–3, 20, 58, 80, 101, 102,
  110, 122, 138, 139, 150, 154, 176,

186, 193, 203
institutional 3, 102, 103, 110, 116,
    180, 183–188, 201, 251–255
private 2, 183, 184
Investor Relations Society 193
ITV 94, 99, 186

Jackson, Eric 196
Jones, Keith 189
Jones, Sir Digby 186

Khurana, Rakesh 250
Kilts, Jim 151

Labour 184
Langone, Kenneth 178
leadership 152, 163, 164, 168, 169,
    171–174, 179, 181, 199, 202
Leighton, Allan 193
life assurance 44, 111, 129, 139
linear 81–83, 85, 104, 117, 255
liquidity 95, 101
listed company 4, 55, 57, 178, 182,
    184, 185, 186, 189, 191, 196, 197,
    203, 205
Listing Rules 45
long term 1–5, 11, 12, 16, 18, 20–22,
    27, 34, 48, 49, 58, 59, 61–68, 73,
    76, 85, 86, 88, 89, 91–93, 96,
    105–107, 110, 120, 122, 129, 138,
    142, 144, 164, 185, 188, 189, 191,
    195–198, 200, 201, 203, 212, 215,
    255
Long Term Capital Management 117
Long Term Incentive Plan (LTIP) 13,
    23, 35, 43, 46, 49, 53, 67, 68, 70,
    71, 72, 74–78, 80, 82–85, 88, 90,

91, 96, 98, 99, 101–105, 107, 110,
    112, 114, 115, 129, 133, 142, 144,
    146, 154, 189, 201, 206, 208, 211,
    217, 218, 255
LTIP see Long Term Incentive Plan
luck 21, 23, 87

manager 5–9, 30, 32–35, 50, 58, 63,
    70, 72, 78, 83, 89, 129, 142, 166,
    169, 192, 214, 255
management 5, 11, 12, 18, 52, 86,
    105–107, 114, 128, 135, 169, 180,
    184, 191, 192, 256
manipulation 78, 116, 126, 142, 201
market level (of pay) 150, 151, 160,
    162–167, 174, 198, 209
Maslow 162
matching share 47, 209
McDonalds 164
McDonough, William 175
McNulty, Dr Terry 251
median 71–73, 75–80, 85, 88, 96, 105,
    110, 146, 157, 160, 161, 165, 174,
    199, 218, 219, 228, 236, 237, 256
MG Rover 171
Morley Fund Management 189
mortgages 38, 39
motivation 13–15, 25–27, 80, 89, 92,
    119, 127, 133, 140, 142, 150, 151,
    160, 162, 166, 169, 171
motivational dead zone 76, 81, 82,
    117, 126, 256
Myners, Paul 102, 103, 185, 186,
    193, 251

National Association of Pension
    Funds (NAPF) 185–186, 193, 250

National Australia Bank 4
New York Stock Exchange 146, 178
Nike 4
nomination committee 166
non-executive *see* director

objective 4, 7, 22, 29, 30, 33–35, 38,
    50, 54, 58, 61, 62, 63, 67, 78, 86,
    87, 101, 153, 171
objectivity 22–24, 27, 50, 53–55, 84,
    107, 195, 199, 200
oil 38, 63, 106, 169, 233
Operating and Financial Review 177
other benefits 43, 44, 111, 139, 195,
    208
out of the money 114
ownership 173, 176, 182, 184, 185,
    187–192, 196, 197, 202, 203

Paddock, Jane 251
Parmalat 4
pension 2, 13, 15, 43, 111, 128, 129,
    132,133, 135, 137, 141–143, 149,
    159, 164, 171, 176, 184, 194, 195,
    202, 208, 209, 253
    fund 37, 38, 134, 135, 149, 164,
    176, 184, 185, 186, 188, 189, 197,
    254
    fund trustees 197, 198
percentile 71, 72, 74, 77, 81, 99, 256
performance 2, 3, 5, 8–13, 17–22, 24,
    26, 28, 29–32, 35–39, 40, 42, 47,
    48, 52, 58, 64, 86, 88, 91, 104, 108,
    110, 111, 118, 130, 149, 160, 168,
    170, 173, 177, 191, 199, 200, 256
performance condition 46, 70, 80, 94,
    103, 105, 114, 115, 117, 125, 126,

145, 146, 180, 210, 230
performance indicator 8, 58
performance measure 2, 3, 12, 17, 18,
    27, 28, 35,48, 54, 57, 58, 64, 66,
    68, 86, 101, 105–107, 112, 116,
    126, 201
performance period 71–75, 79, 83,
    88, 103–106, 115, 207, 218, 228,
    229–233, 256
performance related pay (*see also*
    variable pay) 13–25, 27, 28, 31,
    32, 41, 43, 44, 46–48, 50, 53, 58,
    61, 88, 93, 95, 96, 108, 125, 126,
    128–130, 132, 134, 138, 141–144,
    170, 195, 198, 201, 202, 256, 259
performance reporting 68
performance target *see* targets
Persaud, Avinash 162, 252
personal objective 10, 31, 49, 57,
    61–64
Personal Performance Contract
    (PPC) 9, 10, 12, 23, 51–53, 57,
    58, 60, 61, 64, 66, 86, 111, 257
phased awards 73, 74, 83, 85, 88,
    103–105, 108, 115, 257
Plender, John 162, 169, 175, 252
popular culture 172
power 33, 54, 64, 65, 90, 93, 96, 104,
    190
PPC *see* Personal Performance
    Contract
PRER FILLIP 101, 102, 105, 107,
    111, 112, 143, 195, 201, 202, 236,
    257
presentation 32, 45, 47, 52, 54, 65,
    95, 143–145, 150, 152, 154, 156,
    180

private equity 191, 205
privatised utilities 149
profit 6, 8, 9, 14, 16, 18, 21, 49, 51–53, 57–59, 66, 105, 106, 127, 171, 172, 201, 257
promotion 33, 34, 36, 63, 169, 201
pro rata rule 99, 101, 104, 112, 228, 236, 257
public perceptions 14, 26, 31, 32, 64, 75, 92, 143, 145–147, 149, 153, 146, 163, 171
Prosser, Sir Ian 63, 186

quartile 71, 72, 77, 80, 85, 110, 148, 151, 220, 221, 238, 239, 257

RAC club 186, 189
rate of return 3, 41, 42, 109, 214, 248, 257
recognition 10, 14, 25, 26, 31, 32, 66
recruitment 14, 26, 89, 90, 92, 119, 127, 150, 151, 160–162, 164, 166, 168, 174, 199, 234
red tape 173, 179, 191, 202
regulation 40, 44, 55, 155, 162, 178, 191, 202, 252
relationship 5, 25, 26, 89, 162, 163, 165, 172, 179, 181
relative performance 28, 35–42, 100, 101, 147
remuneration committee 9, 44–49, 53–55, 57, 58, 61, 66, 72, 74, 80, 85, 90, 92–94, 107, 119, 121, 122, 127, 131, 132, 136, 139–141, 143–145, 147–149, 152–157, 159–161, 164–167, 174, 178, 179, 180, 181, 192, 196, 198–202

remuneration consultant 71, 84, 115, 143, 144, 148, 150, 152–155, 157, 179, 180–182, 192, 196, 199, 200
report 28, 45–48, 52–54, 118, 139, 147–149, 151, 152, 154, 157, 160, 161, 180, 258
reporting, external 4, 19–21, 45, 47, 59, 64
retail 37, 199, 233
retention 14, 26, 89, 92, 119, 127, 150, 151, 160, 161, 166, 168
re-test 74, 75, 79, 80, 83, 105, 116, 117, 224, 230
reward 14–16, 21, 22, 29–31, 33, 39, 43, 44, 46, 83, 86, 102, 107, 130, 168
reward for failure 26, 91, 92, 251
risk 1, 2, 6, 7, 14, 33, 39, 62, 90, 91, 102, 106, 109, 118, 121, 123, 126, 127, 129, 163–165, 167, 177, 183, 233
Roberts, Dr John 251
Roche, Gerard 151
Royal Dutch see Shell

Sainsbury 63, 186
Share Option Scheme (SOS) 43, 46, 49, 55, 80, 91, 105, 113–117, 119, 121, 123, 124, 126, 127, 129, 133, 144, 145, 154, 201, 208, 210, 258
share price 1–3, 12, 22, 23, 29, 49, 70, 72, 73–75, 78, 79, 92, 99, 102–104, 106, 107, 118–121, 125, 126, 135, 142, 188, 201, 206, 211, 218, 225, 230, 236, 248, 253, 258
share retention scheme 234
shareholder 2–4, 11, 12, 14–16, 18,

19, 21, 24, 27, 30, 33, 37, 39, 41,
42, 45, 47–49, 58, 59, 63, 68,
72–74, 76–78, 80, 82, 83, 85–88,
92, 93, 95, 98, 99, 101, 104–107,
111, 112, 116, 119, 121, 124–128,
130–132, 138, 140, 143, 145, 149,
150, 151, 154–156, 159–163, 173,
174, 176, 177, 179, 181, 183, 187,
190, 192, 194–196, 198, 200–203,
258
  activism 173, 178, 182–185, 186,
  188, 192, 197, 258
  institutional 45, 74, 92, 178, 180,
  185, 187, 199, 201
  value 3–5, 11, 16–18, 20, 21, 33,
  34–36, 38, 47, 49, 59, 61–63, 65,
  66, 87–89, 94, 96, 98, 99, 101,
  104, 110, 131, 142, 146, 152, 171,
  177, 178, 182, 183, 189, 195, 196,
  200, 201, 258
Shell 4, 63, 64, 169
short term 3, 5, 20, 21, 27, 48, 49, 58, 59,
  63, 64, 67, 68, 76, 78, 96, 102, 105,
  107, 142, 185, 188, 201, 215, 258
single hurdle 80, 258
Skandia 4
Skapinker, Michael 196
sliding scale 23, 80, 81, 85, 115, 117,
  259
Smith, Sir Robert 45
SOS *see* Share Option Scheme
Stakeholder 35, 171, 172, 181, 195,
  259
Standard Life 176
Stiles, Dr Philip 251
stock exchange 45
stock market 3, 63, 102, 152

strategy 20–22, 48, 53, 58, 62, 63, 68,
  106, 161, 162, 171, 173, 177, 178,
  186
stress 34, 68, 162
subjectivity 11, 16, 22, 24, 25, 27, 54,
  96
success 1, 2, 4, 5, 34, 39, 63, 90, 91,
  93, 121, 125, 127
succession planning 89, 93, 164
Sunderland, John 193
suppliers 5, 8, 25
supply and demand 163, 165, 174
sustainability 20, 59, 73, 82, 91, 106,
  110, 111, 124, 138, 165, 171, 191
Sykes, Sir Richard 193, 252

tobacco 4
takeover (*see also* change of control)
  23, 100, 103, 104, 206
targets 5, 7–11, 14, 16, 20, 22, 23, 30,
  33, 36, 40, 46, 48, 49, 51, 54, 58,
  60, 61, 63, 64, 66, 68, 126, 201,
  232
tax 40, 113, 114, 124, 200, 230, 254
team 30–35, 48, 86, 140, 171, 201
Total Shareholder Return (TSR) 2–5,
  18, 20, 21, 22, 29, 48, 50, 71–74,
  76, 78, 79, 82, 86, 87, 96, 99,
  100–103, 105, 107, 112, 122, 126,
  188, 199, 200, 204, 206, 218,
  228–232, 236, 259
total remuneration 47, 128, 132, 133,
  137, 139, 146, 150, 159, 160, 167,
  198, 199, 202, 212
total reward (*see* total remuneration)
Towers Perrin 153
trade association 40, 253

training 34, 89, 168, 197, 198

transparency 4, 22, 24, 50, 52–55, 79, 80, 84, 95, 101, 108, 111, 112, 119, 127, 139, 140, 146, 147, 156, 157, 160, 188, 195, 198–200

trust 4, 22, 24, 29, 31, 80, 95, 111, 112, 161, 162–164, 169, 170, 173, 174, 179, 181, 185, 191, 192, 195, 198, 202, 252

TSR *see* Total Shareholder Return

Typico plc 43, 49, 55, 57, 58, 61, 64, 71–73, 75, 77, 80, 81, 85, 99, 104, 107, 110, 111, 114–117, 119, 123, 135, 136, 218

UK Shareholder Association (UKSA) 183, 184

underlying ownership 3, 12, 188, 189, 191, 198, 200, 203, 258

understanding 6, 22, 29, 61, 62, 64, 140, 147, 185

underwater 114

US Department of Labor 186

valuation (*see also* fair market value) 31, 45–47, 117, 118, 121–125, 127, 133, 142, 145, 146, 162, 208, 210

values, cultural 5, 30, 152,159, 163, 167, 168, 172, 181, 191

value, shareholder *see* shareholder value

value for money 46, 102, 106, 118, 127

variable pay (*see also* performance related pay) 13–25, 27, 28, 31, 32, 41, 43, 44, 46–48, 50, 53, 58, 61, 88, 93, 95, 96, 108, 125, 126, 128–130, 132, 134, 138, 141–144, 170, 195, 198, 201, 202, 256, 259

vested interests 90, 178, 179, 188

volatility 1–3, 12, 49, 73, 74, 76, 77, 85, 86, 91, 101, 110, 119, 121, 124, 127, 142, 145, 201, 207, 219, 223, 224, 229, 237, 241, 242, 259

volatility problem 74, 76, 77, 82 83, 102, 105, 107, 117, 121, 259

Watts, Sir Philip 63

Wellcome Trust 197

WorldCom 4

Printed in the United States
55303LVS00001B/117